The Horse Breakers

The Horse Breakers

CLIVE RICHARDSON

J. A. ALLEN: LONDON

British Library cataloguing-in-publication data
A catalogue record for this book is available from
the British Library

ISBN 0 85131 722 7

Published in Great Britain in 1998 by
J. A. Allen & Company Limited
1 Lower Grosvenor Place
London, SW1W OEL

Typeset by Textype Typesetters, Cambridge
Printed by Dah Hua International Printing Press Co. Ltd

Edited by Susan Beer
Designed by Nancy Lawrence

Contents

Foreword

This book is an excellent history of 'horse breaking' through the ages. It provides the background to modern horse training methods, bringing the reader up to the present day. Clive Richardson has combined a factual approach with fascinating anecdotal reading. It is detailed and well researched.

Horse handling methods have been continually evolving yet after 8,000 years we can still come up with a new system. It is my opinion that we are only scratching the surface; there is still much to learn and, for the good of the horse, every reason to learn it. The early methods outlined in this book were inherited by modern-day horsemen as the only tools they were given to use. While I don't believe they were right or moral, I can't blame anyone for the use of them.

Over the centuries preceding my arrival, man dealt with horses essentially by saying 'you do what I tell you to or I will hurt you'. Horsemen were taught that it was proper to take this position. 'Breaking' was a good term to use for describing the procedure of making a horse accept its first saddle, bridle and rider. The practitioner was to break the animal's will to resist. He would watch his equine student and when he believed the actions were negative he would strike, or in other ways cause pain, in an attempt to discourage these actions.

My method acts in the opposite way. I will not use pain or restraint and I wait for positive actions to occur, for which I congratulate and reward the horse, while utilising active work as virtually the only disciplinary action.

It is my opinion that if we can encourage the horse to do something because he wants to, he will do it far better than if he's doing it because he's forced to. This is a vastly different technique from the traditional approach we have seen through these 8,000 years.

I congratulate Clive Richardson on this book.

MONTY ROBERTS

Preface

When I was about eleven years old, my father bought a house with some land in the country. The previous owner had bought two foals at a sale some years earlier and, at the time the property changed hands, the foals had grown into strong three-year-olds but, since being turned loose as foals, no one had ever handled them and they were quite wild. On account of this and the fact that whoever bought them had first to catch them, they were sold cheaply and I remember their new owner arriving to claim his purchases and my anticipation of the fierce battle of wills I expected to ensue. My only knowledge of horse handling at that time came from what I had gleaned from watching American westerns or reading about cowboy rodeos. Over the next few weeks the man, who came daily, dispelled my preconceived notions as, from a safe distance, I watched with awe and fascination my first experience of a horse breaker at work. Quietly spoken with slow, measured movements, he worked alone and, although there was none of the drama I had secretly hoped for, I was no less impressed by his immense patience and skill, and he inspired in me an interest in horse breaking techniques that would eventually lead me to research the subject and to set out my findings in the form of a book.

Acknowledgements

Over a period of many years I have gathered material for this book from a wide variety of sources including letters, old newspapers and periodicals, as well as from the publications cited in the bibliography. In addition, a great many individuals and organisations have helped me with the research that was necessary before I ever put pen to paper. Whilst it would be impossible to mention everyone, I would like to express my gratitude to the following for their particular help and generosity: The National Sporting Library, Virginia; The British Museum; The Imperial War Museum; The International Museum of the Horse, Kentucky; The Negishi Equine Museum, Yokohama, Japan; Marwell Zoological Park; The National Army Museum; Beamish, The North of England Open Air Museum, County Durham; The Science Museum; The Middleburg Public Library, Virginia, for the use of microfilm facilities; The University of Reading Rural History Centre; The National Cowboy Hall of Fame and Western Heritage Centre, Oklahoma; The Carriage Museum of America, Pennsylvania; Dr Sharon Cregier, University of Prince Edward Island, Canada; the late Ellen B. Wells, Cornel University; Kelly Marks; Bob Langrish; Anthony Dent; Dr Tris Roberts; Jeff Edwards; Tom Ryder; Michael Clayton; Peter Lane; Miranda Bruce; Richard James; Ann Hyland; and Edward Hart. Lastly, I would like to thank the many people who sent me information and photographs, and the innumerable horsemen, travelling people, historians, archivists and librarians who helped me and to whom I am indebted for their guidance and help.

The line drawings and engravings are taken from: W. Browne, *His fiftie yeares practice*, 1624; C. M. Moseman and Brothers Catalogue; *Professor Beery's mail course in horsemanship*, 1908; D. Magner, *The art of taming and educating the horse*, 1987; J. S. Rarey, *The art of taming horses*; Arnold & Sons Veterinary Catalogue; H. Hayes, *Illustrated horse breaking*, 1905; Professor Norton Smith, *Practical treatise on the breaking and taming of wild and vicious horses*.

CHAPTER ONE

The first horsemen

And the fear of you and the dread of you shall be upon every beast
of the earth . . . into your hand are they delivered

Genesis 9: 2

Around 8,000 years ago, the sedentary agricultural people living in
South Turkestan between the Oxus River and the Caspian Sea
became the first horsemen in the world when they successfully captured and tamed the wild horses of the region. Their achievement,
which was soon to be emulated by other tribal groups on the southern Russian steppes and then gradually copied in many other parts of
Asia, was to transform their comparatively primitive lifestyle by
enabling them to travel long distances with ease and speed, opening
up trade opportunities and bringing them into contact with other
cultures. It would also make it possible for them to manage large
herds of livestock and to accumulate wealth in the acquisition of such
herds, to make war on their enemies with greater effect, and to
develop and prosper as the first of the world's great horse cultures
was born. Globally, the achievement of these simple people was to be
dramatic and far-reaching as the synergetic potential of man and
horse combined was realised and exploited across the greater part of
the world.

THE ART OF THE HUNTER

Man's relationship with the horse predates the first horse tamers of
Turkestan by nearly a million years, for since the emergence of *homo
erectus* the horse has been hunted by man as a source of food.
Prehistoric sites in Europe have yielded large deposits of horse bones,
generally the incomplete skeletons of young dismembered animals,
suggesting that these early hunters were selective in what they killed
and that only the choicest parts of the animals were carried back
to camp to be eaten. The bones of thousands of horses have been

discovered either buried in the ground or stacked in caves near Lyons in France, and excavations of other early sites in Europe have revealed similar discoveries. The ratio of horse bones to those of bison or other prey at these prehistoric dumping sites would seem to indicate a preference for horse meat over that of other animals.

By the time Cro-Magnon man was recording the prey he hunted in the form of cave art upwards of 15,000 years ago, the hunting of wild horses had become a highly skilled operation. Like all successful hunters, man had studied his quarry carefully in order to understand its behavioural patterns and habits, and he was aware of its highly developed senses of sight, hearing and smell as well as its use of flight to distance itself from predators including man. Having only simple javelins and spears as weapons, the bow and arrow not being invented until around 10,000 years ago, it was necessary for man to get very close to his prey if he was to have any chance at all of making a kill. Stalking the herd when it was grazing in open ground was difficult and rarely successful, but man knew from his observations that at certain times of the year, such as when migrating, the herd was more vulnerable. Equine behaviour is largely based on the collective experiences of the herd going back many generations, and man would soon learn that successive generations of wild horses tend to follow the same migratory routes and drink at the same watering places along the way. Moreover, at such times their single-mindedness, and their feeling of security in a herd situation surrounded by other horses in close proximity, lowered their guard sufficiently for man, using the accumulated knowledge of generations of hunters, to ambush them successfully. By waiting concealed at narrow places in rocky or mountainous areas, at river crossings, marshy ground, or at the watering holes, man could get close enough to the herd to use his simple weapons.

Other early hunting techniques were to use 'beaters' to funnel the herd into narrow ravines or deep water where individual animals could be more easily speared, or even to stampede them over cliffs. At Solutré in France there is a kill site where generations of hunters purposely chased wild horses over a steep cliff to kill them, and the bones of over 10,000 animals have been discovered by archaeologists at the foot of the cliff. This knowledge of the herding instincts and behaviour of the wild horse would be of significant importance when man first came to capture live horses and tame them.

TAMERS AND DOMESTICATORS

The domestication of animals did not arise until man led a semi-sedentary existence, perhaps only moving with the seasonal migrations of the animals he hunted. The dog was domesticated first around 12,000 BC and it undoubtedly played a role in the hunting of larger prey, including horses, by helping to drive the herds towards the cliffs or the hunters concealed in waiting. Reindeer came next followed by sheep and goats, pigs, cattle, onagers and, finally, the horse which because of its size, speed, sharp senses and flighty nature was the most difficult to capture alive. Although cattle were comparable in size but more aggressive than horses, a cow leaves her calf hidden in long grass while she goes off to graze, so it would have been easy for early hunters to catch the calf and rear it on the milk of other domesticated livestock such as goats until it was big enough to kill for meat. A foal, however, follows its mother from the moment it is on its feet and would therefore be more difficult to catch, so it is likely that any foals captured were either very young or the mare had been killed by hunters or very seriously wounded, permitting her capture as well.

The ability to catch live horses led to the development of a meat and milk husbandry system which had originated following the domestication of cattle. Mares were milked while lactating throughout the summer months and their foals were killed for meat in the autumn or early winter while they were still fat from the summer grass. In the spring the mare was tethered near a watering place to be covered by one of the wild stallions when it came to drink, and the process repeated. The mares, which were unlikely to have lost much of their wildness despite being handled daily for milking, were controlled with simple hobbles made of twisted wool or strips of untanned hide as well as leg tethers. This primitive form of animal husbandry, which formed the basis for the domestication of the horse, was still being practised in parts of Europe in medieval times, and other vestiges of it occur in present-day horse cultures elsewhere. Donkey breeders on the borders of India and Pakistan still tether their in-season donkey mares out away from the village in the hope of getting them in-foal to one of the few remaining Indian wild asses – in the belief that a foal from such a mating will be more vigorous. Hobbles are still used extensively for the control of horses in many parts of the world, and steppe horsemen who catch and milk half-wild mares do so using a traditional method which can be traced back to very early times.

The development of the meat and milk system reduced the reliance on hunting for food and enabled people to live a more sedentary life style as their herds of semi-domesticated animals increased. As more emphasis was placed on their livestock to provide food, the skills of hunting were adapted for the capture of live animals, including equines, as man's relationship with the horse began to move in a different direction.

EARLY HORSE TYPES

Most of the information we have about the wild horses of this period comes from two sources, archaeological excavations of bones which can be measured to give an indication of the size and stature of the animals, and also from the cave art of earlier times which suggests what these horses may actually have looked like. Early cave art, most of which can be dated to between 15,000 and 20,000 years ago, probably had a religious significance associated with the belief that by keeping the images of animals fresh on the rock they would continue to thrive in abundance in the surrounding area. This theory is supported by the fact that the paintings were regularly refreshed with mineral pigments to keep them vibrant, and sometimes additional animals were painted in. The best examples of cave art are to be found in western Europe, and the detail in the work reveals a close study of the subjects depicted. As recently as December 1994 a series of over 500 paintings, including many of horses, was discovered in the Ardeche region of south-east France dating back to the Stone Age, and earlier excavations at the Grotte de Montespan, also in France, produced clay models of horses with javelin wounds. These early paintings and figures not only demonstrate the importance of the horse to man but, more importantly, give clear indications as to what type of horses they were.

Tarpans
Cave paintings from Lascaux in the Dordogne region of France depict wild horses of Tarpan type, as well as open-fronted structures which some archaeologists believe may be corrals into which the horses

Tarpans. (Photograph: Marwell Zoological Park)

were driven before being speared. The Tarpan, whose name literally means wild horse, was originally indigenous to southern Russia, Poland and Hungary. Standing about 12 hands high, it was mouse-grey in colour with a paler under-belly, black legs and tail, a dark dorsal stripe, and a short upright mane. The last true wild Tarpan, a mare, died in the Ukraine in 1880, but some thirty years earlier there were still a few of these animals running wild in the Crimea and in the province of Kherson where one was captured as a foal and sent to the Zoological Gardens in Moscow where it was still alive in 1884. An indication of the nature of the wild Tarpan may be deduced from the descriptions of this animal which was broken to ride and drive as a three-year-old following castration. It was allegedly bad-tempered and uncooperative, a view reinforced by Captain Horace Hayes, an experienced and well-travelled horseman of the late nineteenth and early twentieth centuries, who wrote 'Tarpans are comparatively difficult to tame, and only those which are captured as foals could be broken in. Even then they remained bad-tempered and unwilling workers.'

Przevalski horses

Other examples of cave art, as well as a small carving of a horse's head excavated in one of the caves, clearly depict Asiatic wild horses, or Przevalski horses as they are now more commonly known. Described by Lydekker in *The horse and its relatives* as being 'intermediate in character between the horse on the one hand and the kiang and the onager on the other', these animals once roamed throughout Asia and Europe. The zoologist, J. S. Poliakov, named them after Colonel Nikolai M. Przevalski, an officer in the Imperial Russian Army, who first saw herds of them on the edge of the Gobi desert in 1879. Local Kirghiz tribesmen, who hunted them for meat, presented Przevalski with the hide and skull of one which he in turn presented to the Zoological Museum in St Petersburg. Przevalski horses, which are extant, stand a little over 12 hands and are dun with a yellowish tinge, paler on the flanks and belly, with a short upright mane, no forelock, and a tufted tail. The large plain head with a broad forehead and Roman nose was thought by Przevalski himself to house a large brain indicating superior intelligence, and Colonel Hamilton Smith, an English naturalist who wrote an article about these primitive horses in a leading natural history publication as far back as 1814, also commented on their intelligence. In 1889 Russian naturalists obtained four Przevalski horses in order to study them, and the following year a stallion and two mares were captured and brought to the estate of Friedrich von Falz-Fein, a landowner at Askania Nova in the Ukraine. Even in captivity they lost none of their primitive aggressive temperament and remained essentially wild. Like the Tarpan, they were by repute ill-tempered and difficult to handle, although Captain Hayes claimed 'the supposed untamedness of Przevalski's horse has been disproved to some extent by P. K. Kozlov, and would not be accepted as a fact by any capable horse-breaker without practical proof; although the animal in all probability is much more difficult to break in than an ordinary horse'.

Interestingly, the extinct Tarpan was revived in the 1930s by a German zoologist, Professor Lutz Heck, who noticed that the Polish breed of pony known as the Konik occasionally produced examples showing distinct Tarpan characteristics. The Konik was directly descended from wild ponies kept in Count Zamoyski's private zoological park near Bilgoraj in Poland in the 1700s, and by crossing

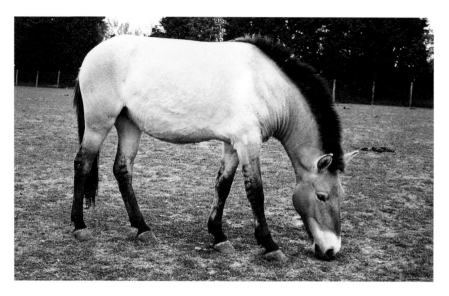

Przevalski horse. (Photograph: Marwell Zoological Park)

Konik mares with a Przevalski stallion Professor Heck recreated something very close to the original Tarpan. Of particular signifi-cance was the fact that the recreated Tarpan displayed the same primitive nature as its wild ancestors.

Asses and onagers

As well as the Tarpan and Przevalski horse, neither of which were evidently amenable to being tamed, the early horsemen were also familiar with wild asses, and in particular the onager or Asiatic wild ass and the kiang of Tibet and the surrounding area. Both were believed to be easier to catch than horses because of their curiosity. Colonel F. Markham in his book, *Shooting in the Himalayas*, pub-lished in 1854, wrote of the kiang: 'When approached they stand gazing at the intruder, until he gets within about three hundred yards, when they will trot off to a little distance, and then turn to look, standing as before, until their pursuer draws near, when they again move off.' Although he adds, 'I never heard of any attempt being made to break them for use', some evidently were caught and used but they proved unreliable and difficult. The onager was more wary to approach in the wild but was more tractable when caught and more responsive to training, but it was still not an easy animal to handle. They were used to draw chariots in ancient Sumeria but, once horses were domesticated, the onager fell from favour and was rarely used after the time of Alexander the Great. The kulan or Mongolian wild ass could, according to R. C. Andrews who studied them in the Gobi desert in the 1920s, reach running speeds of up to forty miles an hour, while the Nubian wild ass, main ancestor of the domestic donkey, was said to be able to out-run a well-mounted horseman.

METHODS OF CAPTURE

Considering the characteristics of all these animals, the achievement of man in capturing and taming them is all the more remarkable. He used a number of methods of catching wild horses and asses with varying degrees of success. Aside from wounding a mare to catch her and her foal, a method which could entail tracking the animal for several days until she became weak enough to catch, steppe horsemen often caught foals by following them for days on end until the foal became too exhausted to go any further. This method has survived the centuries and the Russian naturalists, G. E. and M. E. Groom-Grjeemailo, observed mounted Kalmucks catching foals by this method in the last century. 'At foaling time', they wrote, 'each of the Kalmucks goes with two horses to the desert and having found the herd they follow it up until some of the weak foals fall down on the ground from fatigue and are then secured.' When Carl Hagenbeck, owner of a Hamburg menagerie, was commissioned in 1902 to collect living specimens of Przevalski horses for private collectors, he found it was impossible to capture adults but, using Kirghiz horsemen who followed the foals in the traditional way, thirty-two foals were caught, two of which ended up in the London Zoological Gardens.

Treddle traps and snares were also employed, as evidenced by rock engravings from the eastern desert of Egypt showing the capture of wild asses in these primitive traps. Unfortunately traps often resulted in lame or permanently disabled horses but, further encumbered with hobbles and tethers, such horses were easier to handle and control and under the meat and milk husbandry system unsoundness was of no consequence. It is likely that use was made of corrals like those depicted in the Lascaux cave paintings, including the blocking off of narrow ravines and passes to form natural corrals. Tame decoys may have been used to attract wild herds. A fifteenth-century BC gold cup found in a tomb at Vophio, south of Sparta, shows a wild bull being tethered after being decoyed by a tame cow. The practice was almost certainly of some antiquity then and, as many horse-handling methods were based on those which had proved successful with earlier domesticated cattle, the decoying of wild horses is very likely.

CONTROLLING THE HORSE

At what point more sophisticated methods of horse control were introduced is difficult to determine but in many ways the progress of equestrianism was dictated by the effectiveness of differing methods of restraint. The discovery in the cave of St Michel d'Arudy in the Pyrenees of a horse's head carved from mammoth ivory and almost certainly wearing a halter of twisted material consisting of a head-piece, noseband and throat-latch is believed to date from the period when the horse was first domesticated, and the excavation of moulded and carved figures of horses from sites throughout the area of early horse culture showing ridges and grooves on the head rein-forces the belief that halters were in use at an early stage in horse domestication. As halters, tethers and hobbles were all made of per-ishable materials, no other proof exists as to their design or composition, but most probably they were made of twisted horsehair or wool or strips of rawhide made supple with mutton fat. W. J. Miles, writing in 1868, believed that the halter and bridle both evolved from the tether fastened around the upper neck of the horse. He wrote:

> It must have occurred to the horseman that if this rope was put over the head and over the muzzle or perhaps in the mouth of the animal, he would be more easily fastened or led from place to place, and more securely guided and managed whether the man was on or off his back . . . the occasional struggles of the animal to escape from these tram-mels and the strength which he exerted in order to accomplish his purpose, first suggested the idea of harnessing him.

Some form of head control which would have permitted the lead-ing of horses in hand would certainly have been an important step towards the eventual riding and driving of horses, which probably originated with the biannual uprooting of the settlement when the herds were moved to fresh grazing.

HARNESSING HORSE POWER

The early steppe horsemen left no legacy of art to date their equestrian conquests accurately or indicate what first initiated their getting on to the back of a horse or harnessing it for draught work. Since the middle Stone Age dogs had been used for draught work, harnessed to a travois consisting of two poles tied together in the shape of the letter A, with the point fastened to the dog and the ends of the pole dragging on the ground. The load was strapped to a platform fixed between the two poles. If horses could be led and effectively controlled, even a lame or partially crippled horse could pull a travois, and if part of the load of tent coverings, animal skins, tools and weapons was transferred from the travois to the animal's back the notion of the horse carrying a burden, even a rider, may have been suggested. Alternatively, tired children, the sick or elderly, may have been sat on the horse's back while moving camp, or the boys who guarded the flocks of sheep and goats and the milch mares may have climbed on to the back of a quiet mare for a prank. However it started, further progress towards riding proper would have been hampered by the fact that the horses kept were either older, probably unsound, breeding mares or foals destined to be killed for meat during their first winter. The retaining of filly foals reared in close proximity to man and intended eventually to replace their wild-bred and ageing dams would have made available for the first time young, sound, but not necessarily more tractable animals. The criteria for the selection of those animals to keep on and eventually train would have been founded on the qualities of size, strength and stamina with any indication of amenability being an added bonus.

The small captive herds, which would now include an increasing proportion of youngstock, were prevented from straying off or being tempted away by wild groups of horses by the use of hobbles and tethers, and also by the vigilance of the herders who guarded them against predators or horse-stealing neighbouring tribesmen. Family groups of horses have a tendency to stick together under a dominant stallion, or occasionally a mare, so the presence of the older hobbled mares may have had a herding influence in general. Without these controlling factors, it would have been impossible to tend on foot animals which were not lame, injured, tethered or hobbled. Once riding horses were available, man was able to manage much larger, free-ranging herds which could be safely grazed away from the settlements, as horses are more resilient to attacks by predators than either sheep or goats.

Another possible and valid theory as to the origins of riding and driving horses is that other types of animals domesticated prior to the horse were used as the model. There is evidence to suggest that reindeer not only pulled simple sledges but were used for riding in northern Europe around 5,000 BC, and cattle, which were kept for milk, meat and draught work long before the horse was domesticated, were undoubtedly ridden too. The 'seat' of early horsemen as depicted in art forms of the time was clearly more suited to the riding of cattle or asses which, because of their prominent and bony backbones, compelled riders to seek comfort by sitting further back near the animal's loins. It has even been theorised that the Cretan sport of bull-leaping, popular in the second millennium BC, may have evolved from the breaking in of cattle to ride in the same way as bronco competitions in present-day rodeos in America evolved from the breaking in of horses on ranches.

DEVELOPING MORE ADVANCED METHODS OF CONTROL

Noserings

The advent of riding and driving demanded more precise and effective control devices than the halter, tether and ubiquitous hobbles, and the invention and development of such devices was integral to the progression of horsemanship. Cattle husbandry was well established by the time the horse was first domesticated, and the accepted method of controlling cattle at that time, and which has continued in practice ever since for bovids, was with a cord or bar, later exchanged for a ring, made of bone, horn or metal and passing through the nasal septum. This method was used on horses, as well as on camels, asses and other animals, often in conjunction with a halter of some type. The so-called Standard of Ur, a hollow rectangular box, possibly part of a musical instrument, discovered in one of the Sumerian royal graves and dating back to around 2,500 BC provides evidence of the use of noserings in the scenes depicted on its sides in inlaid shell, red limestone and lapis lazuli. One scene shows a king and his army advancing into battle with chariots drawn by quadrigas of onagers controlled by strong headcollars and noserings.

A baked clay plaque found in Syria and dating to the first quarter of the second millennium BC shows a rider on a horse with the reins, held in his left hand, attached to a nosering, and the Kultepe seal, *circa* 1950 BC, from Cappadocia shows a god standing on a horse which is controlled by a nosering. Other cylindrical seals from the same area and period provide further evidence of the distribution and use of the nosering, and in later times Strabo, the Greek geographer, wrote of horses guided by noserings. The fact that the nosering survived as a means of controlling horses for several centuries would suggest that it was not totally unsuccessful, although it seems likely that its use would make horses headshy and liable to toss their heads about, thus making the saddle-less riders insecure. Syrian plaques showing horses wearing noserings perhaps give an indication of this, for the horses also wear simple girths which their riders hold in their right hands, no doubt to help them stay on.

Lip rings
Lip rings may also have been tried although the one-dimensional perspective in early art forms apparently illustrating lip rings may really have been showing noserings. This is evident in the Standard of Ur where the two wheels of the chariot are placed side by side to make it look like a four-wheeler, and the noserings on the onagers appear to be passing through the upper lip longitudinally. A lip ring would cause problems for a horse, which uses its upper lip when grazing, and it would also tear out easily. Even so, there is evidence of lip rings being used on horses for decorative purposes in later times and this may be a vestige of a functional use. Writing about the horses of Turkey in the 1860s an observer noted 'they have rings of silver hung on their nostrils as a badge of honour and good discipline', and the symbolism of a ring, whether through the nose or not, crops up regularly throughout history to signify taming and ownership.

In Egypt, where the cat was first domesticated and elevated to a position of some regard, these animals were sometimes adorned with rings, and there is an Egyptian bronze of a cat, *circa* 30 BC, with a gold nosering, perhaps signifying it was tame, in the British Museum. In Roman times, a gold ring was the insignia of mounted soldiers and when Severus, the emperor who died in 211 AD, permitted foot soldiers to wear the equestrian's gold ring he was honouring them to seek their favour and support. Even the giving of a metal ring as a pledge of intent to marry, a custom known in Roman times, may have had its roots in the symbolism of possession and subjugation.

Mouth bits

It seems strange that if the horse bit, the most effective and now almost universal method of controlling ridden and driven horses, was known by 4,000 BC or even earlier, that the nosering should have continued in use for so long. Perhaps early horsemen were as entrenched in their views and as pragmatic as many of their modern contemporaries, or maybe new ideas were slow to be assimilated throughout horse-owning cultures.

The horse bit probably evolved from the noseband, which was found to be more effective if adjusted low onto the soft part of the horse's muzzle. Maybe by accident or design the noseband found its way into the horse's mouth, exerting even greater control, and a simple form of jawstrap bridle resulted. A stone relief from Ninevah, *circa* 704–681 BC, shows horses led by a rope around the lower jaw only, which is again surprising when the use of bits was well established and jawstrap bridles were known to frequently cause injuries to the mouth. These early bridles were made of rawhide strips but the mouthpiece was not durable, although twisting it made it harder wearing and also more effective, like the twisted mouthpieces on some modern bits. Excavations of the sites of early horse-owning settlements have often turned up perforated pieces of antler, now recognised as the cheekpieces from horse bits with the replaceable rawhide mouthpiece threaded through the holes and knotted. As late as the early eighteenth century, bits with antler-tine cheeks were being made and used in Sweden. Some antler cheeks had one hole or slot for the mouthpiece and two for the bifurcate reins. Excavations of third millennium BC sites in Romania and Russia have produced antler cheeks with serrations on the inner side, as well as circular bone or antler cheeks with pointed nodules on the inner side to effect more control. Made from the curved browtine or burr ends of red deer antlers, or occasionally from cattle bones, the material was soaked in water and then boiled before being drilled and cut with a knife and chisel to fashion the required shape.

Mouthpieces of other materials were tried too, including bone, horn, rope, wood, and even stone, and the earliest known bit, found on the site of ancient lake dwellings at Robenhausen in Switzerland, was made of stone with a slightly curved mouthpiece with double knobs at the ends to accommodate the headstall. By the fourteenth and fifteenth centuries BC bronze bits were first used in western Persia and northern Mesopotamia, their twisted mouthpieces shaped to imitate the twisted rawhide examples they superseded. Similarly, the cheekpieces of these bronze bits were modelled on the antler prototypes. By the second millennium BC, jointed bits were known with mouthpieces of twisted bronze wire, some having long mouthpiece sections to increase the severity of the nutcracker action, and others having three sections, or rings at the ends like modern snaffles or smooth or ridged mouthpieces. By 450 BC jointed ring snaffles meant that the bridle cheekpieces, which in the absence of buckles were tied and knotted to the bits or fastened with bone or horn toggles, no longer had to end in a Y shape. As the use of the horse bit spread through the horse-owning cultures, the diversity of bit types widened as the extra control they afforded to early horsemen enabled them to put the horse to greater use.

EMPLOYING THE HORSE

For many years historians believed that horses were driven before they were ridden and in some countries like Egypt this was certainly true. The first evidence of an Egyptian rider, a wooden figure of a horse ridden by a groom, comes from a tomb, *circa* 1550 BC, many centuries after the war chariot was well established in that country, and carved monuments of 1400 BC showing battle scenes depict riders escaping on chariot horses, the unusually long reins giving away the horses' true function. There was a belief that the horses were too small to ride, although a harnessed pair could pull two or three people in a vehicle, and traditionally animals had been used for draught, going back to the dog in the Stone Age. In addition, the idea of getting on to the back of a horse and riding it, even though horses were probably used as pack animals, was not something these primitive people came to easily.

Now evidence from archaeological sites at Dereivka in the Ukraine excavated by Dr Dimitre Telegrin of Kiev has disproved this theory. Dr Telegrin revealed that metal bits had been used 500 years before the wheel was invented, thereby proving with some certainty that horses were ridden before they were driven. The dig has provided proof that the people who lived in the farming community on the west bank of the Dneiper River some 6,000 years ago maintained domesticated herds of horses. The people ate a lot of horsemeat, horse bones representing 68 per cent of all animal bones found there, and the fact that most of the slaughtered animals were between six and eight years of age with a high proportion of stallions suggests culling of a managed herd rather than the random hunting of the wild population. Close examination of some of the horse skulls, and in particular the pre-molars, reveals that approximately 3.5 mm of tooth had been worn away from the front surfaces, closely matching the degree of wear on present-day horses ridden in a metal bit. A comparative examination of a sample of wild horses showed only a quarter as much erosion, the conclusion being that the horse remains excavated were those of riding horses broken to a bitted bridle, as poor alignment of the teeth could not have caused such wear. This evidence of horses being ridden in around 4,000 BC explains how a large herd of horses could be successfully managed. It predates the invention of the wheel by around 500 years, although horses were used to drag sledges and the travois before then. It was not until around 3,500 BC that solid wheels came into use, as shown by examples excavated in the Tigris–Euphrates valley in what is now Iraq.

EARLY TRAINING AND HANDLING

Much of what we know about how horses were first tamed and broken to ride is based on archaeological discoveries and informed supposition. The early horsemen were illiterate and left no written and few pictorial records to show how they managed their herds or broke in individual animals, but their oral traditions, handed down from generation to generation, were occasionally commented on in the writings of later historians, giving clues to the practices of earlier times. We know that both horses and asses were selectively bred in domesticated herds to produce bigger, stronger animals, and the skill, or lack of it, of the stockmen resulted in some herds being of better quality than others.

In Cappadocia in the second millennium BC the herds were so large they could not be corralled or contained in any way, and only those animals that were being broken in were placed in enclosures for ease of access during training. A letter from the Hittite king to the king of Babylon, *circa* 1275 BC, comments that in Babylonia the herds were so large 'there are more horses than stalks of straw'. On an ancient Sumerian cylinder document, Gudea, a priest-ruler, reports that the chariot of one of the patron gods was drawn by 'four strong-voiced asses coming from a well-known stock', indicating that some domesticated herds were better known than others on account of their quality. We also know from Assyrian sculptures that the customary method of catching horses was with a lasso, further evidence coming from a stone relief from Nineveh, *circa* 650 BC, showing the capture of onagers with ropes. The slip-knot type of lasso which tightens around the throat depriving the animal of breath and exhausting it, and thereby effecting considerable control, was also used in the breaking of animals. A Hittite site at Boghazköy near the western shore of the Black Sea has yielded a copper rein terret from driving harness, dated around the end of the third millennium BC, which portrays a man training an onager using ropes of this type. Other fragments of evidence from many horse-owning cultures suggest that the slip-knot lasso and hobbles were fundamental to the breaking and basic training of horses. Although relays of riders were probably used to wear the animal down and tire it until it accepted a rider on its back, it is also possible that another of their breaking processes was more gradual and based on regular handling from a very early age.

Berenger, writing in his *Treatise on horsemanship* in 1771, described the Tartar method of breaking which had probably changed little among steppe people since very early times, and began when the horses were only foals. 'When they are six or eight months old they make their children ride them, who exercise them in small excursions, dressing them and forming them by degrees, and bringing them into gentle and early discipline.' This would support the theory that riding began with children riding the milch mares when they were brought in from pasture for milking, for it would have been a small step to begin riding the foals too at this stage. Steppe horses were quite small, even for the tribesmen of the period who were not very big themselves, and they were also slow maturing, so it is feasible that they were not up to much weight as two or three-year-olds. This again is borne out when Berenger goes on: 'The men, however, do not ride them until they are five or six years old, when they extract from them the severest service, and inure them to almost incredible fatigue.' Hard work to keep the animal subdued and to reinforce man's dominance was common to many breaking methods. If a horse went lame or was injured in the breaking process, it was simply turned back into the herd until it was sound again and another animal selected. This was not possible with wild caught animals but was with a managed herd.

Once these people had riding horses and could control semi-domesticated herds of increasing size, they were able to catch selected animals from the herd, or even wild horses, by riding them down and lassoing them from horseback with a running noose thrown either over the head or around a leg. Sometimes two riders would work together to incapacitate a horse after relays of riders had pursued it to tire and weaken it. This method of capture, like the breaking method of bombarding the hobbled animal with riders until it gave in, produced a mount suitable for the needs of these horsemen and the environment in which they lived. Control was learnt rather than taught, and riding the horse in the company of more experienced riding animals would give it confidence and help to keep it under control while it learnt from experience what was required of it.

THE FIRST TRIBAL HORSEMEN

It was possibly the Anau tribesmen who first initiated the catching and partial domestication of horses, although they may not have actually ridden them or used them for draught. More likely it was the Cimmerians, coming from what is now northern Iran to displace the Anau, who developed the skills of horse management, while the Scythians who came in their wake were renowned as highly accomplished horsemen responsible for distributing the skills of equestrianism across much of the ancient world. The Scythians originated in the Volga basin and reached the Russian steppes around 1,000 BC, driving out the Cimmerians whose homeland it had been. Their skills as horsemen enabled them to rule a vast grassy domain from the Black and Azov Seas in the west, across all of what is now the Ukraine, and up as far as the Siberian forests. Their territory included Olbia, Tyras, Theodosia, and all the Greek trading colonies on the Black Sea's northern rim. Although they were largely self-sufficient, by plundering and claiming revenues from neighbours their wealth increased substantially so that by their zenith in the fourth and fifth centuries BC their power and influence was great. As the most accomplished horsemen of their day, they are of particular interest because their horsemanship, including breaking and handling, was evidently based on the accumulated experiences of earlier horse-owning tribes and because, for the first time, their way of life was documented in some detail by Herodotus, a mid-fifth-century BC Greek historian and writer. Although Cicero described him as the Father of History, Aristotle, writing a century after Herodotus' death, called him a 'fable-monger' but, although some of his statements are a little fanciful, Herodotus' writings are nevertheless a valuable insight into Scythian life. Moreover, the discovery of Scythian tombs dating back to 450 BC at Pazyryk in the Altai mountains in western Siberia provides verification of much of what Herodotus wrote as well as much of what had been assumed about these early horsemen.

The Scythians led a semi-nomadic lifestyle, spending their winters in the more sheltered lowlands, and their summers on the cooler mountain slopes where their herds grazed. They lived in settlements of felt tents called yurts which they dismantled and moved to new pastures when their stock had grazed the area bare. When moving camp they did so with their armed cavalry in front, followed by mounted tribesmen driving the herds and flocks of assorted livestock, then the covered ox-wagons carrying the women, children and their belongings, and their slaves bringing up the rear. The men spent most of their time on horseback, tending their herds or hunting boar, deer and hare, and they had the first custom riding apparel of trousers, tunics, soft heel-less boots and even, sometimes, leather or horn armour. Their weapons were bows and arrows, javelins, shields, and long knives with straight blades of iron or bronze. The women never rode at all.

Scythian horses and horsemanship

The Scythian horses came from Mongolian pony stock and were described by J. K. Anderson, an American authority on ancient horses, as 'useful, strong ponies, with coarse necks and shoulders, very low withers and coarse heads'. Standing 13.1 hands high on average, and usually brown, bay or chestnut with few white markings, they were kept in large loose herds with few stallions, as too many would have tended to split the herd up into individual groups of mares around particular stallions, and only a limited number of stallions were needed for breeding as, despite Pliny the Elder's erroneous statement that they preferred to ride mares, they in fact rode only geldings. Surplus colts were gelded at between two and three years of age by crushing the spermatic cord with a wooden mallet. The mares were milked and the milk fermented into a drink called koumiss. Herodotus said they milked mares by inserting a hollow bone tube into the mare's genitals and while one man blew air in supposedly to inflate the veins and force the udder down, another milked the mare into a leather sack or bucket. Curiously, this method is still used today by East African cattle herders. The Scythians were great horse breeders and traders, distributing stock to the Assyrians, Hykos, Cappadocians and Parthians as well as the knowledge of how to handle and break them, and it was at the Black Sea trading settlement of Olbia that Herodotus, who was there collecting material for his history of the Greek and Persian wars, learnt so much about them. Evidence of their trading activities comes from the horses buried in the tombs as they include horses of Ferghana type, a prized strain from Turkestan standing up to 15 hands, which could only have been acquired through warfare or, more likely, trade. By cross-breeding with other strains of horses, hybrid vigour was introduced into the Scythian herds, contributing towards increased size in individual animals. However, if this improved stock was allowed to return to the wild the size gain was quickly lost over a few generations.

EARLY EQUESTRIAN EQUIPMENT

The Scythians were highly skilled at throwing the lasso, and they were probably the first horsemen to use the uraga, a sliding rope of plaited horsehair or rawhide looped on to a long birchwood pole, to catch horses. They employed a variety of hobbling systems including roping one foreleg to the opposite hind leg, and tying a rope from the head to one foreleg, and they continued the established practice of tethering using leg ropes and neck ropes. Their bridles were made of ox or horse hide from which they had scraped the hair before drying it and pounding it with mallets to make it pliable. Sometimes the hide was cured using sour milk or curd, and then animal fat was rubbed in and the leather laboriously kneaded to soften it. The bridles, which

Capturing wild horses using a uraga. (Photograph: Negishi Equine Museum)

often had a lead rein attached as standard, were sewn with sinew thread and fitted with simple twisted rawhide bits with wood or antler cheekpieces. Some of the more ornate bridles were dyed with cinnabar, a mineral pigment mixed with a resinous substance, and decorated with ornamental plates of bronze, silver or even gold. They also had rudimentary saddles comprised of two flat leather cushions, stuffed with stag hair or a type of sedge-like grass, with wooden bows front and back, a felt sweat-pad underneath, and a felt over-covering. The felt was made by beating wool to soften it, wetting it with boiling water, pressing and rolling it to mesh the fibres, then pounding it again before drying it in the sun, after which it could be water-proofed with animal grease. Some saddle coverings were deco-rated with appliquéd cut-outs of mountain goats or mythical beasts, and a girth, which fastened from the near side like the bridle, and was secured with a simple horn buckle, went right around the horse and saddle. A wine amphora of the period shows a Scythian horse wearing a saddle with raised cantle and pommel as well as a breast strap and hindquarter strap. The Scythians did not have stirrups although they may have had simple foot loops sewn onto the felt saddle pad.

Scythian horse breaking

Working either on foot or on horseback and in small groups, they selected animals for breaking which were lassoed in the herd, hobbled and thrown. The latter practice, which probably evolved from casting horses in order to geld them or treat them for injuries or ailments, was soon incorporated into the breaking process as it generally had a subduing effect on the wildest horses and instilled into them the dominance and superiority of man even at that early stage. The animal would be saddled and bridled then mounted and allowed to get used to the feel and weight of a rider on its back while still shackled with the hobbles and restrained by neck ropes held by the other tribesmen. In the wild, predators would leap on to the back of the horse to attack it, so the immediate and natural reaction of a horse to a weight on its back would be to try and dislodge the rider without delay. Only when the frightened horse had recovered from the initial shock and had exhausted some of its energy were the hobbles removed and the animal allowed to go unfettered in the company of several riders on experienced horses who surrounded the young horse to guide it and prevent it going too far. Every few days the horse would be caught and ridden in the same fashion until by constant repetition and hard work it accepted its lot in life. Forward movement was encouraged by the use of whips with wooden handles and leather thongs, while obedience to the reins was simply learnt through experience.

Evidence that the Scythians worked even their young horses very hard is shown by the remains of horses buried in the Pazyryk tombs, many of which show pathological lesions of the teeth, vertebrae and extremities of the bones indicating excessive work especially over rough ground. Once an animal was deemed to be ridable, it had its mane clipped as a symbol that it was a riding horse. This custom stems from the fact that the Scythians were great bowmen and a long loose mane could have got in the way of the bow and caused problems. Draught horses, which were held in lower esteem than riding

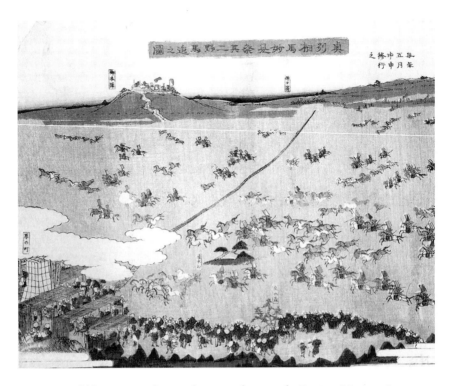

Wild horse round-up. (Photograph: Negishi Equine Museum)

horses, never had their manes clipped and neither did breeding horses nor young unbroken horses. At this stage, if not before, the horse's ears were notched in various forms to denote ownership and the tails docked, knotted, plaited or trimmed short. The presence of horses with quite different ear markings in the tomb of one man would suggest that some of the animals were bought-in or traded, and the poverty rings on the unshod hooves of some of the horses would indicate little or no supplementary feeding even in the severest winters. The exception were some of the horses of the prized Ferghana strain whose stomachs were found to contain grain, but this was unusual. The tomb horses, which ranged in age from two-year-olds to animals of twenty years or more, had been killed with pole axes and were buried alongside their owners to serve them in the afterlife.

Proof of the Scythian method of breaking horses comes from a wine amphora excavated in 1862 at Chertomlyk on the River

Dneiper. Often inaccurately described as a koumiss jug, the famous 28-inch gold and silver amphora with its three seived spouts near the base to filter the sediment from the wine was skilfully crafted around 380 BC, probably by Greek metalsmiths, and depicts in great detail Scythian horse breakers at work. One scene shows men catching a horse with a lasso, another shows a man throwing a horse using a distinct technique common to many horsemen and to be copied for centuries to come, and a third scene shows a man removing the leg hobbles from a saddled horse, its clipped mane signifying its status as a broken riding horse.

Scythian legends abound with references to the importance of the horse in their culture. Herodotus relates an unlikely tale of the Scythian chieftain who was killed in a duel and, when his victorious enemy came to rob the body, the chieftain's horse bit and kicked him to death. While such tales underline the relationship these tribesmen had with their mounts, the influence of the Scythian culture on horsemanship in general is indisputable, and many of their practices survived long after the Sarmatians, possibly inventors of the stirrup, displaced them in the second century. Modern Kazakh and Altaian herdsmen who do not ride a horse again after its owner's death are following a Scythian tradition which began with the sacrifice and burying of the horse in the owner's tomb and which was later transmuted to retiring the horse and referring to it thereafter as a 'widow'. Mongols earlier this century were still using the uraga to catch wild horses as the Scythians had done nearly 3,000 years ago. By distributing their knowledge of how to break and handle horses to others including the Assyrians, Hykos, Cappadocians, Parthians, Germanic Goths and many more, who also got horses from the Scythians, they enabled others to establish their own horse cultures.

Proof of the increasing use of the horse for riding in the ancient world is legion. In the biblical book of Kings II, Rab-Shakeh, the ambassador of Shalmaneser, king of Assyria, says to Hezekiah, king of Judah: 'I will deliver thee two thousand horses, if thou be able on thy part to set riders upon them', implying that the acquisition of trained horses was sometimes compromised by the lack of riders with even basic skills. Such temporary problems aside, the distribution of riding horses was matched only by that of driving horses as the military potential of the chariot was recognised across the ancient world.

THE HORSE IN HARNESS

Up until the invention of the spoked wheel around 1800 BC, vehicles were generally either heavy and clumsily built carts or devoid of wheels altogether, like the hearse-sledges of the Sumerian kings and the travois of even greater antiquity which was used by many early civilisations. The Russian word *drozhky*, meaning a type of primitive vehicle, literally translates as 'that which is dragged', and the travois was still in use in the Balkans during the First World War for transporting the wounded. It was also used in western Ireland earlier this century for harvesting peat. The spoked wheel led to lightweight, swifter vehicles and, in particular, the appearance of the first chariot in Mesopotamia. On the eighteenth-century BC stele of Hammurabi, the king who united most of Mesopotamia around the city of Babylon, there is no mention of chariots for, although they were in existence then, they were very scarce. However, a century later the invaders who crushed the Babylonian empire had developed the chariot as a weapon of war, and other nations were following their example. As well as its military use, the chariot was used for sport, as Egyptian tomb paintings show images of pharaohs hunting ostriches in chariots, while the Assyrian king, Tiglath-Pileser, claimed to have killed 800 lions from his chariot. In China during the Shang dynasty, 1850–1122 BC, the chariot was used in the pursuit and capture of wild horses for domestication, and it also had a processional function as shown by the urgent request from Shamshi-Adad, the eighteenth-century BC king of Assur, to his son, Prince Jasmach-Adad, who was engaged in the breeding and training of chariot horses, to send chariots and trained horses for the New Year processions.

The development of draught harness

When horses were first harnessed to chariots, the model for both the design of harness and the method of attachment to the vehicle was based on that originally used with cattle and later adapted for use with onagers. It comprised a central draught pole with a transverse yoke attached to the necks of the animals, which were driven in pairs. As both asses and cattle have a low head carriage with the neck carried almost horizontally, the yoke sat easily on their necks and was quite adequate for the ploughs or simple crudely constructed vehicles they drew. This harnessing arrangement was unsuitable for horses, however, whose conformation and head carriage is quite different, and the original design had to be modified by making two individual inverted V-shaped yokes which were attached at their apex to the transverse beam of the yoke proper, with their lower points secured down by a girth which fastened just behind the elbows. A throat strap prevented the yokes from slipping backwards but meant that the animals were actually pulling with their necks and not their shoulders. This harnessing arrangement was best suited to stallions with well-developed necks but it tended to produce animals with an upright head carriage and over-development of the underside of the neck causing it to bulge out in front. Depictions of chariot horses in early art show this characteristic clearly. Whatever throat and girth harness, as it became known, lacked in terms of efficient draught was partially compensated for by the control it gave over the horses. A horse can only gallop with its neck outstretched so the constraints of the throat strap, and the artificial head carriage it enforced, meant that animals were virtually restricted to trotting or lateral pacing. Bolters must have been rare, although jibbers were probably common. As the centre of gravity of the chariot was forward of the axle, when going uphill the raised pole must have nearly choked the horses and, in the absence of breeching, downhill travel must have been perilous with the weight of the vehicle taken on the yokes which would have been pushed over the horse's ears but for the anchoring influence of the girth. Fortunately, the chariots were lightweight, and the primitive harnessing arrangement, which was to remain in use for over 3,000 years, even though by then the Chinese had developed the superior breast and neck collar methods of harnessing, was a workable if wasteful method of traction. As the chariot culture radiated to Persia, India, Egypt, Greece, Mediterranean Europe and further afield, the skills of how to break and train horses to harness were communicated and learnt.

BREEDING AND TRAINING THE CHARIOT HORSE

The breeding and training of chariot horses was expensive and time-consuming with the result that well-trained horses were a valuable and much sought after commodity. When King Tushratta, the Hurrian ruler from what is now Armenia, sent his relative, Amenhotep II, pharaoh of Egypt, gifts described in his letter as 'a chariot, two horses, a youth and a maiden', it was the former parts of the gift that would have been held in the greatest esteem. His letter, evidently intended to seek support or strengthen alliances, went on: 'my fraternal gift to thee includes also horses for five carriages', making his gestures especially generous.

Large numbers of personnel were employed in the training of chariot horses as well as the grooms and stable attendants, some of whom did little more than cut grass with a simple reaping hook and carry it back to the stables. The actual breaking was the domain of skilled slaves or sometimes mercenaries from other horse-owning cultures, and was done by repeatedly leading the animals in harness, then as a pair in a vehicle. Although unproven, it is probable that drag sledges were used to accustom the horses to pulling a weight and hearing it moving behind them before being put to a wheeled vehicle. From the outset, training was done in pairs and the horses became so accustomed to working together that if one died or was killed it took considerable re-training to get the survivor to accept a new working partner. Apart from the control resulting from the use of the throat and girth harness, on some chariots, like those of the Assyrians, the reins passed from the bits through terrets on the harness pads and through a rein-slot on the dashboard of the vehicle which gave an element of leverage which aided control. In Egypt chariot horses were driven in a form of drop noseband, sometimes used in conjunction with slit nostrils, and a stone relief of the chariot of Rameses II, *circa* 1400 BC, shows horses driven in drawreins, martingales, and what some historians have interpreted as blinkers on the bridle. The use of drawreins and martingales as a control measure was very probably common in early harness training procedures. Breakages must have been frequent, but the cost of sending inexperienced horses into battle could be great, as a commentator on the battle between the Persian king, Darius II, and Alexander the Great suggests when he wrote: 'The drivers lost control over the shying horses which shook their necks until they freed themselves of the traces, often overturning the carriages . . . ' The word traces has been incorrectly translated here, for traces were not in use at this time, and the writer actually means yokes.

As horse breaking was the work of illiterate and uneducated people, their skills and experiences were passed on and desseminated by word of mouth, but around 1360 BC the first known manual on the training of harness horses was written on six clay tablets and entitled *A handbook for the treatment of horses*. The tablets, which were found in 1917 during excavations of the Hittite capital of Hattusas, now in Turkey, were intended for the chariot corps of the powerful Hittite empire under King Sepululiumas, and were written by a Mittanian called Kikkulis who was in the king's employ. As he himself was probably illiterate, his instructions would have been dictated to a scribe or priest who took them down in cuneiform characters and then read them out aloud to the illiterate Hittite horsemen. Repetitious and detailed, he advises a training programme which begins in March when the horses, having been cossetted all winter, are in a soft and fat condition. Some historians have interpreted the instructions as being an acclimatisation programme for purchased, traded or tribute horses, while others believe it related to horses captured in warfare. When the Assyrian king, Shalmaneser II, had his spoils of war recorded on an obelisk, prominence was significantly given to the 1,121 chariots and 420 horses he claims he took from his enemies. Kikkulis' programme, which lasts for 184 days, was for a pair of horses working together and included a strict diet of barley, cut grass, straw, clover or alfalfa, regular washing in cold or warm water, anointing with oil or butter, rugging, grazing and picketing, swimming, and even details of the distances and paces at which the horses were to be driven. An excerpt advises:

> Pace two leagues, run twenty furlongs out and thirty furlongs home. Put rugs on. After sweating, give one pail of salted water and one pail of malt water. Take to river and wash down. Swim horses. Take to stable and give further pail of malted water and pail of salted water. Wash and swim again. Feed at night one bushel boiled grain with chaff.

The term *pace* is thought to have meant a slow gait, possibly trotting or laterally pacing or even just walking, while *running* either meant fast trotting or even galloping as best they could. The horses were stabled in separate stalls in specially constructed buildings, at first made of reeds or branches but later built more substantially. When Kikkulis advocates the use of muzzles it may have been as much to prevent the horses eating the reed walls of their stables as a precaution against biting, the chariot horses all being stallions, or it may have been an indication of another device for controlling horses especially during training.

The protracted process of domestication which had taken several thousand years to achieve, and which was still on-going, was largely centred around the subjugation of the horse, usually by force, with little understanding of its psychology or its attributes other than speed and strength. With the emergence of new, more advanced civilisations, notably the Greco-Roman empire, a more scientific approach to horse handling was to be considered for the first time as the potential of the horse was exploited on a grand scale. Ironically, the skills of the horse tamer, so esteemed in steppe society, were to be devalued by more progressive cultures, resulting in horse breaking becoming the profession of the lowlier classes, a trend which would persist for centuries to come.

CHAPTER TWO

Horse breakers of the Greco-Roman empire

Neptune, if we may credit give to fame,
First taught with bits the generous horse to tame

Roman poem attrib. Statius. From *Modern practical farriery*
W. J. Miles (McKenzie 1861)

According to Greek mythology, Poseidon, or Neptune to give him his Roman name, the god of sea and horses, created the first horse by thrusting his trident into the ground, and some legends credit him with being the first to tame his new creation as well. In the shared mythology of the Greco-Roman empire, the most famous horse was Pegasus, the fabulous winged creature, reputedly born out of the blood soaking into the ground where Perseus cut Medusa's head off. When Bellerophon set out to kill the chimera, he asked the goddess Minerva for advice and she directed him to Pegasus drinking at the well of Pirene and told him he would have victory on the back of this animal. The myth relates how Minerva invented the bridle to tame Pegasus, making her, at least in mythology, the first horse breaker in the world. As many of these myths were derived from ancient Chaldean fables and folklore which began life as fact and were embellished into legend by successive genera-tions of story-tellers, some truth is probably inherent. Early descriptions of the rhinoceros were so exaggerated that the legend of the unicorn was born, and as far back as 220 BC these fictitious equines with their single twisted horns were being recreated in the royal processions of Carthage with the court's sacred legion of cavalry mounted on white stallions with docked tails, hogged manes, cropped ears and huge ivory horns set in the middle of their foreheads and attached to jewelled bridles. In the case of Bellerophon and his promised victory, the myth is probably based on the early steppe horsemen who not only achieved military supremacy once they were on horseback, but undoubtedly inspired the legend of the centaurs as well.

THE LEGEND OF THE CENTAURS

The steppe horsemen had caused terror among the simple tribespeople they conquered, who believed that these ruthless riders and their shaggy mounts were actually one creature, half-man and half-horse. Both Plutarch and Pliny believed centaurs really existed and they were probably not alone in their beliefs. Wooden figures of centaurs and images of them in other art forms have been discovered in many parts of Greece, and a metope or stone panel carved in high relief on the Parthenon at Athens dating from around 447 BC depicts one of these strange creatures. In legend, a Greek fable tells how Philyre, the mother of the centaurs, cohabited with Saturn on an island in Asia Minor from whence she migrated to the plains of Thessaly – curiously the finest horse breeding area in the whole of Greece – and a book of Chinese mythology called the *Chanhay-King,* dating from the third millennium BC includes a story of centaurs which probably can be traced back to the steppe horsemen too. There are also other vague references to these creatures from other early sources. Poloephatus in his *De incredibilibus historiis* states that the legend of the centaurs was attributable to early horsemen and he cites the tale of Ixion, the king of Thessaly, who, having his country ravaged by a herd of mad bulls which came down from Mount Pelion to cause havoc, offered a reward for the destruction of the bulls. 'Certain adventurous young men' from a colony of Egyptians living in Greece took up the challenge and, although they only had experiences of driving horses in chariots, they trained some horses to be ridden and, thus mounted, charged the bulls, driving them out and even attacking Ixion himself. When they eventually departed, the people, seeing only a rear view of the horses with the riders' upper bodies hiding the heads and necks of their mounts, thought they were monsters and gave them the name of centaurs. The common belief that they were immortal probably stemmed from those riders who fell off their horses and were able to get up and run off, making people believe that even if a centaur was cut into pieces each piece could sustain independent life. Centuries later when the Spanish conquistador, Pizarro, was hemmed in by 10,000 hostile Indians during his exploration of South America and one of his men fell off his horse in the tumult of battle, the Indians fled in fear as, according to the Spanish historian, Herrara, they too believed the horse and man were one. Others were a little more enlightened and Xenophon in his work, *Cryopaedia*, has Chrysantas saying: 'Now, the creature that I have envied most is, I think, the centaur (if any such thing ever existed)'; then, having praised the intelligence, skill, strength and speed of the centaur, adds: 'all his advantages I combine in myself by becoming a horseman'.

THE FIRST HORSES ON GREEK SOIL

The Greeks were among the finest horsemen of their day yet, as no fossil remains of horses have ever been found in Greece, it has to be assumed that horses were introduced from some other country where the skills of horsemanship had already been learnt. Herodotus claimed that the Libyans of Africa taught the Greeks how to harness horses to chariots and this is feasible as the Libyans were superior horsemen who employed Greek mercenaries in their wars with neighbouring Egypt. The Libyans probably learnt their skills from refugees from other lands, or from mercenaries or traders like the Phoenicians, who found a growing market for horses in the lands bordering the Mediterranean, including North Africa, where they sold stock brought from Syria and Cappadocia. Another theory is that around 1730 BC the Syrian Hykos or shepherd kings introduced the horse and chariot into Egypt from whence it was taken to Greece. A close examination of chariots excavated in Egypt supports this, one example excavated near Thebes in 1828 and now in the Florence Museum being constructed of wood from the Caucasus, and the Egyptian words for horse, harness and chariot were Syrian in origin. There are also early records of a colony of Egyptians, perhaps the ones employed by Ixion, who apparently landed in southern Greece and who were reputed to have brought the first horses to Athens. The leader of this band, a man called Erichthoneus, was a horse breaker by profession and famous enough for Virgil in his Georgics to write: 'Bold Erichthoneus was the first who joined . . . four horses for the rapid race design'd', and 'Of bits and bridles; taught the steed to bound . . . to run the ring and trace the airy round.' Whether these Egyptians were actually responsible for introducing horses into Greece is open to conjecture, but the information about Erichthoneus is interesting, for it is the first mention of a particular horse breaker by name and the earliest reference to horse breakers as a profession.

Horses were probably introduced into Greece prior to the eleventh century BC but their distribution was hampered by the fact that these early imports were driven rather than ridden, and the rough terrain of the country was not conducive to wheeled vehicles. Because horses were very expensive – a good animal being worth the equivalent of between ten and twenty oxen, or fifty-five sheep, or 372 suckling pigs – they were owned only by the wealthy and used for racing, hunting or warfare. At the Olympiad of 776 BC chariot races were recorded for the first time, but it was not until the 33rd Olympiad in 648 BC that mounted races were held, which may give some indication of when riding became more common. However, as late as 490 BC news of the battle at Marathon was carried by a foot messenger, presumably because no horses were available. Philip of Macedonia during his reign began transforming his infantry into cavalrymen, copying the example of the Persians, and Alexander the Great continued the trend with great military success.

GRECIAN HORSEMANSHIP

The Greeks adopted the horse with enthusiasm, incorporating it into their culture and making it central to Grecian life. They took the traditional methods of horse management which originated with the steppe horsemen and refined and rationalised them into a philosophy and art. At a time when others cured illnesses with amulets and magic, the learned Greeks were studying physiology and medicine, and they adopted this same questioning, scientific approach to horsemanship and to the breaking of horses.

Greece was not a good horse-breeding country, as it was too rugged and mountainous, but it still sported a number of distinct breeds including the Arcadian, Epidaurian, Acarnanian, and the famous Thessalian from the plains of Thessaly. Oppian, writing in the second century AD, commented on other breeds too including the Orynx which was said to be striped like a tiger or sometimes spotted like a leopard, although it was later discovered that these marks were made with a branding iron when the foal was very young. Generally, the Greeks' horses were not very large in stature, as can be deduced from the position of the riders' feet in relation to the bellies of the horses they rode, as seen in artistic representations of horsemen.

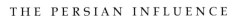

THE PERSIAN INFLUENCE

Although the Greeks were frequently at war with the Persians, some of the knowledge they incorporated into their own style of horsemanship was evidently learnt from their enemies and adapted to their own needs. The Persians counted their wealth in horses, one province ruler owning over 5,000 animals, and so integral was the horse to their culture that at one time a law was passed prohibiting horse owners from walking. Persian horses were highly prized, and even the Chinese, who in the pre-Christian era maintained both a chariot corps and a cavalry, bought horses from northern Persia. They referred to them as celestial steeds and, according to Chinese writers, they sweated blood, although the cause of bleeding was actually a type of skin mite. Herodotus described the Persian mounts as fast, spirited, beautiful, and imbued with sufficient stamina to enable them to gallop for up to thirty miles. The Persians developed the chariot into a machine of war, and even produced a model called a mower with long knives fitted to the wheel hubs. The Persian king, Darius III, used 200 of these lethal vehicles against Alexander the Great's army at one time.

In the fourth century BC Cyrus II introduced a heavy four-poled chariot drawn by eight horses and intended to sweep small enemy vehicles aside, but it was unwieldy, the poles broke easily and there were problems controlling the eight horses. An immense eight-poled chariot bearing an 18-foot tower shielding archers was also tried unsuccessfully, but it did not lessen the overall effectiveness of the Persian army, and by the sixth century BC the Persian empire was the dominant force in the east. Herodotus wrote: 'The armoured Persian horsemen and their death-dealing chariots were invincible, no man dared face them . . .' This military supremacy was centred around the horse and the Persian's skill in managing it. They invented the cavalry picket line which they used in conjunction with hobbles to prevent the horses kicking each other or their attendants, and were using this system prior to 546 BC along with nosebags to feed grain and chopped roughage to cavalry horses. They had special ships designed for the transportation of horses which enabled them to move their cavalry by sea effectively and speedily, and Darius used such ships in 490 BC when he attacked Greece with his horsemen.

The Persians also had professional horse breakers, and it is likely that the Greeks copied their example in establishing this trade in their culture too. Bands of professional horse ropers often accompanied the Persian army on the move, catching and breaking horses for them as well as practising gelding and other veterinary services. The first evidence of such a group of professionals comes in 480 BC when they worked with Xerxes' army. Other groups specialised in branding and ear-notching, a practice that went back to very early times and which was common to others, including the Egyptians who had been branding horses and other livestock from around 2,000 BC.

THE ROLE OF THE CAVALRY HORSE

The Greek writer, Xenophon (430–355 BC), whose works have survived the intervening centuries, reveals much about the attitude of Greeks to their horses as well as their practices and traditions. Perhaps significantly, Xenophon was one of 10,000 Greek mercenaries employed by the Persians to fight in Asia Minor, and he therefore had first-hand experience of the Persian's superior horsemanship. A comparative indication of the status of the horse in the Greek and Persian civilisations can be drawn from the battle of Thermopylae in 480 BC when the Persians fielded 80,000 cavalry while the Greeks, with whom they were in conflict, had none at all. It is likely that when Xenophon returned from the Persian campaign his new-found knowledge of military horsemanship was fairly unique in Greece, putting him in a position to write with some authority on the subject when he retired from military service. In saying, 'It does not seem necessary for me to describe the method of breaking a colt', he appears to be indicating that it was either common knowledge or, more likely, that such an activity was beneath his station in life which is why his writing concentrated on military horsemanship. His comment that those enlisted in the cavalry were people of wealth and political power in Greece underlines the social significance of horse ownership and partly explains why horse breaking was considered a lowly occupation. Because of the high price of horses, only the wealthy could afford them and, if a young man wished to put himself forward for the cavalry, he had to supply his own broken horse. Consequently, the Greek cavalry was comprised of 1,000 of the highest class of Greek citizen, 100 from each of the 10 Attic tribes, under the command of a phylarch, with the entire corps commanded by two hipparchs. Prospective members of the cavalry had to pass a strict entrance examination. An Attic cup found at Orvieto in central Italy and now in the Berlin Museum depicts such an examination with two young Grecian men leading their horses by a lead-rein before two examiners and a scribe with a stylus and writing tablet.

Perhaps one of the reasons why the Greek cavalry was generally ineffective was that it was comprised of men whose wealth rather than horsemanship had secured their inclusion in this *corps d'élite*. Such men delegated the care of their horses, including their breaking, to servants while they attended to matters more appropriate to their social status. Xenophon suggests this when he writes:

> It is also a good deal better than being a horse breaker for a young man to see that his own condition and that of his horse is good, or if he knows this already, to keep up his practice in riding, while an old man had better attend to his family and friends, to public business and military matters, than be spending his time in horse breaking.

He seems to be alluding to the fact that by the fourth century BC, when he was writing, the breaking of horses was the work of servants, a tradition which possibly had its roots with mercenaries, who were merely contract employees, but who taught the Greeks much of what they knew about horses. Agriculture and working with animals, even horses, was considered menial by Greece's aspiring social classes, although the riding of horses was a sign of status. When the second-century BC Greek philosopher, Diogenes Laertius, was persuaded by friends to mount a horse, he did so only briefly lest he become 'horse-proud', and this belief recurs in later civilisations. The Hebrew word for horse, *abbr*, also means strong and valiant.

THE FIRST PROFESSIONAL HORSEBREAKERS

Xenophon was not the first Greek to write on equestrian matters and he quotes the words of an Athenian called Simon who was writing around 400 BC but whose work, with the exception of a few fragments, has been lost. Xenophon's own work, later translated under one title, *The art of horsemanship*, deals only with riding and there is no mention of driving horses at all which, bearing in mind when it was written, means it was probably written for or with the cavalry in mind. If so, his readers would have been the more intellectual and powerful members of society. His comment on horse breaking: 'The man, then, that feels as I do about horse breaking will, of course, put out his colt', is therefore especially apt. This statement is interesting for it recommends the use of a professional horse breaker rather than leaving the job to grooms or servants which would have been a less expensive option. Even so, he seems slightly cautious, for he strongly advocates that a contract be drawn up between the horse owner and the breaker specifying what the horse was to be taught and making a comparison with a man putting his son out to learn a trade.

As Xenophon was writing for what he called 'the younger of my friends', from which may be assumed that they were relatively inexperienced in matters equestrian, probably young men contemplating cavalry service, he must have felt they needed forewarning about these professionals. Xenophon most likely had come across bands of itinerant breakers while he was a mercenary for the Persians, and knew something of their unscrupulous practices. Although the professional would undertake the actual breaking in, Xenophon recommends that the initial handling could be done by grooms and servants. He advises: 'See to it that the colt be kind, used to the hand, and fond of men when he is put out to the horse breaker.' With the increase of controlled and selective breeding, the handling of young stock would be more usual but, as mainly stallions were broken in for either riding or driving, they would have needed skilful handling, the more so as they did not have the benefit of centuries of domestication. Xenophon goes on: 'the groom should also be directed to lead him through crowds, and to make him familiar with all sorts of sights and all sorts of noises', saying that if the horse is frightened he should be taught by soothing that there is nothing to fear. He curtly concludes the brief chapter on horse breaking by saying: 'it seems to me that this is enough to tell the amateur to do in the matter of horse breaking'.

Many of the horse breakers working in Greece at the time of Xenophon were as involved in the teaching of riding skills to the sons of the wealthy as they were in educating horses to be ridable. Depending on their reputation, success, and standing in the community, they would either work in covered sand arenas offering an element of privacy or, at the other end of the scale, in the agora or open market-place and assembly area. Some worked in the open air with the tutor sitting in the shade of a tree while his pupils worked under his auspices, and an Attic vase discovered in the ancient Etruscan city of Vulci shows a lesson in progress with a riding master, two horses and two pupils. Often it was the paying pupils who did the actual breaking under supervision.

Plato believed that riding and gymnastics were essential parts of an Athenian gentleman's education, and the fact that a favourite toy with Greek boys was the hobby horse stick on which they 'rode' would suggest an aspiration to ride at a very early age. Galen, a second-century BC physician, advised that boys should learn to ride at the age of seven, and Plato believed 'we must mount our children on horses in their earliest youth', adding: 'the horses must not be spirited and warlike, but the most tractable'. The first Greek riders may have had to learn as adults, but by Xenophon's time most boys learnt to ride before they reached their teens, as at the age of eighteen they were eligible for consideration for the cavalry.

The age for breaking

The age at which horses should be broken was open to subjective opinion. Simon the Athenian wrote: 'The colt begins to be driven two years after birth', by which he probably meant driven in long reins rather than in harness, and this was most likely the average age for initial breaking, and he goes on to point out, 'he is at his prime for swiftness and courage at six years old', which suggests that Greek horses were slow to mature. During breaking and as a standard precaution thereafter, horses were muzzled to prevent them from biting, and Xenophon writes: 'In fact, the horse ought always to be muzzled whenever he is taken anywhere without a bridle. The muzzle, without hindering his breathing, allows no biting, and when it is on, it serves to keep horses from mischievous designs.' The use of muzzles was something else copied from the Persians but soon adopted into general use. The Temple at Persepolis, built before 500 BC, has a carving of a muzzled horse depicted on one of its facades. The muzzles, which were not worn in the stable, were put on by the grooms whenever they were leading the horses out for grooming or to roll, which was considered an important part of horse care. Because mainly stallions were broken in, the playful nipping of a colt, perhaps encouraged by a groom, could easily develop into a confirmed vice.

Hobbles were also commonly used. In Homer's *Iliad*, Poseidon used them to retain his horses when 'he put golden hobbles around their feet which could not be broken or slipped so they should wait there unmoving for the return of their master'. The breaker also had to teach the horse to tie up, and this was done by fastening the lead rope above his head so that the rope did not tighten when he threw his head up, which may have frightened him, and he had to be taught to lead. A young horse was made to lead at the side of the handler, not in front where he could get out of control, nor behind where he could play up. On general handling, Xenophon's advice was to stroke the colt in those places which he most likes to have touched or which he cannot reach himself, and he emphasises that if the groom knows what he is about the horse will associate solitude with hunger, thirst and teasing flies whereas the presence of man brings food, drink and relief from insects. This philosophy, which may have originated with the Greeks, has been incorporated into methods of breaking horses for centuries.

Bits and mouthing

For mouthing a young horse, the Greeks used a variety of different types of bits and, as curbs were as yet unknown, all had jointed mouthpieces. They were the first horsemen to use 'keys' attached to the mouthpiece to encourage the young horse to play with the bit and salivate, modern breaking bits being very similar in both design and purpose. Xenophon wrote: 'little rings are hung from the joints of the bit in the middle . . .', although a small piece of chain consisting of a few links was sometimes used instead. The Greeks were well aware of the importance of a good mouth and, along with some of the steppe nomads, were unique in that they favoured bits with a mild action. Xenophon believed a young horse should be accustomed to a rough bit to begin with so that it learned to respect it, and by rough he meant a bit with tiny blunt spikes on the mouthpiece. The spikes were usually part of the bit's construction, but sometimes they were simply fitted to it and could be removed if required. The Greek name for bits of this type also meant sea-urchin on account of the similarity in appearance. Some bits had discs on the mouthpiece that fitted between the bars of the mouth and the tongue to prevent an over-enthusiastic horse from seizing the bit and resisting.

To prevent the bars of the mouth becoming hard or desensitised during breaking, oil was rubbed into them with the fingers and, to avoid pulling on the bit unnecessarily while leading the horse, a halter was often worn under the bridle or a lead rein attached to the noseband or to the chin-strap which helped keep the bit in place (but did not function like a curb-strap). The horse could also be tied up with the halter or lead rein which avoided the horse hurting or frightening itself. Donkeys and mules were both ridden and driven in Greece in halters only. Grecian riders were taught to be light-handed, and their practice of riding with the reins passing over the forefingers and down through the hands was believed to encourage this. Horses were bridled from the near side by slipping the thumb into the horse's mouth or pressing its lips against its teeth to encourage it to open its mouth to take the bit calmly. Once bridled, basic obedience to the reins was taught by walking alongside the animal, and it was considered important to lead the horse using both reins, as leading with one rein was believed to cause a one-sided mouth.

Backing and initial riding

Although the Greeks used a form of saddle cloth for riding but no stirrups, young horses were ridden bareback during breaking. Sometimes their young riders were professionals who specialised in this field or in circus riding and acrobatics, which were popular entertainments. An illustration on a Panathenaic vase from the sixth century BC and found at Caminus in Rhodes shows two horses being guided by a rider, probably an acrobat, who has leapt on to the horses using a springboard and is evidently entertaining the spectators, who sat on tiers of benches. A spectator shouts 'Bravo, fine tumbling', while another figure is using a rake to smooth the sand covering the arena. Although equestrian entertainments were well established long before the Greeks had adopted the horse, small-scale entertainments such as that depicted on the vase more probably evolved from the training of both horses and riders in public places which attracted spectators. The athletic feats of the riders handling the partly broken and spirited young horses must have suggested the scope to generate extra income by giving displays of their skill and daring.

An essential part of the breaking process was teaching the horse to stand to be mounted, and this was especially important in a horse destined to become a cavalry mount since if a rider fell off in battle his life might depend on his horse standing to be remounted. It had to learn to be mounted 'Persian-style' by a leg-up, or by a groom or slave kneeling by the horse as a human mounting block, and some were taught to lower their backs by stretching their legs out front and back or bending the knees or dropping one shoulder. A horse lowering its back or 'settling' is shown on a frieze on the Parthenon, as are mounting blocks which were common in Grecian streets. Other mounting methods taught at the initial breaking stage included mounting from a spear used as a vaulting pole with a foot loop part-way up the shaft, or even from a light rope ladder thrown over the horse's back.

Although Xenophon's instructions are more concerned with the further schooling of the horse than the initial breaking, his advice of 'reward him with kindness after he has done as you wish, and punish him when he disobeys' could be equally relevant to both. The voice was used extensively to calm the horse if he became excited or anxious, or to 'rouse him by clucking', although if this was insufficient the Greeks had simple rowel-less goad spurs which fastened to the heel by straps over the instep and under the sole. The heel goad was used by most horse cultures from the Etruscans to the Persians, as a whip would have been awkward for a mounted warrior carrying weapons. Pointed hand prods derived from the ox goad of earlier times were sometimes used when training horses from the ground, and the Greek kentron may have taken the form of a bident or trident, the latter being traditionally carried by Poseidon, the god who according to mythology created the horse. Armenian graves of this period have yielded socketed bronze bidents, and even earlier pit graves and catacomb graves were found to contain simple hooked goads when excavated.

PSYCHOLOGY AND EQUITATION

The Greeks' studied approach to horse breaking is revealed in stories from their folklore and history which suggests an understanding of equine psychology applied to dealing with problem animals. Thales, one of the seven wise men of Greece, reputedly had a pack mule which carried salt and which had to cross a wide but shallow river on its daily journey. One day the mule stumbled and fell while crossing the river, and lay long enough for the salt to dissolve. Thus relieved of its load the mule got up and went on its way, and having learnt this ploy to unburden itself began lying down in the river every time it crossed. Having considered the problem, Thales loaded it with sea sponges which, when the mule lay down, absorbed so much water that the animal could hardly struggle to its feet afterwards, curing itself of the habit.

More famous is the tale of Bucephalus, a fourteen-year-old black stallion with a white star and a wall eye, purchased from a Thessalian horse dealer called Philoneicus by Philip of Macedonia in 343 BC. According to both Plutarch and Pliny, the purchase price was the equivalent today of over £10,000, but the absurd price they quote was probably merely intended to imply that it was a horse of great value, well trained for warfare and, because of its age, presumably very experienced too. The horse had evidently not been tried before purchase and, according to Plutarch, when brought before the king, 'He would neither allow anybody to mount him, nor obey any of Philip's attendants, but reared and plunged against them all, so that the king in a rage bade them take him away for an utterly wild and unbroke brute.' The king's twelve-year-old son, later to become Alexander the Great, noticed that the horse was afraid of its own shadow and, turning the animal's head towards the sun, ran along-side him as he moved off and leapt on when he was in motion. Plutarch, writing of Alexander's success said, 'Feeling the bit gently with the reins, he restrained him, without whipping or hurting him, until he saw that the horse had giving up all threatening behaviour . . .' The king took what he had seen as a premonition of his son's greatness while Bucephalus, whose name meant ox-head but referred to his type rather than his conformation, carried Alexander for much of his military career and eventually died at the age of thirty in 327 BC. Apparently, the horse would permit a groom to ride him bareback but when 'saddled' with the thick saddle cloth and girth of the period would only permit Alexander on his back, bending his knees without command to help Alexander mount. He was suppos-edly unmanageable by any other.

THE HORSE IN THE ROMAN EMPIRE

The Romans were not as skilled horsemen as the Greeks and even appeared to show some reluctance to adopt the horse, preferring to use the services of horse-owning mercenaries as cavalry rather than train their own. In 176 AD, for example, a contingent of Sarmatian horsemen, the tribe who had driven the Scythians from their home-land, were recruited along with their own mounts to serve in Britain. The Roman empire incorporated some of the best horse-breeding regions of the time and so they had access to a wide variety of horses as well as to the knowledge and skills of the horsemen of the countries they annexed to the empire. After the Punic wars, Roman horse breeding escalated in response to the demand for horses for sport, and by shipping horses of Numidian breeding to the Iberian peninsular this region of the empire became the centre for the production of the best quality horses. Vegetius himself said the Spanish horse 'excelled all others for the circus'.

Following the example of the Greeks, the first Roman cavalrymen had had to supply their own broken horses but as the cavalry grew in size horses were requisitioned from all parts of the widening empire, Germanicus taking all suitable horses from Gaul and others emulating him elsewhere. Size was a quality much prized by the Romans in a horse, even though the riders they sat on them were not especially tall. Vegetius said that cavalrymen were not to measure less than 5 feet 8 inches although shorter men were sometimes recruited. The best warhorses were Friesan, Burgundian or Thuringian which could stand up to fifteen hands high. Roman writers affirmed that some breeds were 'gentle to ride, obedient to the bit' while others were 'high mettled'. North African horses were renowned for their quiet nature, and Strabo, a geographer by profession who often commented on equine matters, described them as 'small, obedient and swift'.

During the Punic wars the Romans commandeered and confiscated huge numbers of horses from Gaul, the Iberian peninsular and other parts of the empire, while Livy wrote of 4,000 Apulian horses rounded up for breaking by the opposing Carthaginian cavalry. Such figures may seem exaggerated but the mortality rate for cavalry horses was very high and it was only because the herds from which such animals were drawn were so large that the use of cavalry was able to expand so rapidly. As early as the third century BC a Syrian ruler called Seleucis Nicator maintained a royal stud of 30,000 mares and 300 stallions and employed horse breakers full time to transform the wild young colts into cavalry mounts. There were herds of vast size throughout Parthia, Media, Armenian and Persia, and Herodotus wrote of a provincial governor in Assyria who reputedly

had 16,000 mares and 800 stallions plus warhorses, the latter probably meaning broken young horses from the herd ready from the
battlefield.

HORSE BREEDING AND EARLY HANDLING

With the selective breeding of horses in maintained herds, it was
usual to breed from a mare every other year only, and Columella, a
gentleman farmer and writer, verifies this by saying 'a well-bred
mare should be mated on alternate years, so the foal produced will be
stronger from the milk received'. Common working mares, however,
were bred from annually, the foal running alongside the mare as
soon as she was returned to work. Another Roman writer, Varro, in
his work on farming techniques and management, said that foals
should not be weaned until they were two years old, adding that foals
should be regularly handled 'so that they may not be wild after they
are separated', and evidently advocating the frequent handling of
youngstock. Mares were often foaled in stables but, according to
Varro, should be turned out when the foals were around ten days old
or the dried horse manure pulverised into powder and used for bed-
ding, and to help give the horse a shiny coat, could burn the foal's
hooves. Stabling often took the form of stalls bedded with powdered
manure, straw or chaff, and fitted with mangers and tying rings on
the walls. In cold weather the doors were shut and a brazier lit to
keep the building warm. Loose boxes were also used as well as loose
yards. Hard feet were highly prized in any horse, as shoeing was just
in its infancy and a footsore horse would be unable to work. Leather
shoes made from rawhide soaked in water, pulled around the hoof,
tied and left to harden to shape, were known to have been used by
Alexander the Great's Companion Cavalry, among others, and both
Pliny and Catallus described their use, suggesting they were quite
common. Hipposandals made of reeds or tough Sparta grass were
also used but with poor results, although leather boots with metal
soles were a little more successful. Pelagonius, a veterinary surgeon,
emphasised that 'the soundness of the feet is of prime importance'
and recommended a floor of wooden planks for the stable. Some
horse breeders sent their brood mares and foals to graze on dry rocky
high ground in summer in the belief that the terrain would help to
harden the foals' feet.

ROMAN HORSE BREAKING

At five months old the foal was brought into the stable regularly to be fed 'a ration of barley meal whole with its bran, or any other produce of the earth which he will eat with appetite'. Grain in Roman times had a very high nutritional content. Cereals in Roman times produced a much smaller crop but on longer stems than present day much-improved grain varieties, but the nutritional content of each grain was higher than is the case today.

Varro recommended that bridles were hung in the stable for the young horse to see so that he 'may get accustomed to the sight of them', and he expected the horse to be well handled when it came to be backed as a three-year-old, for he says: 'when the colt has learned to come to an outstretched hand you should put a boy on his back, for the first two or three times stretched out flat on his belly, but afterwards sitting upright'. Like many others, Varro advised giving the horse a purgative prior to breaking, which may have been to cleanse the system or possibly worm the horse but more likely was to quieten the horse by making it feel temporarily ill or debilitated. A common purgative consisted of pulverised pannax root, honey, mustard and oil, with the horse's barley sprinkled with salt water afterwards.

Varro disagreed with those who broke their horses at eighteen months of age on the grounds that they were not mature enough for work, and Virgil shared this view, believing that training should be undertaken gradually, beginning with putting a soft rope bit in the horse's mouth when it was weaned as a two-year-old but before it knew its own strength. Pelagonius also thought a horse should not be broken until it was three but he was speaking of race horses which were not raced until they were five-year-olds, and he thought horses for general riding, driving or pack work could be broken as two-year-olds. Palladius, whose advice was often as outlandish as it was baseless, contradicted the logic of most Roman writers when he said that horses should not be handled at all until they were two-year-olds, at which point they should be broken. Although it was customary to leave horses for war entire and to encourage them to be aggressive, as Varro said, 'we prefer to have them quiet on the road. Castration effects this.' Those animals that were gelded were operated on prior to breaking.

Although much of what these writers said was basically sound and showed some empathy with and consideration for the horse, the Romans were generally inclined to be cruel and rather brutal in their treatment of animals. Virgil, having emphasised the need for a soft bit for a young horse so as not to hurt his mouth and frighten him, contradicts his sympathetic approach by advising that the young horse be put on half-rations during breaking, saying: 'when they're broken in, fill out their bodies with coarse mixed mash, for until you break them, their hearts are too high flown, they jib at handling, refuse to bear the lash or obey the cruel curb'. Many breakers disregarded Virgil's advice about mouthing and broke their young horses with curb bits fitted with high ports, long cheeks, and discs and spikes on the mouthpieces. Even Roman snaffles could be very severe with harsh twisted mouthpiece sections and attachments to increase their severity, and some Roman bits were so fanciful that some of the horse's teeth had to be drawn to get them into the mouth. Another control device the Romans favoured was a type of hackamore of metal construction called a psalion, from the Greek word for scissors, which resembled a drop noseband but was strapped to the bit, bringing great pressure to bear on the horse's nose. Such devices resulted in animals which were under absolute control but which carried their heads almost vertically to alleviate the pressure from the action of the curb and psalion.

Young horses were often broken in a large circular outdoor ring called a gyrus which had high sides to help focus the animal's attention and block outside distractions. Virgil credited the Greeks with the invention of the gyrus, and mentions them more than once in connection with the training of cavalry horses. They were certainly used in many parts of the Roman empire. One discovered and excavated at Baginton in Warwickshire was over 1200 square yards in size and therefore large enough to accommodate several animals being broken at one time. Its box-like entrance was also large enough to hold a number of horses, presumably all awaiting training, and its circular shape would have encouraged continuous forward movement while offering the animal no corners to seek refuge in. It is possible that the Romans practised a form of early lungeing using these round breaking pens, and they certainly long reined horses in them, with the long reins passing between the two pommel horns on the saddle.

Different styles of breaking

Horse breakers themselves fell into a number of discrete groups whose work was specifically for either the army, the circus, the race track, or other more mundane employment. Varro implies that horses were sometimes broken by their intended user, so the experienced cavalryman broke his horse one way while the circus rider broke his another.

Military breakers were either members of the cavalry who were assigned to this important but very time-consuming work, or they belonged to a band of professional breakers working for the cavalry on a contract basis. Like all army nagsmen they had to work with all types of horses as well as draught and pack mules, producing acceptable results within stringent time scales. As such, their methods were necessarily often rough and ready, but they usually did not break animals until they were between three and four years of age as, once backed, the animals would be required to go into work immediately, and to learn while they worked.

Virgil, writing of cavalry and race horses in his *Georgics*, says that before breaking really gets underway the trainer should get the horse used to 'bear the squeal of dragging wheels, and hear the jangle of harness in stable'. It was also necessary to get young horses used to unusual sights and sounds, for the battlefields of the time were extremely noisy and frightening places. During the civil wars both Pompey and Caesar had problems because their horses were frightened of elephants, and they had elephants specially brought in so that their horses could get used to their appearance and smell. This was not a new practice, for when Perseus of Macedonia fought the Romans his horses were terrified of the Roman elephants and, being unable to acquire the real thing, he had life-size model elephants constructed which his horses were paraded past until they lost their fear. Saturating a young horse with the thing that it is frightened of is common in many forms of horse breaking, and the Romans accustomed their young horses to drums, waving weapons, shouting, and other aspects of mock battle scenes as part of their education. Cavalry horses also had to learn to stand in a picket line for this was the accepted method of securing horses when an army was on the move. A watchman was posted not only to keep an eye open for the enemy but to check that no fights broke out between the horses – a not uncommon occurrence when most of the animals were stallions – and that none of the horses became entangled in their tethers. Because of the high injury rate for cavalry horses, there were special veterinary hospitals for sick and wounded animals maintained by the army as well as veterinarians working privately. Minor injuries would be treated by the cavalryman himself using specially prepared salves and ointments or traditional cures like grated pomegranate rind for abrasions.

Private owners sometimes left the breaking of young horses to their own grooms, some of whom must have been reasonably well-educated, for Varro comments that grooms should keep diseases and their treatments written out for reference. Thus, grooms had to be able to read, which means they could have read the works of the great Roman writers on equine handling, although it was not always sensible advice. Secundus in his *Natural history* recommended: 'a mule can be checked from kicking by rather frequent drinks of wine'. Many breeders sold their youngstock at riding age and if an animal was broken and relatively quiet it would have commanded a higher price. Although the Greeks taught their horses the walk, trot and gallop as riding gaits, the Romans called trotters *tortores* meaning torturers or *successatus* meaning shakers, and preferred the lateral pace or amble which they taught by hobbling the horse's near fore to its near hind, and the same on the other side, preventing the animal from moving diagonally.

According to Berenger, writing in 1771, the Romans also tied rollers of wood on the pastern joints to compel horses to lift their feet so they were 'sufficiently high-stepping for desired elegance of form'. There was a tendency to overwork young horses to keep them manageable, and many writers commented that ailments were often caused by hard work after periods of idleness. Columella recommended the excessive hard work and repetitive routine of work in a mill as a cure for unruly stallions. Roman law decreed that damages were payable for negligence on the part of a horse breaker resulting in an animal getting out of control, even if the breaker was not negligent, but simply not strong enough to hold on to the animal. Once broken, horses were sold under a warranty, which was a legal document similar to that covering the sale of slaves, which for legal purposes were classed alongside horses. The Roman deed of sale included a clause indemnifying the purchaser against any claims for damage the horse may have done prior to purchase. As both Varro and Pelagonius wrote about these warranties, it can be assumed they were in common use at the time.

THE HORSE IN SPORT

The most lucrative field of horse breaking was for use in the circus and race track, both of which employed thousands of horses every year. Most horse-owning civilisations had used the horse in some form of sport, and the Persians had hippodromes for mounted games and races from the sixth century BC, possibly having copied the idea from India. The Persians introduced the idea into Greece, and Blundeville, writing in 1558, said: 'Xerxes, on hys comming into Greece, made a runnyng of horses in chariots to be proclaymed in Thessalia, because hee wolde have hys horses to runne wyth the best in Greece.' Such challenges led to organised chariot races and their inclusion in the Olympic games in 776 BC, the first year the winner's names were recorded. The races were run in the open air with the two ends of the track marked with piles of stones or wooden markers, and the prize was the honour of winning, as only garlands of laurel, olive leaves, pine or parsley were presented to the winners although in later times the winner might receive an amphora of olive oil. The opening spectacle of the games was a chariot race of nine miles in length in which up to forty chariots drawn by quadrigas of four horses driven abreast competed, although few finished the gruelling race. There were shorter races for young horses, a synoris or race for harnessed pairs, and in 500 BC a race for mule carts was introduced at the meeting at Delphi but discontinued after 444 BC. In addition there were baton races, and relays involving foot runners and chariot horses. The Romans copied chariot racing from the Greeks, turning it into a national sport. Their brutal circus entertainments, encouraged and popularised throughout the empire, involved large numbers of horses, both completely wild as well as broken and trained, and the breaking and supplying of animals for these gory spectacles made many dealers into rich men.

The Roman circus
The magnitude of the Roman circuses is hard to imagine but, as one ancient chronicler commented, Rome's 150,000 unemployed were

only interested in 'dole bread and circuses'. In Rome alone the Colliseum could accommodate 50,000 spectators, while the famous Circus Maximus which originally had capacity for 150,000 in Caesar's time had extended its provision to 380,000 by the fourth century AD, with the arena measuring 2,121 by 404 feet and incorporating a central raised bank called a *spina* around which the track ran. On the *spina* seven huge bronze dolphins, a tribute to Neptune, the god of horses, which spurted water through their mouths were used as lap markers by being tipped forward each time the runners had completed a full circuit of the track. Twelve starting gates called *carceres* and operated by a lever were arranged at one end of the arena, and Ovid wrote of chariot horses impatient behind the *carceres* door. The track, which was covered in a mixture of yellow sand and cedarwood sawdust, was raked between races by teams of mules pulling harrows. As Suetonius wrote: 'Such a throng flocked to all these shows that many strangers had to lodge in tents pitched along the road, and the press was often such that many were crushed to death.' Once in the stadium some spectators got so excited that, according to Dio Chrysostomos, a second-century AD writer, some would sink to 'flinging their clothing at the charioteers and sometimes even departing naked from the show'.

Under the Emperor Augustus twelve races were run each day, but this was increased to twenty-four by Caligula, the mad emperor, with races for from two to ten horses driven together (although four was the usual number). Sometimes even the emperors drove. Nero once took the reins of a ten-in-hand at a race meeting in Greece but fell out of the chariot and slaves had to heave his overweight body back into the vehicle so that the race could continue.

Even the young were obsessed with chariot racing, and children were reported driving around the courtyards of their fathers' villas in toy chariots drawn by sheep, goats and dogs, while Horace wrote of small boys 'harnessing mice to a little cart'. Tacitus, decrying the decadence of Rome, said youths were more interested in chariot racing than study, adding: 'Really I think the passion for horses is all but conceived in the mother's womb . . . few indeed are to be found who talk of any other subject.' Other parts of the Roman empire also had their race tracks and circuses, there being around twenty-five in Roman north Africa, and another twenty-one in the Iberian peninsular. The Byzantine empire had its arenas too, the most palatial being the hippodrome in Constantinople which was based on a Roman design and constructed of imported marble with seating for 60,000 and a spina adorned with ancient works of art like the obelisk from the Temple of Karnak put in place in 390 AD.

Many of the large-scale professional horse breakers who supplied the race tracks and circuses were also dealers, and we know from the writings of Pelagonius that dealers from Sicily and elsewhere were very active, especially at these sporting events where they congregated to solicit business. Their biggest customers were generally members of the ruling senate who were responsible for staging the games to entertain the masses and drum up support for themselves. Because of the wastage and subsequent high cost of such events, large numbers of cheap horses were required and the dealers responded by breaking quickly and inadequately any horses they could get their hands on. Their methods were not surprisingly rough, but as people wanted to see thrills and spills, the terrified boltings of half-wild teams which ended in accidents and collisions delighted the crowds. There were even cases of wild horses turned loose in the arena where slaves had to rope them and try to harness them to chariots, usually with dire results, and wild-horse hunts in the arena were another popular entertainment. The professional animal catchers across the empire were kept busy rounding up wild herds to supply the demand, and a third-century AD mosaic, now in the Museé Archeologique d'Hippone in Algeria, shows mounted catchers chasing wild horses with lassoes.

Charioteers and horse breakers

Many of the men who broke horses for these sporting spectacles were ex-charioteers or circus riders who because of age or injury were no longer able to continue in their previous career. At the height of the Roman empire, the average lifespan for a charioteer was between twenty-five and thirty years. Few survived as long as Diocles who, beginning at the age of eighteen in 122 AD and for the next twenty-four years, drove in 4,257 chariot races, winning 1,462 of them. As Juvenal said, a teacher had to work for a year to earn what a successful charioteer got from one race. Many charioteers were of very humble birth, sometimes even slaves who won their emancipation through their skill as horsemen. For example, Basil the Macedonian was found naked and starving on the steps of the temple and presented to a wealthy citizen for whom he 'tamed fierce horses', earning his eventual freedom. Social status in the Roman world could be gained by skill as Pliny commented when he pointed out that the official who supervised Rome's grain supply 'was descended on his father's side from a tribe that went about in skins'.

Some charioteers, having enjoyed success on the race track, were fortunate and progressed to breaking and training horses for wealthy owners who could afford to lavish great care and attention on their prized animals. Owners who sent their horses to such people for breaking were perpetuating the tradition of putting horses out for breaking rather than doing the job at home, and in class-conscious Roman society horse breaking was always deemed a lowly occupation. The chance to better themselves in life was a great motivator for slaves who had any aptitude for working with horses, but it also made them ruthless and cruel in their methods although this generally was only a reflection of the treatment they were used to themselves. Pliny was sure that 'the love of glory and the desire to win inhabited the bodies of even slaves and criminals', both of whom could win freedom through sporting success, but those who were successful became conceited and arrogant. The epitaph for one young charioteer at Delphi reads: 'I am Scorpus, the pride of the noisy circus. But alas! short was the time Rome could applaud me; when I reached thrice nine years, I was carried off by a jealous Fate who, counting my victories, believed that I was old.'

Training the Roman chariot horse

The Campus Martius, a mile from the Circus Maximus, was where most of the horses destined for this arena were picketed. The camp incorporated the Trigarium where animals were trained and exercised, and in the run-up to major events the camp bristled with activity. Slaves employed by many of the trainers to break horses eagerly awaited opportunities to help in the main arena as mounted *jubilators* with whips who urged the chariots on, or as *agitators* who did the same job but on foot which was more dangerous, and even more perilous was the work of the *sparsors* who were required to run into the path of the racing chariots to throw water over the smoking wheel hubs. A third-century AD Gallic mosaic, now in Lyons, shows these personnel at work. More usually, these slaves worked with young horses, preparing them for the track which, in the case of the well-bred and highly prized teams of the wealthy owners, involved a training period of several years. Race horses began their harness training as three-year-olds but did not make their first appearance on the track until at least two years later. Aulus Teres, a charioteer who listed forty-two successful chariot horses and their breeding, described thirty-seven of them as African, meaning they were probably of Numidian or Libyan breeding. Wealthy owners spared no expense in the training of their finest teams, selecting horses from the best bloodlines, and sending them to the most successful breakers and trainers where they were fed on the best grain with their feeds dampened with honey and wine. Their breaking was carried out slowly and with care, the grooms leading them about to accustom them to everyday sights and sounds before harness was ever put on them. It was a far cry from the sketchy breaking of the scratch teams hastily put together by unscrupulous dealers for less prestigious race meetings.

The breaking harness for all horses was strongly made in special factory-like establishments from the hides of sacrificial or meat cattle and horses and was less ornate than that used for the actual racing, but often incorporated very severe bits. Sometimes the horses had the muscles of their tails nicked to prevent them from flicking them over the reins, and often the tail was docked or bound up out of the way. In a quadriga, only the two middle horses were actually harnessed to the vehicle, the two outside horses being attached only by the reins to the central pair which needed to be very steady and well-trained as they pulled the actual vehicle. The off side horse on the outside (the track always racing anti-clockwise) needed to be a little faster than the rest as he had to go farther, but it was the near side inside horse, called the funalis, who was most esteemed as he had to be able to slow down and corner carefully then speed up quickly so he took most of the strain and had literally to control the rest of the team. Because of his position, he was also in the most danger of being crushed. The teams were trained to obey verbal commands and a flick of the whip so that their transitions were crisp and synchronised, and Homer in his Odyssey writes of 'a team of four stallions on the plain who start as one horse at the touch of the whip, and break into their bounding stride to make short work of the course'. Trained horses for racing or other work were sometimes obtained in other parts of the empire and shipped to Rome, like the 'well-trained horses' Julius Caesar saw in Britain, some of which he brought home, where they found favour with jugglers and other entertainers on account of their small size, docility and intelligence.

Despite the trouble and expense lavished on top-class sport horses, the standard of breaking generally in Roman times was poor, especially for those horses destined to work pulling carts, as pack animals, or turning grain and olive mills. The empathy and understanding the Greeks had for their horses was soon eclipsed by the harsh brutality which characterised much of the Roman's attitude to animals in general, and as horse breaking remained the province of the lowly, ruthless and ignorant, the prognosis for it being elevated to anything more was not promising.

CHAPTER THREE

The Middle Ages

Scarce anything awakens attention like a tale of cruelty

Samuel Johnson

By the time the Roman empire was in serious decline, the ascending powers throughout Asia and into Europe all owned horses and had become skilled at the breaking and riding of them. In common with horsemen from very early times, control was the kingpin around which their horsemanship developed and although the horse bit was, and has remained since, the most effective way of managing a ridden or driven horse, it did not prevent them experimenting with other devices in the hope that such an invention might enable them to achieve the greater control they strived for. For a mounted warrior to use his weapons effectively, especially the bow and arrow, he had to be able to let go of the reins altogether without losing control of his mount, and even with spears, javelins, lances and swords which only necessitated one hand it was imperative that the horse could be stopped and easily turned with the other.

DEVELOPING MORE ADVANCED CONTROL

The Persians had bits with metal cheekpieces that extended down and joined under the jaw, forming an early type of curb, which would explain the overbent head carriage of Persian horses in early art. Although the Greeks never used curbs, the Romans had them after the time of Julius Caesar and some, like the bronze curb bit found at Pompeii, had twisted mouthpieces to add to their severity. As well as a whole variety of bits of varying design and action used by civilisations from the Egyptians to the Etruscans and ranging from crudely made plain snaffles to the bits described by Homer which had purple-stained ivory cheeks, some innovative devices of restraint were tried and tested. Headstalls reinforced with long metal plates with sharp corners which pressed into the sides of the horse's face were used by some horsemen around the Mediterranean, but they probably caused the horse to toss its head and were ineffective. More successful were the nosebands with small metal studs or barbs on the inner surface used by the Parthians and Persians. Any tendency for the horse to raise its head to evade the action of the noseband studs was checked by the use of a martingale, and there is evidence of both martingales and even draw reins used by the Egyptians as far back as 1400 BC, as a depiction of the chariot of Rameses II shows. Arrian, a second-century BC Greek historian, mentioned the use of spiked nosebands by the horsemen of India, saying: 'Their horses are not saddled, nor do they use bits like the Greek or Celtic, but a band of stitched rawhide is fitted around the muzzle of the horse, with bronze or iron goads, not very sharp, turned inwards.' Wealthy people used ivory studs on the noseband. It is likely that the use of such nosebands developed from bit cheekpieces with sharpened nodules on the inner side to encourage the horse to turn when the rein on the opposite side was pulled. An early form of drop noseband was used by the Egyptian charioteers, fitted low on the nose to impede the horse's breathing, although in some depictions it was used on animals with slit nostrils. The practice of slitting a horse's nostrils is very old and is represented on an ancient stone relief from Amarna. The purpose was to allow the animal to breathe more freely as it was believed that, since a horse cannot breathe through its mouth, wide distending nostrils were a sign of sustainable speed and stamina.

North American Indians slit the nostrils on their racing and war ponies, and the Arabs also followed the practice and occasionally still do today. As late as the eighteenth century Hungarian cavalry-men slit the nostrils on their horses to prevent them neighing and giving away surprise attacks. Evidently, slit nostrils did not negate the effectiveness of a drop noseband or the Egyptians would not have used them on animals disfigured in this way. Very broad tight-fitting nosebands were used by the Turks, and muzzles with reins attached were experimented with on particularly unruly stallions, while hobbles remained in constant use with most horse cultures.

HORSEMANSHIP WITHOUT TACK

Against this backdrop of ornate and varied devices for managing horses, it is surprising to find that many horsemen broke their animals using the minimum of equipment and even jettisoned that once the horse was ridable. Lucan in his *Pharsalia* praised the Massylians, who controlled their warhorses with nothing more than a stick, when he wrote: 'Without a saddle the Massylians ride, and with a bending switch their horses guide.' It seems to have been a north-African practice for Livy (59 BC – AD 17) said the Carthaginians, Numidians and Mauretanians all rode with no saddlery and only a stick with which to tap the horse on the face to guide it. Their neighbours, the Libyans, were similar, for Nemesian said of their horses: 'No need to repine at their ugly head and ill-shapen belly, or at their lack of bridles . . .' The Numidians, living in what is now Algeria, Berber neighbours of the Carthaginians, were very skilled horsemen who, according to Strabo, rode small, spirited horses. Numidian mercenaries comprised the bulk of Hannibal's 10,000 cavalry when he defeated the Romans in 218 BC and they were famed then because they rode with neither bridles nor saddle cloths, using instead just a neck collar with a lead rein which they used for tying the animal up or catching it when it was loose. They guided their horses with a light stick and taught them to turn to the right when the stick was applied to the left-hand side of the neck, and vice versa. This early form of neck-reining was augmented by tapping the animal on the nose to stop it, although the command was probably reinforced by the use of the voice and pulling back on the neck collar which fitted high up the neck around the throat. In one military operation in Liguria, eight hundred Numidian mercenaries were used by the Romans, and Livy commented on them in his work, *The history of Rome*. 'Both men and horses were of a small size and thin make, the riders unaccoutred and unarmed, excepting that they carried javelins in their hands; and the horses without bridles, and awkward in their gait, running with their necks stiff and their heads stretched out', he wrote.

Arrian in his *Cynegetica* wrote that Numidian children rode as soon as they could walk and by the age of eight could successfully hunt onagers, riding bareback and guiding their mounts with a 'whip' although the guide stick was never actually used to strike the horse. The children lassoed the onagers after they had tired them by riding after them. The horses of north Africa were renowned for being quiet to handle, which may partly explain how this curious method of control originated. Claudius Aelionus said the horses of Barbary, the coastal area of north Africa conquered by the Arabs in the seventh century, were 'so tame that they can be ridden without a bit or reins and can be guided simply by a cane, so that only a lead rope is necessary on the halter'.

Breaking and training horses to be ridden without any tack had many advantages. In battle, enemies often tried to remove their opponent's bridle by slashing at the poll of the horse with a sword so that the bridle fell off, taking the rider's control over his mount with it. Also, only riders conversant with this unique method of riding could handle horses trained to be ridden without tack, making such animals difficult for enemies to steal in battle and not a lot of use to them when they had got them. As many of the Numidian horsemen were professional mercenaries working for the Romans, Carthaginians or anyone else who would enlist their services, horses which did not have to be saddled and bridled meant a saving in time if the mercenaries were called to arms at very short notice.

NUMIDIAN HORSE BREAKING

The Numidians and their neighbours broke and trained their horses initially with bits and bridles, and there is plenty of evidence to show this, including a fourth-century BC vase bearing an illustration of Numidian horsemen riding with conventional tack. Mules were always worked with bits and bridles, and it was only the esteemed horse which received the specialised additional training so that it could be guided with only a stick. The system was to use a tap from the stick in conjunction with the voice and reins during training, eventually dispensing with use of the reins although they remained in case of emergencies, and only when the animal was obedient and responsive to the stick was the bridle dispensed with altogether. As a style of riding it continued in use for centuries, and Plutarch wrote of Julius Caesar riding without a bridle. Geoffrey Gambado, riding instructor to the Doge of Venice, writing in 1787, alluded to this when he wrote: 'How Julius Caesar stopped his horse, when he rode with his hands behind him, I am at a loss to divine.'

At the time of Muhammed (570–632), Arabs were reported to be riding with neither bridles nor saddle cloths, using only a short stick and neck strap, and Richard Berenger in *The history and art of horsemanship*, published in 1771, spoke of Turks riding with a three-foot long stick used to tap the horse on the left or right to direct it. It is possible that the tradition, which was Arabic in origin, began with the carrying of a stick or staff as a symbol of honour or status. For eighteen-century Bedouins it was the mark of a sheik, but in early times it probably denoted a person of wealth and position who owned livestock as the staff had another more functional purpose. The staff was originally quite long with a crook end which was used to catch the noserings or halters of camels and horses, so only a person of wealth and status would have carried one. A decorated Greek drinking cup dating back to the fourth century BC and depicting cavalrymen and their mounts being examined shows a hipparch or phylarch, possibly of the troop being examined, carrying a staff with a crook end, the length of the whole stick being at least four feet. When riders began to carry staffs, probably to catch loose horses at first then as a means of guidance, the length of the stick was reduced to manageable proportions.

At the time of the Norman invasion of Ireland in 1172, the invaders were surprised to find the Irish riding with no saddles or bridles, only a simple halter with a lead rope and a stick with a crook at the upper end uncannily similar to those used by the Arabs. Giraldus Cambrensis said of them: 'They drive on and guide their horses by means of a stick with a crook at its upper end which they hold in their hand.' This apparent Arab custom was assumed to have been introduced into Ireland by the Phoenicians who, in the opinion of Julius Caesar, had preceded the Roman invasion of Britain in 55 BC by some years. Many believe the Phoenicians, who were great horse traders, also brought horses of eastern blood to Britain. The tradition of riding with only a stick has survived to the present day and north-African donkey riders can still be seen guiding their bridle-less mounts with nothing more than a short length of cane.

THE EVOLUTION OF SADDLES

Developments in the design of saddles greatly strengthened the effectiveness of horsemen as riders, giving them greater security of seat when breaking and riding young horses. The Scythians had a form of primitive saddle without stirrups and Herodotus wrote of them suffering swelling and discomfort in the legs as a result of riding. Most other civilisations had only saddle cloths of sufficient thickness to protect the rider from the discomfort of sitting on the horse's spine, although the statue of Alexander the Great sculpted by Lysippus around 334 BC shows him sitting on a saddle cloth fitted with a surcingle and a breast strap. It is likely that both the Greeks and Romans began using saddle cloths with girths, breast straps and, sometimes, quarter straps, around the fifth century BC, although on the one hundred and twenty-seven feet high column erected by the emperor Trajan in AD 114 no saddles are shown at all, but this may be artistic licence. Galen, writing about the Roman cavalry in 170, said that the men complained of pain in their legs, the stirrup not yet being in use.

Roman riders evidently felt less secure on horseback than their more skilled contemporaries, including the Greeks, which may have explained why they preferred to use mercenaries rather than ride into battle themselves. Roman race riders gave themselves more grip on horseback by tying themselves to the girth, a practice which bears some similiarity to the charioteers who tied the driving reins around their waists in races and carried a knife with which they hoped to cut themselves free in case of accidents. The Romans eventually developed a simple wooden framed saddle, covered in leather and girthed over a thick saddle cloth, which they termed a *sella* from the Latin word for seat. Later Roman saddles had four horns, one at each corner of the seat, to give the rider something to brace himself against when handling weapons.

As the word 'saddle' has often been used to translate the term 'saddle cloth' in ancient documents, such records can be confusing. The reference in II Samuel 17:22 where Ahithophen 'saddled his ass' referred to the thick saddle cloths donkey riders used. They also sat well back on the animal's croup as it was more comfortable and gave the rider a little more height, which was often necessary if the rider was tall and his mount rather undersized. Xenophon commented that 'a double-back is easier to sit upon', signifying that a horse with the muscles on either side of the spine raised above it was more comfortable. Nigerian riders of more recent times were known to slit their ponies' backs with a knife so that calloused ridges formed, giving the rider something to grip to.

Nomadic invaders from the steppes are generally credited with introducing the saddle into the Roman and Byzantine empires where the idea was soon developed, and the first true saddle made its appearance in the fourth century. Some historians believe the riding saddle may have developed from the camel or pack saddle, but whatever its origins it was quickly adopted by most horse cultures.

Stirrups
Of equal significance to horsemen, and horse breakers in particular, was the invention of the stirrup. It began life with Asian horsemen who sewed loops of leather to their saddle cloths to support their legs on long journeys and to give them greater security and grip. Long before saddles were invented, the Magyars of what is now Hungary were using heavy saddle cloths without girths but with stirrups attached by short leather straps. Indian sculptures of the second century BC depict the use of foot loops which may have been used for mounting only or may have been for general riding, and others used simple toe loops or even a knotted rope which was gripped between the toes and which eliminated the danger of the foot becoming entangled in the loop and the rider being dragged. An early Roman poem tells of a man dragged to his death with his foot in a leather loop, from which it is reasonable to assume that the man was a foreigner and most likely a mercenary, as the Romans did not have stirrups of any type at that time. Early in the first century the stirrup as we know it was in use in China, but it was not until five centuries later that Attilla's Huns introduced it into Europe where it was in general use by the ninth century.

Little, if any, tack was specifically developed just for the breaking of horses, with perhaps the exception of keyed breaking bits by the Greeks. Lassoes, hobbles, drawreins, studded nosebands, martingales, muzzles and other devices were as much a part of general horse management as the tools of the horse breakers who also used them.

STEPPE HORSE BREAKING

The steppe horsemen from the Cimmerians, Scythians and Sarmatians through to the Quadi, Alans, Huns, Goths, Slavs, Avars and Bulgars all broke their horses by a similar method handed down through the generations and little changed as their lifestyles

Some horses were so vicious they had to be muzzled during breaking.

remained comparatively constant over the centuries. Vegetius, writing in the fourth century, said the horses of the Huns were quiet, learned easily, and were not difficult to break, although he also said they were thin and ugly but endured cold, hunger and wounds well. His words suggest animals that were not particularly fit and which were hard worked to keep them tractable. The Magyars, active around 800, were still breaking their horses using methods developed by the Scythians over 2,500 years earlier, and it was not until the emergence of the Mongol empire, which at its peak stretched from China to the Danube making it the largest empire in the world, that strict rules were laid down governing the breaking of horses and other aspects of horse management.

Genghis Khan (1167–1227) became the supreme ruler of the Mongols around 1200, and under his ruthless jurisdiction the empire prospered and grew. The Mongol way of life was similar to that of the Scythians in many ways with the horse central to their culture. They used ox-carts for transporting their possessions when they moved camp, with their vast herds of livestock, including stocky Mongolian ponies now known to be descended from Przevalski horses, under the control of mounted herdsmen. Genghis Khan's Code of Laws stated that horses should be broken as two-year-olds, or even yearlings, then turned away until they were four or five years old as

Mongolian ponies were slow to mature. This method, traditional among steppe horsemen, taught the horse obedience at an early age and before it was strong enough to put up much resistance. Meng Hung, a writer of the period, said this practice resulted in civil behaviour and no kicking or biting. Before being turned away the colts were gelded, one contemporary writer saying this was done as soon as the horse had four permanent teeth. Only the best horses were kept as breeding stallions, one to each herd of 50–60 mares, with the rest being gelded as this made them quieter to handle, less inclined to stray from the herd, and less prone to neigh during ambushes, a major consideration for warring tribesmen. When the horses were rounded up and caught again two or three years after initial breaking, they still remembered their early lessons and were soon ridable again. This protracted system of breaking resulted in horses which stayed sound for longer. This was important for the Mongols who often rode up to eighty miles a day, so an unsound horse could be a liability. Moreover, their horses, which were never shod, also never received any corn or supplementary feed. Through their military conquests the Mongols increased not only the size but the quality of their herds as well. When they ransacked Peking in 1215 they seized most of the Imperial horse herds which included animals of the Ferghana strain first introduced into China by the Emperor Wu Ti in the seventh century BC and described in an official Chinese document of the first century as standing up to sixteen hands high.

Training the warhorse

As the Mongols' military strength grew, they trained their horses specifically for war by getting them accustomed to having a bow and arrow fired from their backs. This was done first by making a slapping sound to simulate the noise the bow makes when released, and when the horse was quite used to this the actual weapon was substituted. The Mongols never used a whip on their horses as the arm movement of drawing an arrow from its case might make a horse think it was going to be struck and leap forward, putting the bowman off his shot. Horses also had to become accustomed to having a javelin or a lasso thrown from their backs.

The Mongol tack was simply a bridle with a thin jointed ring snaffle bit, and a leather and wooden saddle fitted with stirrups and worn over a thick felt pad. The riders never washed but smeared themselves with animal grease instead with the result that writers of the time said the army could be smelled twenty miles downwind. Each mounted warrior had five horses, exchanging mounts as soon as one was exhausted, and the large herd of loose horses which accompanied them on their travels often had dummies stuck on their backs to make it appear to enemies that the army was much larger than it really was. Although dummy horses had been used by the Romans for teaching riding skills, the Mongols appear to have been the first to use dummy riders, and their use on horses broken and turned away would have helped to prevent these animals lapsing into wildness again.

HORSEMEN OF THE BYZANTINE EMPIRE

Byzantine horsemen from the sixth century were also breaking their horses specifically for warfare. Buyers from the cavalry purchased young unbroken horses from their breeders during the winter months, although some were bred at the Imperial stud farms, in readiness for breaking in the spring. Because there was no grazing in winter for an army on the move, cavalry were least active at this time of year when the horses were lean and unfit, and spring was a traditional time for horse breaking before the animals grew fit on the new grass. The early Byzantine empire was rich in horses, but not all were suitable as cavalry mounts as some breeds were noted for their uncooperative or vicious natures. The book of Dede Korkut, compiled in the fifteenth century but commenting on a period up to seven centuries earlier, said that the Kazilik breed from Armenia was not an easy ride and needed a skilled horseman to master it, while the Chahri breed from Khorasan, according to one Turkish writer, 'was very risky to approach' because of its aggressive temperament. Another Turkish writer believed all foreign horses needed harsher handling than home-bred stock. While some horses were bred in loose herds and managed by skilled herders using lassoes and uragas, both of which were still being used as weapons to drag cavalrymen off their mounts in the ninth century, many horses were bred in close proximity to man. Turkish horsemen, who according to a ninth-century writer spent more time in the saddle than on foot, raised and trained many of their horses from foals, and because they rode mares as well as stallions, if a mare was taken hunting her foal followed on behind. Thus the foal became accustomed to the sights and sounds it would encounter in its later working life from a very early age. There are even instances of horses used for hunting which were required to carry cheetahs like pillions behind the saddle, the big cats being used to bring prey down during the hunt.

When the young horse was of breaking age, it was backed and ridden on in a designated breaking ring, similar to the Roman gyrus, which was either covered in soft sand or which had the surface ploughed and harrowed to make it soft to ride on. Deep going was harder work for a young horse and contributed to tiring it sooner.

For breaking, the young horse was initially taught to lead. Abou Bekr, a fourteenth-century Turkish writer, said that a horse would learn to link being led by a groom with being ridden, in that it had to go forward freely in the presence of man. He emphasised gradual training, and believed a cavalryman should train his own horse, as he said a rider could never be safe on an ill-trained horse and that if he did not personally train his charger he courted death. The horse was then fitted with a bridle and a thick pad saddle with stirrups and, if appropriate, was accustomed to wearing armour of chain-link type by first wearing a heavy blanket on its back.

Once the horse was broken and in cavalry service, a large saddle-bag was strapped to the saddle containing essential items for life on the move, including basic rations, spare bowstrings, an awl and strips of fine leather for saddlery repairs, hobbles for grazing the horse in, and a lasso for catching it or other loose horses. It would also be shod with special shoes which had a solid sole with a small airhole. These were designed to help protect the horse's feet from enemy caltrops, three-spike objects made of iron strewn on the ground with the intention of laming the horse by puncturing the sole of the foot.

ARAB HORSE BREAKING

Throughout medieval times and beyond, the Arabs developed their skills of horsemanship to parallel their abilities as breeders of the very finest stock. From around the seventh century, they developed a style of breaking that began with the weaning of foals at three to four months of age, at which time they were tied using a collar and lead rein, similar to that used by the Numidian cavalryman, to one of the tent poles and fed on ewe or camel milk, being weaned on to hay or even dates as they grew older. Unruly foals were hobbled. Men would boast proudly of rearing their horses as members of the family, which was true, for by bringing their foals into the tent and securing them therein the risk of loss through theft was minimised. Perhaps the quietness of Arab horses is in part attributable to living so close to man for so long. An army remount buyer who wrote a book, *Horse buying in Syria*, in 1854, following a visit there to purchase horses for the Crimean war, said of Arab horses: 'being very docile they are easily broken in properly'. Training was gradual, beginning with children scrambling on to their backs as yearlings although the Sahara Arabs left this stage until the young horses were eighteen months old, when children would sit on them when they were led to the watering places to drink. As two-year-olds they wore a saddle and bridle for the first time, and a year later they were ready for proper work. Barbs broke their horses as two-year-olds but, like most muslims, did not castrate their colts as it was prohibited by Islamic law.

Lady Wentworth, writing earlier this century but reviewing the handed-down traditional breaking methods of the Arabs, believed they were good horse breakers as they were patient but, while Arabs valued their horses highly, they worked them harshly once broken and demanded much of them. Miles, writing around 1850, said they broke them after their second year when the horse was mounted for the first time and ridden at full speed for up to forty miles over sand and rock in the heat of the day. It was then swum and if, after all this it would eat as if nothing had happened, it had proved itself. A veterinary surgeon called Osmer, writing in 1761 and comparing other breeds of horses to Arabs wrote that no other breed could 'bear fatigue with equal fortitude as our severe discipline of training will in some measure help to show'. Although Arabs gave their horses little water during breaking as they believed it spoiled an animal's shape and affected its wind, they fed them well on cut grass, corn, dates, and even meat, boiled or raw, which the horses grew accustomed to and ate. During the 1600s, racing horses in Arab countries were sometimes fed oysters and raw eggs to condition them, and they had vinegar spurted into their nostrils to clear the sinuses, a practice still followed today in Indonesia with racing bulls.

During breaking spurs were never used but, once the horse was broken, vicious spurs were worn by the riders. Sometimes shovel-shaped stirrups with sharp corners were used which worked in the same way as spurs. From the very start of breaking, very severe bits were used including ring bits with a short spike or even a shank on the mouthpiece with a circular iron ring attached which pressed up against the roof of the mouth when pressure was applied through the reins. The severe action of the curb bits tended to cause their horses to throw their heads about in resistance to the discomfort they suffered. Some Arabs used a studded noseband instead of a bit for control, and this was adapted into the chain noseband from which the hackamore eventually evolved. Travellers wrote of the highly coloured woollen headstalls, chain nosebands, and single woollen rein passing from the back of the noseband along the left side of the horse's neck to the rider's hands. Some early writers spoke of metal-covered nosebands, which sounded similar to the Roman psalions in action, used by some Arabic tribesman. The Arab saddles were deep seated, giving the rider considerable security especially when riding young horses.

Specialist training

Arabic breaking was focused on producing a riding animal which had confidence in its rider and which was very responsive, as this suited the Arab style of warfare. They trained their horses to halt abruptly and turn sharply, which is why they favoured severe curb bits and never used snaffles, but the prized characteristic of bounding into a gallop from a standstill was achieved through training to respond to the voice as much as through the use of spurs. The verbal command 'ha' which was used as both the signal to burst into a gallop as well as a warcry has been used by horse cultures since very early times. In the biblical book of Job it says of the horse: 'He saith among the trumpets, ha, ha; and he smelleth the battle afar off, the thunder of the captains, and the shouting' which refers to the courage of the horse and the command war horses were trained to respond to. In a cavalry charge the horse is encouraged and emboldened as it is akin to galloping in a wild herd, and military men knew this and used it to their advantage. The Arabs had a wide vocabulary of words connected with breaking horses and the individual processes therein. They also taught their horses to stand still when the reins were thown over their heads to the ground, and to wait to be remounted if a rider fell off. Lady Ann Blunt, an authority on Arab horses and

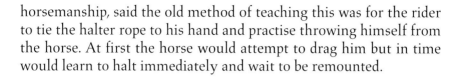

horsemanship, said the old method of teaching this was for the rider to tie the halter rope to his hand and practise throwing himself from the horse. At first the horse would attempt to drag him but in time would learn to halt immediately and wait to be remounted.

THE HORSE IN ANGLO-SAXON BRITAIN

In Anglo-Saxon Britain, horses were considered too valuable for the menial work of ploughing, which was left to oxen, but they were used for general riding, hunting and warfare. Breeding stock and young unbroken animals were grazed on marginal land on the edge of village settlements with the land nearer to the village being used for crops, hay, milch cows and sheep. Only those animals used for riding were kept in an enclosure in the heart of the settlement for ease of access and, as only stallions were usually ridden, place names like Stony Horse Close signify the site of an enclosure for 'stoned' or entire riding horses. Animals for cartage or pack work were invariably gelded. Young animals being broken in were also kept in the 'close' and, as youngstock was grazed away from the village centre in a semi-feral state at all other times, the horse breaker would have been dealing with largely unhandled animals. Winter forage in the form of browse – the collected leaves of deciduous trees – was reserved for sheep, pigs and cattle, so horses were left to fare for themselves all year round with the result that stock was neither large nor robust, and the absence of any form of selective breeding other than survival of the fittest only contributed to the indifferent quality of horses bred. By the end of the winter, the traditional time for horse breaking, animals for training would have been very lean and the actual breaking would have been minimal with the animal put into full work immediately and kept quiet with a regime of hard work and poor keep.

Wealthy people kept their horses in a similar manner with their youngstock little handled prior to breaking. The will of Wynflaed, a land-owning woman who died around 950, stated: 'she bequeaths to Cynelefu her share of the untamed horses which are with Edmaers . . . and Eadwold and his sister are to have her tame horses in common'. Another will, that of Wulfric from about fifty years later, included the grant of 'a hundred wild horses and sixteen tame geldings' to the monastry at Burton, and the estate of Aelfhelm from a similar period includes what are described as harnessed and unharnessed horses. These documents signify the difference in status and value between broken and unbroken horses.

The first royal studs

From the seventh century the horses belonging to successive kings came under the auspices of a supervisor who was employed to maintain the stud, handle youngstock and undertake all breaking with the help of grooms. Most of the horses were kept in loose herds under the eye of a man called a horsewatcher who was responsible for keeping the herd together and protecting it from, among other things, wolves, which were common throughout western Europe, posing a real threat to young or new-born foals.

The Welsh king, Hywel Dda, who died in 950, drew up a set of laws reflecting the importance of the horse in medieval society and giving approximate values of horses at the time. A foal was worth about 6 pence, a two-year-old 48 pence, and a three-year-old 96 pence, although once it was caught and brought to the 'close' for breaking its value increased by another 20 pence implying that this was a time-consuming or skilled task to warrant the extra cost. 'Bridling' a horse, which meant breaking it, only cost 4 pence in comparison. Under the royal laws, if after sale a broken horse was found to be difficult to manage or ride, then the vendor had either to take the horse back or to refund a third of the purchase price. The king himself, like many of his predecessors, kept a sort of Master of Horse who was responsible for all the king's horses including the breaking and training of them. Like other grooms he slept above or very close to the stables or pens where the horses were kept to protect them from possible theft and to monitor their well-being. The first mention of a Master of Horse occurs in the reign of King Alfred (871–901), showing the existence of royal studs even then. A prerequisite of the job was that the Master of Horse, like others employed elsewhere in a similar capacity, received for his personal ownership all unbroken horses amongst those taken in spoil by the king, suggesting that unbroken horses were plentiful and not greatly valued in the wild.

The advent of the knight on horseback

The changing face of warfare transformed horsemanship throughout Europe and led to the introduction of the armoured knight on horseback in the wake of the Norman invasion. Successive defeats at the hands of the Persian and Parthian bowmen had forced the Romans to change from infantry to cavalry centuries earlier, while further west mounted swordsmen had proved their superiority over foot troops time and again. Beginning with the Roman trooper clad in a mail tunic to offer some protection from arrows, the heavily armoured knight of the Middle Ages evolved. The transition had been gradual. Mongol horsemen had worn silk tunics which wrapped around the arrow head and enabled it to be pulled from the wound with the minimum of tissue damage, and Sarmatian horsemen had developed a type of armour in the fourth century consisting of pieces of hoof steamed and straightened and sewn onto a leather body garment. Trajan's column shows Sarmatian warriors wearing such armour, and the Persians had armour consisting of small metal plates as early as 490 BC. By the time of the Norman invasion, the evolutionary process was almost completed, and the Bayeux Tapestry commemorating the Norman victory at the Battle of Hastings in 1066 shows knights on horses of comparatively light build ridden by men carrying their spears overarm. It would have been impossible to carry the spear or lance underarm so the weight of the horse gave it momentum, as the shallow-seated saddle would not have given the rider enough support and he would have been lifted right off the horse. Although deep-seated saddles with high pommels and cantles had been used in earlier times, a fourth-century Roman mosaic from Lincolnshire showing officials' mounts at a chariot race wearing such saddles, they did not come into general use in Europe until the twelfth century, when knights were wearing heavier and more sophisticated armour and their spears had been discarded for lengthier lances. The increased weight of the riders and a very different form of combat meant that a different type of horse was needed, and their breaking and training had to change as well.

The manufacture of saddlery for the knights was a highly skilled operation using only the very best hides which were carefully tanned using dog and pigeon dung until the improved system using oak bark was adopted. Saddlery was expensive, and the importance of the manufacturing trades was recognised by the awarding of a royal charter to the Loriners Guild, who made bits, stirrups and spurs, in 1269, and three years later the Saddler's Guild received its royal charter from Edward I.

The significance of the great horse

A knight in full armour weighed over 400 lbs (30 stones) so a substantial horse was needed to carry him. Although William the Conqueror had ridden an Andalusian at the Battle of Hastings, the more favoured types were the ancestors of the Ardennes, Flemish, Flanders, Percheron, Friesian and Holstein breeds, as size and weight were of great importance. Although contemporary artistic representations of heavy horses suggest they were bigger and heavier than excavated bones would testify, most standing around fifteen hands, the idea was for these horses to intimidate and trample the enemy and they were even shod with heavy studded shoes in front to facilitate this. In the belief that military success in future would depend upon heavily mounted knights, the breeding of 'great' horses became of paramount importance throughout Europe. In Britain where the breeding of such horses was a crown monopoly, it fell upon the ruling monarchs to set up royal studs and breeding programmes with the bulk of the foundation stock being imported from the Low Countries. Along with these imports came the knowledge from more skilled horse cultures of how to manage them. William the Conqueror brought over horses of the Flanders breed, and King John continued the trend by importing one hundred Flanders stallions. Edward II also brought Flemish horses into the country as part of a policy to produce Britain's own breed of 'great' horse, eventually to be known as the Old English Black and on which Henry VIII mounted his cavalry. Other continental breeds imported included Friesians and also Brabançons, a Belgian draught breed, examples of which had been imported since the time of Richard the Lionheart. The horses were bred under the care of the Custodes Equorum Regis or Keeper of the King's Horses in large royal parks like Windsor, Woodstock and Guildford, and used mainly for military purposes but also to a lesser extent for personal use. In 1326 Edward II used six 'great' horses to draw his carriage when he travelled from London to York to go hunting, and Queen Elizabeth I's 'firste chariott' was drawn by six 'great' horses harnessed nose to tail in a single line.

Great horses because of their 'cold' blood were generally much quieter to handle than other breeds, especially those with eastern blood. The Roman chronicler, Tacitus, had noted this when he wrote that Friesian horses were sufficiently docile for unskilled men to be able to handle them successfully. Because of their quietness, they were relatively easy to break, and the type of riding they were required for did not demand skilled or precise training. They were only needed to 'gallop' in short bursts, and this really meant little more than a canter, and for the most part they just trotted or walked. Because of the encumbrance of armour and the weight of the lance carried along the left side of the horse's neck, the knight had to ride with long stirrups and his legs thrust forward so he needed spurs with shanks of up to eleven inches even to reach the sides of his mount. Having little mobility in his armour-encased upper body, stopping or turning the horse was achieved with the aid of very severe curb bits, some of which had cheeks of up to fifteen inches in length, although snaffles were used for most other spheres of horse-manship. The horses were broken and given basic schooling in enclosed arenas or schools where the standard of horsemanship was generally poor.

The controlled breeding of horses led to better handled young-stock and coupled with the inherent quietness of these horses breaking required less skill than it once had. With no literary guid-ance, as none was available and most people were illiterate, and a demise in the handing down of accumulated knowledge as the steppe horsemen had done, ignorance, superstition, fear, witch-craft and cruelty flourished. Many horse breakers had little or no skill at all, and the prevalent belief was that horses had to be subdued by force, with the result that cruelty and bad practice became the norm. Restive colts were sometimes secured in a wooden framework, like a modern cattle crush, called a trave, travus or trave house and left thus imprisoned to settle down before breaking lessons. These narrow stalls were much used, especially on the continent, for securing oxen and horses for shoeing, and were used in Japan and other western countries to hold horses still for grooming or veterinary operations. Chaucer in his *Canterbury Tales* alludes to their popular use when he wrote, 'She sprung as a colt doth in the trave.'

When in order to protect pilgrims from attack in the Holy Land and to try and take Jerusalem back from the muslims, the Crusades began in 1095, the demand for great horses increased. The Knights Templar had their own farms on which they bred horses, broke and trained them for battle. In many cases a knight was allocated a partic-ular horse as a foal and he was responsible for rearing it and eventually breaking it to suit his way of riding. Even if a knight did not break his own horse he was responsible for supervising the person who did, and this system helped develop the special relationship it was deemed a knight should have with his horse. The Rule of the Templars prohibited a brother from loaning among other things muzzles or hobbles, indicating that these pieces of equestrian equipment were still standard to both the breaking and general management of horses at that time. A knight who had a difficult horse could request a change of mount, and this was usually agreed to. Once broken and ready for service, the horses were shipped out to the Holy Land in specially built boats which held twenty-one horses in stalls fitted with ringbolts for tying and under-belly slings for stabilising the horses in heavy seas. Access was through a large ramped opening in the stern, and hay and fresh water were carried for the long journey. Even with these arrangements, many horses were lost at sea and equine contagious diseases affected many others, increasing the pressure on the breeding farms and breakers to maintain the supply.

OTHER ROLES OF THE HORSE IN MEDIEVAL SOCIETY

As the breeding and training of great horses proliferated, so did that of other classes of horses which in the Middle Ages included coursers or racehorses, rouncies or general riding cobs, sumpters or capuls (which were packhorses) and palfreys or light riding horses. The great horse, always a stallion, was only ever ridden in battle. At all other times it was led by a squire mounted on a rouncy while the knight rode a palfrey. Each of these classes of horse was broken and trained differently. The sumpter or capul was usually a gelding, sometimes referred to as a 'curtailed' horse inferring that they were invariably docked. They worked in loose-headed droves of between ten and twenty animals, each carrying up to two hundred weight of goods, and led by a mounted supervisor on a bell mare who wore a brass bell around her neck. Horses of this class were also used in treadmills and for turning capstans. The rouncy was the lowest order of riding horse, being suitable as a mount for servants as well as for the 'wolvers' employed by the great monastic houses to protect their sheep flocks from attack. The palfrey was the most common riding horse and they were used for general travel as well as hunting and hawking. Although trotting horses were stronger and faster if less comfortable to ride, animals which paced laterally were more highly esteemed.

Training the horse to pace

The knowledge of how to train horses to pace had been known from early times. The Chinese and Persians taught horses to pace using cord hobbles, adapted from breaking hobbles, and the Romans also had knowledge of laterally gaited horses, as Secundus wrote of Spanish horses which 'have not the usual gaits in running – but a smooth pace, straightening the near and off-side legs alternately, from which the horses are taught by training to adopt an ambling pace'. Tacitus, writing about first-century mercenaries from Germanic tribes, said they taught their horses to pace by tying the legs together on one side. Before the invention of the stirrup it was a more comfortable riding pace than trotting and even after the advent of the stirrup it continued in popularity. A sixteenth-century English saying was: 'How can the fole [sic] amble when the horse and mare trot.' Although some horses showed an inclination to pace naturally most were taught the gait, and Nicholas Morgan in his *Perfection of horsemanship*, written in 1609, included a chapter devoted to 'The manner to teach a colt to amble without handling' which relied heavily on the foal's natural preponderance to pace. William Browne in his book, *Browne his fiftie yeares practice*, published in 1624, advised teaching the horse to amble with the use of hobbles which he called side-lanyells, the name derived from lanyard or a length of rope and a term still used by north-country shepherds to describe a type of hobble used on sheep to prevent them from jumping out of fields.

Gambading horses

Horses were also broken and trained for processional mounts used for riding into vanquished cities or in celebratory parades. On such occasions the monarch or military leader needed a horse with height, style and great presence to draw the attention of all on-lookers, and the modern term describing someone as being 'on their high horse' derives from this use. An inventory of horses belonging to Algernon Percy, the fifth earl of Northumberland, *circa* 1512, includes 'a curtal for his lordship to ride on out of townes. Another trottynge gambaldynge hors for his lordship to ride on when he comes into townes.' The term 'gambading', which comes from the Italian word *gambado* meaning a curvet, was common in the later Middle Ages but it described a practice dating back to the pre-Christian era. Xenophon advised that the quality of high-stepping and showy action necessary in a parade horse was not present in all animals, and he believed a horse needed supple loins to 'be able to gather the hind legs well in under the fore'. A horse with a light mouth when held back will come back onto its hocks in a prancing manner, he said, adding: 'There are, to be sure, some persons who teach this movement either by tapping the hocks with a rod, or by directing someone to run along by the side and strike him with a stick under the gaskins.' This age-old system was copied by generations of successive horse breakers preparing animals for this specialist work. In ancient times the people of Sybaris in southern Italy trained their horses to dance to flutes, which proved to be their downfall when their enemies, the people of Croton, played flutes as battle was about to commence, making the horses dance and their enemies fall off, leaving them vulnerable to defeat. Arabs in the seventh century, who preferred mares to ride as they believed they had more endurances and also because Muhammed advocated the riding of mares over stallions or geldings, taught their mares to prance for festivals as well as for warfare. They trained them by holding them up on the curb so that they leapt forward, rose on their hind legs a little, backed and leapt again. The horsemen of late medieval times tapped the horse's legs with a stick while the music played so that later, like a dancing bear, the horse associated the music with the stick and danced to cue. At the ascension of Queen Elizabeth I, her henchmen, the name derived from the old English word *hengst* meaning horse, gambaded around her doing high school airs, while in September 1668 Samuel Pepys went to see a dancing horse at St Bartholomew Fair, commenting that the 'dancing mare forgot many things and was beaten by her master who was mightily vexed'. Some dealers and breakers specialised in the breaking and sale of horses for this particular market.

The jousting horse
Alongside the role of the mounted knight in warfare was the tournament, which set off as a training exercise and progressed into a popular sport. It was an opportunity for knights to show off their

skills and the training of their horses, and it followed a long tradition going back to the ancient Greeks. A vase found in southern Italy and now in the Louvre shows a contest at the Panathenaic Festival, around the fourth century BC, with a shield set up and riders galloping past and hurling javelins at it. The tradition continued on through the Roman circuses and into medieval Europe where military training practice became the joust, a sport with blunt weapons, special jousting armour, and lists or central planking to avoid head-on collisions. Professional jousters could make a good living from the sport as they claimed the arms, saddlery and even the horses of the defeated, and a good horse for jousting was worth the equivalent of up to six palfreys. Some jousters also did a little horse dealing or broke animals for other people, and there was an excellent market for them, as even old or injured horses found buyers at the many horse sales and fairs beginning to appear around the country. In 1154, a monk, William Stephanides, wrote of the sale at Smoothfield (Smithfield), saying: 'Every Friday there is a brave sight of gallant horses to be sold. Many come out of the city to buy or look on . . .', and a year later William Fitzstephen commented on the same sale where he said well-bred unbroken young colts were offered for sale. Although jousting survived long after the military value of the great horse was fading, the death of King Henry II of France in a joust in 1559 caused the sport to fall into disrepute and it soon lost popularity.

It was the introduction of gunpowder which caused the demise of the mounted knight and by the end of Elizabeth I's reign the great horse in warfare was virtually obsolete with many studs closed and the horses sold off. The reduction began after the Battle of Poiters in 1356, and carried right on through to Elizabethan times. William of Wykeham, Edward III's Surveyor of the King's Work at Windsor Castle, used the proceeds of the sale of the Windsor great horses to part-fund construction work at the castle. So great was the reduction nationally that in 1588 when England was threatened by the Spanish armada, only 3,000 cavalry could be mustered in the whole kingdom to suppress the expected invasion. Another reason for the disbanding of the heavy cavalry was that a knight on a great horse was a slow and not very manoeuvrable unit, and the heavily armoured crusaders were no match for the swift saracens who rode with short stirrups and bent knees, unencumbered by heavy armour, on well-trained fast horses which were light in hand and mobile. This style of light cavalry was common to tribes all along the north African coast, including the Moors and the Mamluk rulers of Egypt who trained their cavalry horses in special hippodromes while the cavalrymen learnt their skills on model horses before they were even allowed to mount the real thing.

THE MOORISH INFLUENCE ON HORSE BREAKING

When the Moors invaded Spain, they not only brought their style of cavalry to oust the old-fashioned and out-dated knights, they also introduced the Arab style of breaking horses into Spain and also into the French Camargue, a marshy region on the south coast where black cattle and horses are still reared in the old Spanish Moorish tradition. Camargue horses are believed to be descended from Numidian horses introduced into southern France by Flavius Flaccus in the early Christian era, and other horse blood was brought in by the Moors who occupied Provence in 732. Camargue horses were too small for armoured knights, but they were used and still are by the cowboys or *gardiens* for herding cattle. Their riders use a trident, a legacy of Roman influence, which they carry and wield in the style of a lance to help with the herding. They also use a long horsehair lasso which, being too light to use from horseback, they throw from the ground. Their horsemanship is steeped in tradition and includes breaking horses with a hackamore, later changed for a severe curb bit, which shows a strong north-African influence. They also use a snubbing post, a stout wooden post set into the ground to which the young horse is tied in the initial stages of breaking, which derives from the Arab system of tying young horses to the tent pole, and their bits and style of riding show a strong Arabic influence. The Arab style of breaking produced an agile horse ideal for cattle herding which was becoming well established in Spain at that time. Bull-fighting, which had been introduced into the Iberian peninsular by the Romans, quickly gained popularity and was eventually 'exported' to the new world along with the Moorish style of breaking and also cattle herding which developed into ranching. The Arabs also introduced their style of horse breaking into India, which began importing horses from north Africa towards the end of the Middle

Japanese warrior breaking a horse. (Photograph: Negishi Equine Museum)

Ages. The Indian horse breakers copied many practices from the Arabs, and an attendant of Sir T. Roe, writing in 1615, reported on a long-established practice he saw used by the horsemen of eastern India. 'They tye not down their horse-heads when they stand still, as we do, with halters, but secure each horse by two ropes, fastened to their hind-feet, which ropes are somewhat long, to be staked down behind them in tents, or other places where they are kept.'

In other parts of Asia, the method of breaking was closely akin to that of the steppe people from whom it originally evolved. In Tibet, where mares or geldings were preferred for riding, the breaking was done by young men who introduced the young horse to the bit by tying ropes to the rings of the plain snaffle and pulling the horse from side to side, halting it and sending it forward again. This primitive form of long reining was followed by putting a rider up bareback, and then in due course saddling the young horse and riding it with two helpers on foot to assist with controlling it. This method of breaking was common to many parts of Asia, and an eighteenth-century visitor to Siam commented that even on quiet broken horses the officers who rode them needed a slave on either side to prevent them from falling off. In Korea, servants broke the horses to ride but, once quiet, they were ridden only by noblemen, and in Japan it was customary to tie the horse's tail to the girth when breaking to help prevent bucking.

Making the great horse redundant in both war and sport meant that a supply of big, strong and quiet horses was suddenly made available for other purposes including cartage, pack work and agriculture. Although oxen were still more widely used on the land than horses because of relative values and the general esteem in which horses were still held, horses began to be used more extensively. Harnessing methods had improved, but there were still plenty of examples of abysmal horsemanship. In Ireland, the Hebrides and parts of England, ploughs were still tied to the horse's tail as late as the seventeenth century, the overloading and overworking of horses was commonplace, and there were even cases of horses being harnessed to living trees to test their strength.

DECLINING STANDARDS OF HORSE BREAKING IN EUROPE

In Europe, the cruelty of the age extended to horse breaking which was increasingly conducted with little skill or kindness but with a surfeit of abuse and brutality. Severer curb bits, longer spurs, whips, overwork and callous subjugation were the means of instilling obedience into a young horse, and at times such treatment was supplemented with red-hot bars, burning torches, and poles with sharpened tips for the use of assistants when trying to teach the horse forward movement. In his book, *Hippiatrica Sive Marescalia*, first produced in manuscript form in the middle of the fifteenth century and printed as a book for the first time in 1486, Laurentius Rusius recommended:

> The nappy horse should be kept locked in a stable for forty days, thereupon to be mounted wearing large spurs and a strong whip; or else the rider will carry an iron bar three or four feet long and ending in three well-sharpened hooks and if the horse refused to go forward he will dig one of these hooks into the horse's quarters and draw him forward; alternatively an assistant may apply a heated bar under the horse's tail, while the rider drives the spurs in with all available strength.

A French edition of the book was produced in Paris in 1533 and reprinted in 1541, and the book was in circulation as an accepted manual of instruction for nearly two centuries. Rusius also advised the use of a hedgehog skin wrapped around the end of a whip as encouragement for a hesitant horse. He was not alone in the cruelty of his methods for Thomas Blundeville, writing in 1565, suggested that the way to cure a horse that lies down when crossing water was to:

> Cause a servant to ride him into some river or water, not over deepe, and appoint three other footmen with cudgels in their hands, to follow him hard at the heeles into the water, to the intent that when the horse beginneth to lie downe they may be readie to leape upon him, and with the help of the rider to force him to ducke his head downe under the water, so as the water may enter into his eares; not suffering him to lift up his head againe of a good while together, but make him by maine force to keepe it still under, continually beating him all the while with the cudgels, and rating him with lowde and terrible voice; that done, let him onely lift up his head to take breath and air. During which time, cease not also to beate him still upon the head, betwixt the eares; which done, ducke his head with like violence once againe into the water, and then let him rise up upon his feet; and whilst he is passing through the water, let the men follow after, beating him, and rating him all the way, until he be clean out of the water, and then leave, for otherwise it were disorder.

When it seemed that horse breaking was regressing into an abyss of dire cruelty, accepted as good practice and perpetuated through the written word and casual indifference, the Renaissance burst upon Europe, elevating horsemanship into an art, even if breaking was to be slower to emerge from the Dark Ages.

CHAPTER FOUR

New thinking

The colt that's back'd and burden'd, being young, loseth his pride
and never waxeth strong.

Venus and Adonis
William Shakespeare

THE BIRTH OF SCHOOL RIDING

In early sixteenth-century Europe, a whole new philosophy on
breaking, training and riding emerged which was to have a huge
impact on horsemanship for centuries to come. School riding or
training a horse and rider in an enclosed arena evolved partly
from the jousting or tilting yards in which knights had practised
their horsemanship and armed skills, but school riding did not immediately replace tilting. On the contrary, the two appear to have been
practised side by side. While jousting as a sport was going out of
favour, interest in equitation appeared to have been increasing
and, in the spirit of the Renaissance, it was suddenly seen as an
art alongside literature, music and painting. Schools were set up
aimed at teaching riding skills to the European aristocracy, and later
the wealthy, with riding instructors and horse trainers becoming
professionally attached to many of the great households. School riding centred around a high degree of collection, something neither
necessary nor required in a jousting horse, but known and admired
in the Moorish style of riding which had made the armoured knight
redundant.

The foundation of the European schools of equitation heralded a
new approach to training horses, with more emphasis on understanding the aids and how to apply them, more precise control, and
the use of reason and well thought out principles. It necessitated
gradually rethinking over a period of time the age-old methods of
breaking, examining the equipment used, and modifying some that
had been in use for years. The schools offered, for the first time in
centuries, quality training by competent instructors for those who

could differentiate between the genuinely skilled and the inevitable imposters. In addition this period saw the beginning of written instructions, in the form of manuscripts and books being made available after a protracted period when there had been very little, and much of that poor. Even so, it was to take some time for the benefits of the Renaissance to filter down to the unfortunate horses, and even many of the classical riding masters not only practised, but advocated, methods that would be unacceptable today because of their blatant cruelty.

The turning post

Some of the equipment used was well established, such as curb bits, which were essential to get the degree of collection they sought, and they were used in conjunction with rowelled spurs, a riding whip or rod, and a deep-seated saddle to give the rider security of position. One essential and new piece of equipment was the turning post, which was used for both breaking and further training. It comprised a stout post driven into the ground in the centre of the riding manège to which the horse was tied by a length of rope and made to trot or gallop around. While it may have evolved from the snubbing post introduced into Europe by the Moors around 710, there are references to the use of a turning post much earlier.

In India in quite early times a traditional method of breaking a horse was to tie it to a post by a long piece of rope then chase it round until the rope wrapped itself around the post and the horse was brought to a halt. This strange practice bears similarities to the system used in some countries of tying a horse to a tree and compelling it to move in ever decreasing circles until it ends up fast to the tree. In both cases the purpose was to wear down an unbroken animal with the minimum of effort on the part of the horse breaker, as well as teaching it to go forward in response to verbal commands. The turning posts used by the European schools were different, for the posts had a deep ridge cut under the bulbous top of the post into which the end of the rope was tied in a fixed loop so that it slid around. The horse breaker then had both his hands free to walk behind the horse armed with a whip to keep it moving forward. An anonymous instructor writing in England in 1674 said:

> The next thing we shall speak of is the turning-post, which must be smooth and strong, and very well fixt in the center of the straight ring,

Lungeing with one foreleg strapped up, circa *late* 1500s.

then causing some person to stand at the post, give him the right rein of your cavezen to hold about the post, and to walk or trot your horse about the same as oft as you think fit on your right hand; then change your right rein for your left, and do as before; continue this doing till your horse be perfect in every turn.

Evidently this early form of lungeing was well established by that time, and the horsemen of the period were well aware of the importance of working a horse equally on both reins. William Browne, writing in *Browne, his fiftie yeares practice,* published in 1624 but covering a period beginning in 1574, advocated the use of a turning post around which the horse was lunged, but he also advised tying one foreleg up to restrict the animal if it played up and to tire it out more quickly. Two hundred years later American horse tamers used this method with difficult horses, lungeing them with alternate front legs strapped up and sometimes even with bags of sand tied across their backs.

Lungeing and dumb jockeys
Lungeing without the use of a turning post became more widespread in the eighteenth century but it was not an innovation as Aelian,

Long reining a horse fitted with a dumb jockey.

writing in Roman times, said when the Indians broke their horses they 'compel them to go round and round returning to the same point. Now if a man would do this he requires strength of hand and a very thorough understanding of horses. Those who have perfected this try the same method of driving a chariot in circles.' By 1835 when J. G. Peters published his book, *A treatise on equitation*, lungeing was 'recommended by all the best authors on horsemanship as the first and most important lesson for a young horse'. He advised lungeing in a riding house or covered arena of at least sixty yards by twenty yards, 'lofty in proportion, with a good light, and of course very airy', and he emphasised the importance of delegating the job to someone conversant in how to lunge or the exercise would be 'nothing else than merely flogging the poor animal round, until it is perfectly tired'. Whereas in earlier times it had been customary to have the horse tied to the turning post or held by one man while two or three others brandishing whips kept the horse moving, Peters recommended one man on the reins and one on the whip.

Less than twenty-five years later, J. H. Walsh, editor of *The Field*, was advising his readers that the purpose of lungeing was to give the horse exercise in little space while accustoming it to some pressure on the bit by means of a 'dumb jockey'. These controversial apparatuses were originally made of wood with a crupper and fixed side-

Blackwell's patent whalebone and India-rubber dumb jockey and breaking cavesson.

reins, and were left on the horse in the loosebox, yard or small paddock with the intention of developing a good mouth and a pleasing head carriage. Too often they caused horses to lean on the bit and become heavy on the forehand with an insensitive mouth, but the introduction of gutta percha or whalebone examples with flexible arms was believed to minimise this happening. One user wrote:

> We can bear testimony to their valuable action in producing an easy mouth, and checking that tendency to resistance produced by the common leather rein and clumsy wooden apparatus. The yielding nature of the reins and checks is admirable . . . they are also serviceable in frosty weather, in looseboxes, to teach easy and graceful carriage.

Since the late sixteenth century when the original crudely made examples were first used, they were especially popular with dealers and those who needed to break large numbers of horses as quickly as possible, and many stables used one when breaking young horses. Other horsemen abhorred them. J. G. Peters, writing in 1835, insisted that 'To tighten or buckle up the poor animal very short with the snaffle bit rein to the saddle, wooden cross or *l'homme de bois*

Bitting harness fitted for the field.

Bitting harness fitted for the stable or field.

forcing it to a bend of its neck, which it has never been accustomed to before, is opposed to all true principles', and J. Boniface, writing in 1903, supported this view of the dumb jockey, saying: 'This contrivance, advocated by some very expert practical horsemen, is well calculated to ruin the mouth of the new horse.'

Later horse breakers endorsed the criticism, including Captain Hayes who remarked: 'Horses tied up in this manner will seek to relieve the muscles of the head and neck by abstaining as much as possible from bringing the hind legs under the body', while Henry Wynmalen, a twentieth-century dressage expert, deplored them for forcing the horse's head by means of bearing and side-reins into what resembles a position of well-schooled collection, although he conceded that it was understandable why dealers used them. A dumb jockey was seen as a great labour-saving device as its use could save hours of long reining in the breaking process to achieve a horse which at least looked as if it carried itself correctly.

Long reining

Long reining had been practised since Roman times as a means of teaching a young horse to accept the bit and at the same time to respond to verbal commands. Roman tombstones have been excavated depicting images of long reining, suggesting that it was a common practice at the time, and showing that it was done with the long reins passing between the two pommel horns on the front of the saddle and back to the hands of the breaker who walked behind the animal. Such training was probably reserved for valuable horses, like racehorses, and the majority of animals 'mouthed' by having a severe

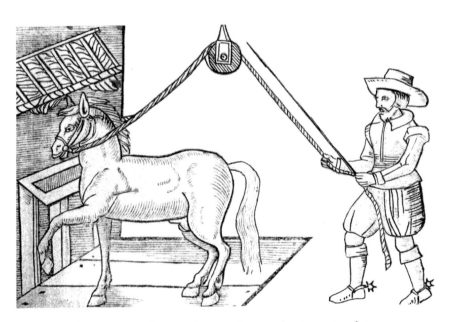

Mouthing a young horse using a pulley mechanism, circa *late* 1500s.

curb bit forced into their mouths at an early stage in breaking and they learnt from experience. Browne used a mouthing apparatus whereby the rope reins went from the breaker's hands through a pulley attached to the ceiling of the stable and down to the rings of the bit in the horse's mouth. The breaker stood behind the horse holding the reins and whip, a position very similar to that used in long reining, and encouraged mouthing by driving the horse forward into its bit. He used a snaffle, but Browne was training horses for general riding and not school work. Two hundred years after Browne, an English horse breaker was still advocating, for the haltering of difficult colts, 'a pulley firmly fastened to one of the rafters in the ceiling' over which the long halter rope could pass and be tied or played like an angler plays a fishing line. It seems curiously similar to Browne's recommended method.

Training pillars

The use of two turning posts spaced a few feet apart between which a young horse was tied by pillar reins from the cavesson or bit rings was another method of mouthing a young horse with the minimum of effort. It could also be used to teach certain high school movements in later training and as a system is still used today by the Spanish Riding School in Vienna among others. Humbler horse

George Bowman, international driving competitor, keeping a watchful eye on young horses being 'mouthed' in pillar reins. (Photograph: Sally Taylor)

Long reining using a riding saddle with the stirrups as rein bearers.

breakers sometimes turned the horse in his stall and tied him between the stall ends with his quarters toward the manger to emulate the effect of training pillars.

School riding demanded absolute control of the horse which needed to be collected to such a high degree that today it would be considered over-bent and behind the bit. Artistic representations of horses of the period in schools emphasise this level of collection but probably show the horses both bigger and more muscular than they actually were although many were literally 'great' horses. By severely over-bitting horses, free forward movement was often difficult to achieve and, even though neither speed nor extension was required, forward movement could often only be attained through the use of sharp spurs and whips. Most breaking and initial training in these schools was not done by one person but by a riding master assisted by two or more helpers, all armed with whips. These whips, or rods as they were more commonly called, apparently only lasted a very short time, evidence of their considerable use, and Lady Aspley in her book, *Bridleways through history*, published in 1936, comments that stable boys in illustrations of the period are often shown carrying whole armfuls of whips. In fact, it was probably one of their main jobs to cut fresh birch and hazel switches for the purpose.

GRISONE AND THE ITALIAN SCHOOL

The first European riding school was founded in Naples by the Italian riding instructor Frederic Grisone whose book, *The rules of riding*, was published in 1550 to great acclaim. Although many of his principles were very sound, his contribution to improving the standard of horse breaking was not great and he believed that 'correction' was central to training a young horse with reward being merely cessation from correction. Grisone wrote: 'In breaking young horses, put them into a circular pit; be very severe with those that are sensitive and of high courage; beat them between the ears with a stick.' Such recommendations were included in his book, which was approved by Pope Julius III and which ran to eight editions between its publication date and 1600, and were practised by breakers for centuries afterwards.

A French newspaper article of around 1860 reported on the success of a horse breaker who in 1846 had made a good living from buying vicious horses, which the article noted were more common in France than in England, and selling them on after a few days by which time they were perfectly quiet. His remedy lay in the use of a lead-weighted whip which he applied liberally between the ears of the horse at any hint of trouble.

Grisone's use of a circular breaking pit is interesting for it sounds similar to the gyrus used by his countrymen in earlier times for horse training. Like his Roman forebears, he used blocks or platforms to facilitate mounting, but advised: 'If your horse refuses to approach the mounting platform because of fear of work or excessive high spirits, hit it with a stick between the ears or elsewhere on its body except in its eyes, and then it will do your bidding wonderfully.' Other cures for problems he suggested included tying burning straw or a live hedgehog beneath the tail of a nappy horse, and arming helpers with sharpened spikes to use on horses showing a reluctance to move forward. 'If your horse comes to a halt or goes backwards', Grisone wrote, 'place a man behind it, provided with a vicious cat tied to a long pole in such a way that she lies belly upward with the free use of her claws and teeth. The man should hold the cat close to the legs of the disobedient horse so that she can bite or scratch it.' These drastic measures were backed up with verbal threats, for Grisone added: 'I would advise you, when your horse is behaving badly, that you chastise him in a loud and frightening voice, addressing him angrily, threatening him with any harsh word that comes to mind.'

Using such methods it is hardly surprising that Grisone had a dramatic effect on the horses he trained and that they were sub-serviently obedient, even if history does not record what their attitudes and temperaments were like. The Duke of Martina's brother, commenting on Grisone and another prominent horseman of the time, wrote: 'They with a most perfect judgement had this spe-cial grace given them, that every horse at the first riding seemed to obey unto them even at their becke [sic], so as the bystanders were astonied [sic] thereat.'

Through his work as an instructor, as well as through his writings, Grisone encouraged others to adopt his ideas and follow his example, and one such emulator was Count Cesar Fiaschi from Ferrera. The count was an innovative horseman and one of the first of the Renaissance masters to understand and appreciate the importance of the voice and even music as an aid to training horses. Like many of his contemporaries, he wrote a book in which he recommended train-ing exercises, many of which are still practised today.

One of Fiaschi's pupils, Giovanni Baptista Pignatelli, became the most famous of the riding masters of the Neopolitan schools which were enjoying patronage from all over Europe. Cited by some as the greatest horseman in the world, Pignatelli was a progressive thinker who favoured the use of milder bits, as he believed a bit 'should serve to inform the horse of the rider's wishes rather than force them upon him', and his methods were influenced by a group of circus riders from Constantinople whom he patronised and whose light and ath-letic style of riding he incorporated into his own horsemanship having learnt 'their art after long study and experiment'. According to Berenger, Pignatelli invented the single training pillar, originally using a tree because 'from want of covered buildings for the purpose of riding and breaking and to save holding them on the longe [sic] he used to tie his horses and work them around it'. Although Berenger's statement is easily proven inaccurate, it probably indicates that Pignatelli was an advocate of the use of the turning post. Although he never wrote a book, he was a renowned instructor and charged the highest fees for teaching his skills to others. He was very selective of his pupils and, even if accepted, they were bound to train with him for a period of six years, spending the time either under instruction or breaking and training horses under the auspices of their mentor.

THE FRENCH SCHOOL

Among the many pupils who trained under Pignatelli at his school were two Frenchmen, Saloman de la Broue and Antoine de Pluvinel, who later returned to France to introduce the new ideas of the Italian masters under the patronage of the French court. They founded the very influential French school while the Neopolitan school, which had instigated the whole movement, slipped into demise. Saloman de la Broue, who died towards the end of the sixteenth century, shared Pignatelli's view that a horse should be broken and trained initially with a mild bit like a simple snaffle or bridoon, even if he did resort to severe curbs in later training. At a time when most horsemen knew only the concertina-like effect of constraining a horse between a severe curb bit and whip and spurs to get the shape and elevated movements they sought, the Frenchman's theories on bitting and correct mouthing were quite radical.

Antoine de Pluvinel, who was born in 1555, studied with Pignatelli for the mandatory six years as a young man and soon after his return to France opened an academy in Paris for the education of young noblemen in not only riding but literature, painting and music. With equitation now classed as an art, the breaking of school horses had been elevated to a pursuit worthy of educated people, although the majority of working horses throughout Europe were still broken by those of the lowest social orders and using methods virtually unchanged since medieval times. Pluvinel's own contribution to breaking was above all a more humane approach and a distancing from the long-standing and entrenched belief that the horse was by nature vicious and potentially dangerous and had to be subdued by force. Pluvinel recognised the intelligence of the horse and how to use this to advantage during breaking, and he taught that a horse resists more often out of lack of understanding than malice. He, too, favoured the use of milder bits, and he made full use of pillars in both breaking and further training, giving rise to the claim that, like Pignatelli, he had invented them, although this was untrue. When Frederigo Mazzuchelli, a renowned Milanese teacher, advocated the use of 'driving reins' in his book, *Elementi di Cavalerizza*, published in 1805, some readers made the erroneous assumption that he had invented long reining; attributing the invention of equipment to those instructors who used it was nothing new.

Pluvinel made use of a number of established artificial aids including the *chambrière*, a whip used for lungeing and work between pillars with a four-foot cane stock and a leather thong of around six feet, and a *houssine*, a rattan switch of at least three feet in length, used by riders and always carried in the right hand. Traditionally the reins were always held in the left hand as weapons were held in the right, and when school riding was introduced the whip replaced the weapon. Pluvinell also used a *seguette*, a type of training cavesson with teeth or notches on the inner surface, and also a plain cavesson which fitted over the bridle with the reins laid on the neck for lungeing. During training lessons, Pluvinel often used 'blinders' or circular blinkers to cover the horse's eyes, as he said: 'It is a fact that horses learn better when they cannot see, and are more inclined to obey the bridle and the spurs in that they are less apprehensive and less inclined to be distracted.' As regards the most suitable environment for training, he suggested an open or roofed manège about thirty-six feet wide and a hundred and eight feet long, and although Pluvinel was much involved in the actual breaking of horses himself he did so with the assistance of a retinue of whip-bearing helpers. In the tradition of the time, Pluvinel wrote two books on equitation, *L'instruction du roi* being the better of the two and taking the form of a discourse between himself and the French king, Louis XIII, who was one of his pupils. Saloman de la Broue had also written a book, the first book on equitation to be written in French even though the writings of Fiaschi and Grisone had both been translated into French in response to the growing demand for literary instruction on this new art.

Pluvinal's successor in terms of carrying forward a more enlightened and humane approach to breaking and training was a man called de la Guerinière whose book, *Ecole de Cavalerie*, published in 1733, met great acclaim. Like Pluvinel, he was a skilled teacher and communicator as well as a great horseman. Despite the success of his Paris academy where he taught riding, and his appointment in 1730 as riding master of the Academie des Tuilleries, impecunity dogged his life. He was one of the first instructors to move away from the repressed over-collection of horses and he brought a freedom of movement to the way his horses went which began at the breaking stage. Like many of his predecessors in school riding, he was a fervent believer in the use of pillars and said: 'I regard the pillars as a means whereby not only to bring out the resources, the vigour, the

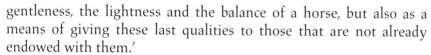

gentleness, the lightness and the balance of a horse, but also as a means of giving these last qualities to those that are not already endowed with them.'

The popularity of racing, which was attracting a large following in France towards the end of the eighteenth century necessitated a very different breaking method to that being expounded by the classical riding masters whose manège-based equitation was as far removed from the freedom of the race jockey as was possible. Riding in general, which was still the main form of transport as the widespread use of the carriage had yet to come, was influenced by both the classical school, which appealed to the pretentiousness of some, and the more business-like approach of the racing fraternity and the military. A succession of military commanders in the period following the French Revolution attempted to adapt the skills of classical riding to the needs of the cavalry, and many published books on the subject. Le Comte d'Aure, who became commandant of the prestigious cavalry school at Saumur in 1848, recognised the two styles of equitation and, instead of the traditional method of breaking cavalry horses by teams of rough-riders whose methods were frequently as uncouth as they were, he introduced a less harsh system of breaking to produce troop horses suited to all aspects of work including cross-country riding and jumping and yet with a degree of collection.

THE OTHER EUROPEAN SCHOOLS

While Italy instigated the discovery of riding as an art, and France developed it into dressage as we know it today, other countries also had their schools of equitation. The Spanish school, with which Imperial Austria started its Spanish Riding School, was based on Moorish methods and originated with the Spanish Court Riding School founded in 1572 to provide riding education for the nobility and using horses of Iberian parentage. There was a German school too, and in 1680 an academy opened in London in the French style to teach social skills including riding. Prior to that Italian instructors had been brought over to teach the young King Henry VIII horsemanship. While school riding was therefore known in Britain through the work of continental instructors, some of whom brought horses with them, and also through training with foreign instructors at their home establishments, one man is credited with popularising school riding in England. William Cavendish, later Duke of Newcastle, was a wealthy and influential supporter of Charles I who had been an incompetent cavalry commander during the Civil War and who, on the king's deposition, was forced to seek exile in Antwerp where he acquired a number of horses and established a classical riding school. As one-time instructor to the king, he said: 'I had the honour to be the first to sate [sic] him on horseback', and in 1658 his first book, *A general system of horsemanship,* was published. He returned to England after the restoration, publishing a second book in 1667, *A new method to dress horses.* The term 'dress' in this context gave rise to the modern word 'dressage'. While Cavendish was evidently influenced by his experiences on the continent, his general beliefs were original for he was a horseman of great skill as well as a learned and influential man in national affairs. Although he could handle his horses roughly at times, his general philosophy on breaking and handling was one of empathy and understanding, elements that had been noticeably missing in the writing of Grisone only a century earlier.

WILLIAM CAVENDISH'S METHOD OF BREAKING A HORSE

Cavendish believed in handling a young horse thoroughly prior to breaking, and advised stabling him in a stall where he was tied up for two or three successive winters in order to make him tractable before he was brought into work. 'For by this means', Cavendish wrote, 'he will not be wanton, apt to lie down, or be guilty of any extravagant actions common to young horses, and thereby endanger the rider. By this method you will avoid the trouble of working him upon ploughed lands, morasses, etc. before you mount him; by which exercise he is in danger of breaking his wind, or at least of spoiling his genteel air.' Lungeing a horse in soft ploughed or marshy ground was a commonly recommended cure for over-exuberant or problem horses but it could cause lameness or even respiratory problems.

'When you have made him tractable by these means', he went on, 'the first saddle you put upon him should be quilted, or one made of chaff or straw, well fastened by a surcingle, that it may not hurt his back, but leave his shoulders liberty that he may trot freely, as every colt should do.' The term 'colt' meaning a young unbroken horse, irrespective of whether it was a colt, filly or gelding, had been in general use since the early Middle Ages and originated from the fact that for centuries only uncastrated male horses were used for riding, so an animal being broken to the saddle would automatically have been a colt. Even after fillies and geldings were used for riding, the word colt continued still for all unbroken animals.

Cavendish advised leaving a young horse unshod during breaking, or shoeing it with only lunettes or half-shoes on its fore feet, to reduce the risk of it accidentally injuring itself.

> Nothing more should be put upon his head than a halter, or cavesson, with reins to it of the same kind. Moreover, he ought to have nothing in his mouth; should there be anything in it, it ought only to be a small piece of whip-cord, with a headstall without reins, as this is an improper time to put a bit in his mouth.

In saying this, Cavendish evidently put great emphasis on protecting the mouth of a young horse, and broke with tradition by not bitting the horse until it was backed and had been ridden for several weeks. Prior to actual backing, he advised that:

> the rider ought to mount himself upon a gentle horse, and lead the colt behind him three or four days, till he follows the horse freely. Then the master ought to mount him for two or three days successively, and afterwards suffer him to go alone. But the rider must at this time take care to manage his head by degrees,

and he reiterated the importance of not stopping the young horse suddenly 'since such practice may occasion a violent pain in the reins of a young horse' implying that the reins were probably attached to a cavesson of some description. These early breaking lessons were conducted in an enclosed manège which helped to focus the horse's attention and effectively contained and controlled it while it was being taught the aids. During the month of walking and trotting the young horse, following mounting him for the first time, Cavendish recommended that it was important to 'leave him at last as vigorous as you found him', which was another move away from the traditions of wearing a horse down through excessive lungeing or other work as part of the breaking process. At this stage the horse was bitted for the first time but a curb was recommended rather than a snaffle, although Cavendish advised rubbing the bit with honey to make it more acceptable to the young horse. He also advised using him continually in the same manner, managing him with the cavesson, and not with the bridle, so that he may be only just sensible of it: use him likewise sometimes to move gently backwards, and, when he seems to comply, caress him. During this time, which will require a month, or more, you must keep him trotting. After the expiration of two months, put his saddle on.

Throughout his instructions on breaking, which comprise but a small part of his writings, Cavendish constantly comes back to the importance of a good mouth and correct head carriage as it was integral to the more advanced training that was his real interest. 'The main point', he emphasised,

> is to manage a horse's head, and to give him a proper weight upon the hand; for it is very easy to manage his haunches . . . If the head of a horse is well regulated, you may afterwards manage him as you please, provided his nature and strength will admit of it; for should you not secure his head, it is impossible ever to make him a compleat horse, since you have only your hands and heels to manage him otherwise the most essential parts will fail you.

Cavendish concluded by writing: 'Hitherto I have succinctly and clearly shown my new method of breaking a colt, hoping you readily comprehend what I have said upon this subject.'

THE CLASSICAL INFLUENCE

While Cavendish's method was certainly new in some respects as it included some innovative elements, only a small ratio of the horses broken and trained in Europe were broken in riding schools. The bulk received their training in very different circumstances, although the teachings of the great masters were beginning to filter down to less enlightened breakers. A truer picture of how riding horses were broken in general life may be gathered from some of the less erudite, cheaper, and more accessible books on the subject, of which many were written from the seventeenth century onwards. A typical example was *The compleat gamester*, published in 1674, which included a chapter on horse breaking under the title 'The art and mystery of riding, whether the great-horse or any other'. It begins: 'As an introduction to the art of riding, I think it requisite to treat of the taming of a young colt', and it advocated bringing the colt home and giving him eight to ten days to get used to his surroundings and to being handled before placing the saddle in the manger that he may grow acquainted with it and 'so that he may not be afraid either at the sight thereof or at the noise of the stirrops [sic]'. Having girthed the saddle on, the writer advised taking a simple snaffle bit, washing it and anointing it with a mixture of honey and salt and placing it in the horse's mouth so that it hung directly about his tushes, the presence of which would indicate that not only was the horse male but that it was aged between four and five years. This was done in a morning and the horse led out in hand and watered. On bringing him in, he was to be left to mouth in the bit for an hour or so, then unsaddled and unbridled, and left until evening when the process was repeated again. 'The next day do as you did before', then fit him with a sharp cavesson and martingale,

> which you must buckle at that length that he may only feel it when he jerketh up his head; then lead him forth into some new plow'd land or soft ground, and there having him trot a good while about in your hand to take him off from wantonness and wild tricks.

The next stage was to try and mount him, but if he acted up then he was to be trotted again before trying to mount him once more by half-mounting, leaning over his back and dismounting.

> If he seems distasted at it, about with him again, and let him not want correction, but if he takes it patiently, cherish him and place yourself in the saddle, but stay there a very little while, then cherish him again and give him bread or grass to feed on.

The writer then recommended checking that all was 'fit and strong', meaning the saddlery, before mounting 'carrying your rod inoffensively to his eye' with someone to lead him on, occasionally halting and moving on again.

> Observe this course every day till you have brought him to trot, which will be but three at the most, if you observe to make him follow some other horseman, stopping him now and then gently, and then making him go forward, remembering his reasonable cherishings, and not forgetting his due corrections as often as you find him froward [sic] and rebellious, and when you ride him abroad, return not the same way home, that you make him take all ways indifferently, and by these observations you will bring him to understand your will and purpose in less than a fortnight's time.

The writer's advice on schooling included ridden work in a circle about a hundred paces in circumference, and the teaching of high school airs. He evidently believed that the use of a cavesson and a standing martingale were 'an excellent guide to a well-disposed horse for setting of his head in due place, forming of his rein, and making him appear lovely to the eye of spectator'. His writings appear to have been based on the teachings, perhaps read, of the great riding masters and his whole approach is generally kind and considerate, with few exceptions such as when speaking of the aids, or 'helps' as he calls them, of which the spurs' chief use, he claims, is for correction 'which must not be done faintly, but sharply when occasion shall require it'. On teaching the half-rear as a showy action and one 'that carrieth much grace and comeliness therein', he wrote:

> After you have stopped your horse, without giving your hand any ease, lay the calves of both your legs hard to his sides, shaking your rod, and crying up, up; which though he understand not at first, yet by frequent practice, with helps, cherishings, and corrections as aforesaid, he will come to understand your meaning.

The writer knew the dangers of teaching this movement to a newly broken horse and warned that 'his advance must not be too high, for fear of his coming over upon you . . . he must not advance for his own pleasure (for that is a great fault) but for yours, according to your will and command'. Should the horse rear too high the rider was to 'give him not only your spurs both together, but lash him twice or thrice with your rod between the ears'. A combination of severe bitting and repressive over-collection in school riding often resulted in rearers, and the standard remedy was still in use two hundred and fifty years on when a French writer recommended dealing with the vice by 'administering a hard blow between the ears with a strong stick . . . or by the old method of smashing a full bottle of soda water between the ears'.

THE CIRCUS TRADITION

School riding was also influenced by the circus tradition that went back to very early times with Scandinavian rock carvings from the Bronze Age showing figures performing handstands and acrobatics on horseback. Horses trained to perform tricks were a part of Persian,

Greek, Roman and Byzantine circuses, and there were many notable horse trainers and performers including Philoroeus, a humble stable boy who in the tenth century captured the approval of the Byzantine public by galloping around the arena standing on the back of a horse and juggling a razor-sharp sword. Circus horsemen broke and trained their animals and performed in enclosed arenas like the manèges of the riding masters, and their feats were sometimes quite extraordinary. Strutt's *Sports and pastimes* commented on such unlikely equestrian circus attractions as horses which carried oxen on their backs, and even horses which danced upon tightropes. Goya reputedly based his sketch of a similar and quite incredible feat on what he had witnessed at a Spanish circus. Other arena entertainments included horses trained to fight men, something the Arabs had taught their horses to do in warfare since the seventh century, dance, feign death, walk on their hind legs, and much more. All this took specialised training but the circus horsemen were highly skilled. In 1758, an Irishman, Thomas Johnson, known as The Tartar, had amazed onlookers by riding astride two, three or even four horses at once, and two years later in a field enclosed by boards, to which admittance cost one shilling, another trick rider had entertained spectators by standing on horseback or vaulting on and off while the horse galloped round.

Some circus breakers and trainers had more serious aspirations including Philip Astley, a sergeant-major in the 15th Light Dragoons, who on demob in 1768 hoped to become a riding master to the nobility. He gave public demonstrations of horsemanship, and eventually set up a circus called Astley's Amphitheatre which was essentially equestrian. He trained the horses himself from scratch, following a regime that was strict and hard, for his livelihood depended upon it. As he told the manager of Covent Garden when discussing the training of his horses, 'Mine know that if they don't indeed work like horses, they get no corn.' One of Astley's horses, Billy, could count, having been trained to stamp one forefoot every time Astley clicked his thumb and finger nails together; could mark the name of Astley letter by letter in the dirt floor; tell gold from silver, ladies from gents; take a handkerchief from its owner, unfasten his own saddle; wash his feet in a pail of water; and even serve tea by lifting a boiling kettle from the flame. Like Astley's other horses, Billy was trained under a simple reward and punishment system.

Astley was continually on the lookout for new and imaginative equestrian acts for his circus, one of the most bizarre he ever booked being David Wildman, a bee-keeper and the author of a treatise on the subject, who first appeared at a venue in Islington in 1770 exhibiting bees on horseback. He stood with one foot on the saddle and the other on the horse's neck with a swarm of bees covering his head and face. When he fired a pistol, part of the swarm left him and marched over a table! When appearing at Astley's Amphitheatre, Mrs Astley rode around the arena with a swarm of bees on her arm like a muff. Bees can be prone to attack horses, more so if the horses are sweating, and during the American Civil War a confederate cavalry troop lost several horses to bee stings when they accidentally disturbed a wild swarm in a wood, so it was an astonishing arena entertainment.

After Astley's death, his partner, Antonio Franconi, continued to stage equestrian arena entertainments although the term 'circus', derived from the Latin word for circle or ring, did not come into use until 1782 when Charles Hughes, an ex-Astley employee, set up his Royal Circus. Many of the people who broke and trained horses for circuses were very secretive about their methods although one, a man called Davis who trained Covent Garden's four-legged stars, apparently did so by staring at them, shouting, and pulling faces!

In France the riding master of the circus became as popular as the opera diva or popular actor, and the great nineteenth-century circuses like the Cirque d'été in the Champs-Elysées became tremendously popular. This surge of popularity helped dispel the travelling show stigma of horsemen training animals to entertain the public, and ultimately spawned some of the world's finest and most innovative horsemen.

BAUCHER AND FILLIS

François Baucher (1797–1873) was an extraordinarily gifted horseman and trainer whose equestrian interests were confined to school riding and who was believed to have never ridden outside a school. Born too late for the hey-day of the classical schools of equitation, he was obliged to demonstrate his skills in a circus environment. He was in many ways the link between classical riding and public entertainment; the round circus ring was clearly reminiscent of the lungeing arena where the circumference of the ring was marked by the hoof prints of the horses as they worked around a central turning post.

Baucher believed that a horse had little intelligence or memory but that it could be programmed like a simple machine to produce a performance. He demanded absolute obedience from the earliest stage of breaking, and claimed that a horse that would accept the application of the spurs was three-parts broken. Certainly the performances of horses he trained, like Partisan, were outstanding but, while he had many ardent supporters, his methods and achievements had little practical use outside of the arena. Although he wrote on the subject of horse training, he was not a skilled writer and failed to communicate his vast knowledge to his readers, but he was an excellent teacher in person.

Baucher trained Pauline Cuzent, the actress, to ride and mounted her on Buridan, a Yorkshire Coach Horse, which he had broken and trained to a high level. Following in the tradition of lady circus riders like Caroline Loyo who appeared at the Circus Olympique in Paris in 1833, Pauline Cuzent was a great success and she eventually bought both Buridan and Partisan from Baucher and performed with them extensively, including before Czar Nicholas I at the Russian State Circus. Unfortunately her health gave out and she died in 1855, the same year in which Baucher suffered a serious accident when a chandelier fell on him as he was about to mount to give a demonstration at the Cirque Napoleon. He never rode in a circus again.

Baucher's successor in many ways was James Fillis, an Englishman, born in London in 1834 and, like Baucher, primarily interested in school riding and the training of horses for public exhibition. He established his reputation giving public demonstrations daily at the Champs-Elysées Circus in Paris, and ended up as chief cavalry instructor at St Petersburg from 1898. He claimed to have trained 150,000 horses in his lifetime, while his book, *Breaking and riding*, first published in Paris in 1890 was, and still is, a respected reference book. It was actually 'ghosted' by Georges Clemenceau, presumably in close collaboration with Fillis. Although both Baucher and Fillis were largely concerned with training horses for public demonstrations and achieving the spectacular, like the horse Fillis trained to canter on three legs or another which he trained to canter backwards, they both did much to influence future generations of horse breakers by demonstrating the horse's scope for learning and helping to raise the profile of the professional horse trainer.

BREAKING A HORSE TO DRIVE

Significantly, very few books on the breaking and training of harness horses were written prior to the nineteenth century although Prizelius, a German, writing in 1777, knew of 178 works on riding and horse management at that time. The reason for this was that in the early years of equestrian writing there were relatively few driving horses, since the state of the roads discouraged the use of wheeled vehicles and also, while riding was seen as an art during the Renaissance, driving was not. The traditional method of breaking a horse to drive was to harness it alongside a quiet schoolmaster and just work it. Like many other breaking methods, the horse learnt by experience, not by teaching, but it was effective and relatively quick. In the early years of the last century when the number of horse-drawn vehicles in daily use increased, a new type of vehicle specially designed for the breaking of horses and appropriately called a 'break' first made its appearance in the streets of Europe and North America. The early breaks were built on very simple lines with a high boxseat to accommodate two people set over the forecarriage which was connected to the rear axle by a heavy perch. A small platform bolted to the perch immediately behind the boxseat was provided for a groom to stand on, and the four large dished wheels

Breaking a horse to drive.

Breaking pit ponies using an unusual three-wheeled breaking cart. The ponies' full tails show they are not yet in work. (Photograph: Beamish Open Air Museum)

A skeleton break. The high box seat was raised out of the way of kicking hoofs, and a groom stood on the platform behind ready to jump down and help in case of trouble. (Photograph: Science Museum)

were set wide apart to give the vehicle stability. The high boxseat was raised out of the way of kicking hooves, and the heavy, crudely built and sometimes unsprung body frame was strong enough to withstand assault by the most uncooperative of horses. Although a few breaks were used in private stables or by those companies who broke and trained large numbers of horses for their own use, most breaks were found in dealer's yards. So much so, that for many years these unique vehicles were commonly known as dealer's breaks to distinguish them from the other types of breaks which came into popularity in later times. The growth of the mail-coach system and the insatiable demand for coach and carriage horses for both private and public use, not to mention horses for cartage and heavy draught work, made rich men of many dealers. Their busy yards were usually full of young horses, the breaking and training of which was virtually a full-time job for the dealers and their nagsmen. The system was to harness the young horse alongside the schoolmaster or break horse and just set off, with a groom standing on the platform on the perch ready to jump down and assist in case of serious trouble. Very strong heavy-duty harness was used, and the pole and splinter-bar were often padded and leather covered. The young pupil wore protective knee-pads in case he fell down and injured himself, which was not uncommon. Recalling the breaking to harness of a promising young horse, a well-known Victorian horse dealer wrote: 'the first time he was put in the break he threw himself down, blemished his hocks and broke his tail'.

Dealers and nagsmen

The dealers and their employees were also frequently injured in the business of breaking so many young horses, and George Talkington of Uttoxeter, an early nineteenth-century dealer, suffered a succession of mishaps during his long working life. These included a broken right shoulder, three broken ribs each side, a fractured skull, two serious back injuries, the right kneecap kicked off, a dislocated ankle, seven broken ribs, dislocation of the right shoulder, two broken ribs and a collar bone, a broken arm, another seven broken ribs, dislocation of the left shoulder, two more broken ribs, and serious bruising of the leg. That aside, he lived to be eighty-three, sired eighteen children in fifteen years, and died of natural causes.

Most of the dealers broke their horses in the cities where they

A long-shafted breaking cart for training young horses to go in harness.

would spend their working lives, and in Victorian times London's Piccadilly in early morning was often busy with dealer's nagsmen working young horses in breaks. First light not infrequently saw fierce battles between nagsmen and their reluctant pupils, and any nagsman using his whip too freely would be subject to cries of 'shame, shame' from passers-by on the pavement. One experienced nagsman advised that the safest place to put a young horse in harness was in a busy street where it would be too distracted by all the activity around to try and kick its way out of the vehicle. It generally took around eight months to train a harness horse fully so that it could be considered safe to drive in the city streets.

By the end of the nineteenth century, breaks had evolved into several designs with the original form of the vehicle distinguished by being called a skeleton break on account of its minimal construction. Many superior examples were built with high dished wheels, turned perches, and more elegant lines to the boxseat and supports. A rumble seat sometimes replaced the groom's platform, a handbrake was often added, and fully elliptical springs were fitted to the forecarriage, although the rear of the vehicle remained unsprung which caused it to bounce on rough roads due to the lack of weight over the back axle. This problem was often partially remedied by placing a 'lead box' over the axle which was filled with blocks of solid lead to minimise the excessive rattling.

Breaking a pit pony using a coal tub on rails. Once broken, the pony would spend its working life underground. (Photograph: Beamish Open Air Museum)

Two-wheeled breaking carts

The skeleton break was suitable only for pairs of horses or possibly teams of four. For breaking a horse in single harness a two-wheeled breaking cart was used, and there were several designs. All were strongly built with a low centre of gravity, firm suspension as a bouncy vehicle was dangerous, rigid shafts of sufficient length to prevent the horse from kicking the vehicle, and a forward-facing seat with adequate purchase for the feet to facilitate control should the horse play up. Some horsemen preferred to use a long-shafted flat cart for breaking while others liked to start their young horses in a wheel-less vehicle which dragged along the ground like a travois. In America a distinct design of vehicle known as a Kentucky breaking cart was developed. The seat for two people was raised on twin cantilevers angled from the platform-style floor which was set on side or dennett springs above the two large wheels. The extra-long straight shafts had a metal arch between them and in front of the low dashboard to keep the reins up high and prevent any possibility of the horse getting his tail over a rein. On some examples the seat was railed all round to help secure the position of the driver, but on

Miners trying to teach a pit pony to carry a rider. (Photograph: Beamish Open Air Museum)

others a padded backrest or even just a broad leather strap supported the driver. If the vehicle did not have a footboard, an adjustable footrest was often fitted.

Traditional harness training

Youatt recommended that a carriage horse should be broken after its second winter, having been well handled from birth, then bitted and 'suffered to amuse himself, and to play, and to champ it for an hour, on a few successive days . . .' The horse was then accustomed to the harness, piece by piece, concluding with the blinkers, and a few days later was put in the break, and it was generally acknowledged that a young horse was less likely to kick or play up if it was kept moving. 'No great time will pass, sometimes not even the first day' Youatt advised 'before he will begin to pull.' Some horses were less cooperative, and J. H. Walsh recommended that in double harness 'it is a safe plan to have the whole space between the forecarriage and the splinterbar made up with iron rods so close together that if a horse kicks he cannot get his legs hung over the bar'. Some break horses were so experienced that if a young horse kicked and got a leg over the pole,

Kentucky breaking cart. (Photograph: C. Richardson)

the break horse would press against the offender's leg and hold him quiet until the matter was sorted out. According to Walsh the break horse should be 'an animal of good courage and free from vice who will draw steadily off on the slightest notice and will stop firmly when required'. An assistant called a breaksman helped when required by leading the colt in turning, and it was traditional always to have the young horse on the off side and the break horse on the near side.

R. W. Dickson, in his book *An improved system of management of livestock and cattle, circa* 1822, wrote that a method of breaking

considered very excellent is that of putting such young horses in their full harness in the middle of other team horses, letting them have no weight to pull, so that they may be dragged round by the teams without any sort of interference by the drivers, such dragging being continued until they are become quite gentle and tractable. They are then to be mounted and ridden in such situations where they cannot be unruly so as to dismount their riders, on account of the other horses in the teams keeping them in order. By these means such young horses soon fall into good and tractable courses, and move with the same ease and regularity as the other horses, being thus broken in almost without difficulty or hazard.

Mounting a rider, like a postilion, on an unbroken horse harnessed as a member of a team was a novel if dangerous idea and not one that was extensively practised. Never the less, there was a great divergence in breaking methods, particularly in the breaking of horses for saddle work, with practitioners offering conflicting and often misinformed advice.

STRANGE PRACTICES

Charles Thompson in his book, *Rules for bad horsemen*, published in 1830, noted 'there is in this country, more than any other, an almost universal fondness for horses, and the exercise of riding them; yet few, in comparison, out of this multitude, make even tolerable horsemen, and still less number do the thing as it ought to be done'. Incompetent and inconsiderate horse breakers abounded at that time but the correlation between cruel handling and the vicious horses such methods produced was rarely made. In his *Philosophical and practical treatise on horses*, published in 1810, John Lawrence advised the owner of a 'restiff' horse to 'knock him on the head with all speed before he causes an accident' and he cited the case of two vicious mares he knew of and said 'besides a number of inferior accidents, one of them tore out the entrails of a boy'. After twelve months' work on them 'the greatest severity, instead of breaking their spirits, served only to enrage and render them worse', and he concluded weakly 'If there be any safe method of approaching vicious animals, it is to warn them with a somewhat loud and severe voice.' Other breakers used more dramatic methods and another writer in *The housekeeper's handbook of tips and wrinkles*, under the title 'How to handle a savage, vicious horse', said:

Approach the horse firmly, fixing your gaze upon his eye. Have in your hand a six-chambered revolver loaded with blank cartridges. The moment he attempts to savage you, fire, not point blank at him, but directly in front of his face. This will give the horse a sudden shock and take his attention. If he is in a stall this is your opportunity. Before he has time to recover himself, rush in and seize him by the headstall, and again discharge the revolver close alongside his face, saying: What do you mean? How dare you!

Henry Hall Dixon summed up the prevalent attitude towards difficult horses when he commented: 'In Ireland as in England, the accepted modes of taming a determined colt, or a vicious horse, are either by a resolute rider with whip and spur, and violent lungeings, or by starving, physic and sleepless nights.'

There were a few prophets in the wilderness including R. W. Dickson who, in 1822, was advising his readers that breaking 'is best and most effectively done by mild and gentle treatment' following careful early handling of youngstock to accustom them to being haltered and led, tied up, have their feet lifted, and groomed. He had strong views on mounting bits which he believed

> should be of the plain, snaffle, slabbering kind, but much thicker than those in common use, in the centre hinges of which should be fastened small plates with moveable beads, so as to lie upon the tongues, and induce the horses to move their jaws, and prevent them from bearing hard upon them so as to deaden their mouths.

He went on

> being bridled in this manner, they are to be reined up to the large girths or surcingles that pass round their bodies, but which should not be done in too tight a manner, or too great a length of time in the beginning.

Although he recommended the use of a cavesson for leading and lungeing, he advised care with this 'very rough and severe contrivance' and warned the breaker to be vigiliant when leading horses in and out of stables and to leave the reins unfastened in case they caught on the door frightening the horse. Care was also to be taken in bridling a horse to avoid any risk of head-shyness.

> The first step in the breaking of young horses is that of lungeing them well in a circle, by having a long, thin, small portion of cording fastened to the cavesson, and held in the hands of the breakers, round whom they are made to trot in as full a circle as it will allow; which has the benefit of

Wright's patent developer for bitting the horse and developing style to the head and neck, circa 1900.

giving ease and pliability to the shoulder and other parts. In order to produce the most advantage from this practice, the heads and necks of the
horses should, however, be left at full liberty without being reined up, as
is the common method.

This aversion to the use of dumb jockeys and side-reins was contradictory to common practice, and it is interesting that the writer never
mentions long reining although in other respects he follows well-
tried methods. 'With some, the animals are taken to proper pieces of
ploughed or other ground' he wrote

and made to walk sharply round in the halters or bridles, as held in the
hand, and, when somewhat exhausted and tamed by such means, sham
efforts are to be made to mount them, in a slow deliberate manner, till
they appear quite patient in bearing them, when they may be fully
mounted, being led carefully by other persons. The riders should cherish
and encourage them at every step as they pass forward, and should then
move themselves well in the saddle or on the backs, the leaders removing
their hands further from the mouths of the horses, until they go readily
forward of their own accord by the mere direction of the persons on their
backs.

Green's patent dumb jockey for breaking and training horses. The reins were attached to springs in the arms of the dumb jockey which gave and took with the motion of the horse's head.

Dickson also commented on the breaking method whereby the pupil was saddled and led alongside a quiet schoolmaster, and ultimately backed and ridden in the same manner. This idea evidently originated from the breaking of driving horses alongside a reliable schoolmaster, and Dickson was convinced that 'In this mild way very obstinate and refractory horses may often be broken with great ease and facility with little expense or trouble.'

Thirty years after Dickson had expressed his views on horse breaking, Youatt evidently shared many of his beliefs. He advocated the breaking of horses for hunting or general riding at between two and a half and three years of age, with the task undertaken by a man 'who will never suffer his passion to get the better of his discretion'. The breaker was to be assisted in teaching the horse to lead and lunge by a steady boy with a whip, something reminiscent of the horse breakers of the Renaissance period, and he too is scathing of the use of dumb jockeys, saying 'There are many curious and expensive machines for this purpose but the simple reins will be quite sufficient.'

MILITARY HORSE BREAKING

The military across the world broke vast numbers of horses and mules, especially in times of war, and, for Britain, hostilities like the Crimean and Boer wars necessitated importing cavalry horses, most of them unbroken, from as far afield as South America. Requisition and request were the least expensive ways of acquiring horses, and Charles I at the onset of the Civil War sent out a proclamation asking that 'horses, geldings, mares or naggs be sent in to be used as dragoon horses and with them saddles and bridles'. Men presenting themselves for the dragoons or heavy cavalry customarily brought their own horses, although one could be requisitioned for a man if he could not provide his own, and his pay sheet debited to its value as the animal then became his personal property which encouraged him to look after it properly. As only broken horses were requisitioned the army had no professional horse breakers on its payroll, but when the Crimean war started in 1854 it was a very different picture. Remount officers and buyers were charged with finding fit, young horses at a competitive price which the government set at a maximum of £40 for a troop horse and £42 for an artillery horse, provided the animals were between five and nine years of age and fully trained. Twelve

Hobbles and lassoes used to restrain a young horse in the early stages of breaking (Indian Army). (Photograph: National Army Museum)

Catching wild horses in India, circa 1910. *(Photograph: National Army Museum)*

months into the war the army were so desperate for remounts that the buyers with their fixed budgets were scouring dealers' yards and horse fairs on the lookout for anything they could afford. Many bought unbroken three year olds, for which the government price limit was £26 5s 0d, and passed them on to army nagsmen to break. By 1870 when the British cavalry consisted of thirty-one regiments, although the availability of horses was greater, the maximum purchase price was still only £40, forcing remount officers to buy a larger percentage of unbroken horses and establishing the importance of army breakers.

By the time of the Boer war an extra £10 on the purchase price limit did little to make the remount officers' job any easier as with an average of 336 army horses lost each day, a total of 326,000 for the entire war, the supply could not keep pace with the demand. The remount depots, which were often little more than horse-breaking centres on a very large scale, worked round the clock as the government was forced to resort to buying unhandled wild horses abroad. During the Boer war, 87,000 horses were shipped to South Africa from Britain, with another 23,028 from Australia, 14,621 from Canada, 5,611 from India, 110,000 from America, 3,220 from

Throwing a horse (Indian Army). (Photograph: National Army Museum)

Rhodesia, 64,157 from Hungary, and 26, 544 from Argentina. Many of these horses arrived loose-headed in the holds of boats and, after a brief acclimatisation period, became the charges of the army breakers whose methods were through necessity often harsh but quick. Throwing the horse down was standard as, according to one experienced cavalry officer, the practice 'convinces the horse of the ascendancy of man'. He recommended standing on the horse's near side and lifting the near fore with the left hand while with the right hand drawing the headstall rope to the horse's right by leaning over his back so that the horse comes down onto his near side knee and can be pulled over onto his side.

Some nagsmen were less refined and simply used lassoes and leg ropes to disable the horse. Backing was done by rough-riders who rode the animal in a high-sided breaking pen until it gave in either through exhaustion or resignation. According to one commentator, many of the rough-riders had 'a roll of cloth buckled firmly in front of their saddles, and with this precaution, even if the colt bucks or kicks, it is almost impossible for him to dislodge them'. Some adopted the dangerous practice of mounting the unbroken horse while it was tied head to tail, while others tied the head down to the

Difficult horses often had to be thrown in order to subdue them.

girth, strapped one foreleg up, or rode it in tight side-reins. It was hard and risky work with many casualties, and men were generally only assigned to the job for a limited period of time. During the First World War, one of the three main British remount depots was at Romsey, near Southampton, where forty full-time rough-riders were included in the personnel who were responsible for the 5,000 horses stabled there.

During the American Civil War, one remount depot had 7,000 horses on its premises and the team of rough-riders were breaking huge numbers of horses weekly as the wastage in combat was high, one conferate general having thirteen horses shot from underneath him although he himself escaped death. The depot also had to retrain spoilt or difficult animals, many of which had been prematurely put into service when they were little more than 'green broke' although others had been ruined by incompetent cavalrymen. One commentator wrote: 'The success of the Cavalry Bureau during the Civil War

Accustoming a young horse to the feel of a sack on its back (Indian Army).
(Photograph: National Army Museum)

was remarkable for fitting for further service thousands of temporarily incapacitated horses that had been broken down through
inexperience and careless abuse by hastily enlisted men.'

The bulk of the depot's work, however, centred around breaking
horses, including the herds of mustangs brought in by rail from further west where they had been purchased by remount officers.
Described as small, ugly, fine-boned with the appearance of being up
to little weight, and 'queer tempered', mustangs were conceded to be
strong and hardy with great stamina, and moreover they were available in large numbers and very cheap. Even the British remount
officers went to America during the Boer War to buy mustangs, but
the criteria laid down by the British Commission in 1900 of seeking
horses of between 14 and 15 hands, 5 to 9 years of age, and broken in
were loosely interpreted by the American vendors. After a number
of the 'broken' mustangs proved to be unridable, the British
demanded to see all prospective purchase saddled, bridled and ridden
before they were accepted, vetted, branded and shipped to South
Africa.

The governments of some countries bred their own cavalry horses
including Russia, which at the end of the last century had seven

Accustoming a horse to a dummy rider (Indian Army). (Photograph: National Army Museum)

major breeding establishments, and Hungary with four state breeding farms. The horses were broken at three and a half years of age to both ride and drive before being handed over to the army. The Prussian cavalry in the early part of the nineteenth century had at one point been mounted on wild steppe-bred horses from the Ukraine and Moldavia, and Sohr in his *Riding manual* published in 1825 for the benefit of the Prussian military had recommended an 'accelerated method of forcible breaking' claimed to be quick and effective. Such methods were tried by most cavalries at some stage but with poor long-term results, and by 1886 troop horses of the Prussians, which were by then broken more conventionally, were reported as being 'of worse quality than the British, worse fed, groomed and equipped, but a long way better broken'.

Horses destined for the use of officers in the French cavalry, and consequently animals with more size and quality than standard troop horses, had their breaking spaced out over a twelve-month period, while the British cavalry's *Manual of horsemanship* suggested ten weeks for the breaking and initial riding of a troop horse and advised, 'However tractable a horse may be his training should on no account be hurried.' The breaking programme comprised two

Hobbles on a saddled horse (Indian Army). (Photograph: National Army Museum)

weeks leading the horse about and getting him accustomed to strange sights and sounds; two weeks trotting on the lunge or long reins to teach the horse to respond to the voice; two weeks lungeing, long reining and getting used to the saddle; two weeks during which the horse was backed; and a final fortnight of riding the horse on at walk and trot only.

Pack and artillery horses went on for specialised training, but the breaking and initial handling of young mules was a specialised business from the very start requiring great patience and skill. 'Young mules are naturally timid and easily startled', the Manual warned, 'but they are, as a rule, docile and easily broken in, if treated with great kindness and patience . . . men must be carefully selected to break remount mules'. According to one seasoned mule-skinner, the secret was to let the mule see everything before it was placed on its back from the surcingle to the pack-saddle, and to take plenty of time and progress slowly and quietly. Only when the mule was quite used to being led around wearing the pack-saddle should he be introduced to a load, in the form of two 80 lb bags of sand, which he must be allowed to see and smell beforehand. A badly broken mule could be a liability and, according to a retired sergeant who had worked with mules during the First World War, a kicking mule was hated more than the enemy.

ZEBRAS AND QUAGGAS

If breaking mules was a challenge, the ultimate test of skill was reputedly breaking zebras, which many people believed were untameable, but several adventurous horsemen tried to disprove the pundits. In the early 1800s, Mr Sherriff Parkins of London drove a pair of quaggas about the city in a phaeton to the astonishment of people who had never seen examples of the rare partially striped species of zebra. Lt Colonel Hamilton Smith emulated his example and drove one in a gig at about the same time, commenting that it had a very light mouth. Once common in South Africa, quaggas became extinct in around 1870, the last specimen in England dying in the London Zoological gardens in 1864 and now preserved in the Natural History Museum in London. Contemporary reports would suggest that the quagga was not particularly difficult to break, although the same could not be said of the other species of zebra who retained the unpredictable temperament and wild attributes, including a reluctance to be trained, that at one time must have marked all wild horses in general. Zebra breakers found that if as little as one day was missed in the training programme the animal was as wild as ever, and at no point did it show any willingness to cooperate.

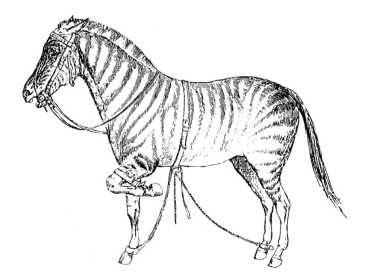

The zebra from the London Zoological Gardens wearing the foreleg strap and throwing gear used by John S. Rarey when he successfully broke it in 1858.

*Head ropes and leg ropes control a young horse while it is first mounted.
(Indian Army). (Photograph: National Army Museum)*

*Leading a newly backed young horse. The pupil's tail is tied to foreleg hobbles
to discourage bucking (Indian Army). (Photograph: National Army
Museum)*

Captain Horace Hayes, a very experienced breaker whose book,
Illustrated horse breaking, published in 1896, was for many years
the definitive work on the subject, disputed this and in 1892 in
Pretoria, capital of the Transvaal, broke a young Burchell's zebra in
one hour to carry a rider, commenting, 'In doing this, I did not throw

the animal down, nor did I resort to any of the usual heroic horse taming methods.' He was probably referring to American horse tamers whose spectacular methods he was sceptical of. On another occasion Captain Hayes, while in Calcutta, broke an old zebra stallion at Frank Fillis' circus, taking less than an hour to have it amenable enough to be ridden by Steve Margaret, a noted Australia rough-rider, and later by Mrs Hayes who once even hunted a zebra in Leicestershire. Hayes believed the Burchell's zebra was compara-tively easy to break, and recommended the taming and breaking of this species for saddle and harness work because they were immune from the Tsetse fly bite. The Swedish Zeedenburg brothers evidently agreed with him as they ran a coaching service in South Africa which lasted until after the Boer war using zebras and imported South American mules. Travellers wrote of seeing spans of eight mountain zebras, reputedly the most difficulty of all zebra species to break, being used for draught work in South Africa. The fascination for dri-ving zebras in harness was taken up by many horsemen as a gimmick, including Leopold de Rothschild, a member of the wealthy banking family, who drove a four-in-hand of zebras and was pho-tographed with them outside the Albert Hall in London in 1896. Although they were regularly driven in Hyde Park, they had to be taken out early in a morning as the sight of them apparently fright-ened other horses.

Prior to the First World War, the Mazawattee Company main-tained two four-in-hand teams of zebras for promotional purposes. Although based in London, the teams travelled as far north as Leicester. Unfortunately, no other details of the zebras can be found, as the Tea Company's records were lost in the London Blitz.

CATCHING WILD PONIES

In mid nineteenth-century Britain, where the horse was fundamen-tal to almost every aspect of commerce, industry, transport, war and sport, and a complex interdependence of occupations based around it, it is surprising that the hunting and capture of wild horses was still being practised as it had been thousands of years earlier. An article in the Cambrian Quarterly Magazine, published around 1850, reported 'Pony hunting used to be one of the favourite amusements of the Welsh farmers and peasantry, a century and a half ago, and it has not,

The Mazawattee Tea Company's team of zebras, circa 1910.

even now, fallen altogether into disuse.' It went on to relate the story of a farmer called Hugo Garonwy who supplemented his income from farming with the capture and sale of wild mountain ponies or *merlyns*. 'He set out one morning with his lasso coiled around his waist, and attended by two hardy dependants and their greyhounds. The lasso was then familiar to the Welshman, and as adroitly managed by him as any gaucho on the plains of South America.' Having come across a herd of ponies, they cooped them up

in a corner of the hills where perpendicular rocks prevented their escape. Already had he captured three of the most beautiful little fellows in the world, which he expected to sell for four shillings or five shillings each at the next Bala Fair – to him a considerable sum . . . there remained, however, one most untameable creature, whose mane, and flowing tail, and wild eye, and distended nostril, showed that he was a perfect Bucephalus of the hills; nor indeed was it safe to attack him in the ordinary way. Many of the three year olds had been known to break the legs of their pursuers. Garonwy was determined to give the noble fellow a chase over the hills and so overcome him with fatigue before he lasso was flung . . . Vain was the effort to tire the merlyn. Hugo, naturally impatient, and without waiting to ascertain that the coils were all clear, flung the lasso over the head of the wild horse. The extremity of the cord was twisted around his own body, and tightening as the animal struggled, the compression became unsupportable, and, at length, in spite of every effort to disengage himself, Garonwy was dragged from his horse. The affrighted merlyn, finding himself manacled by the rope, darted off with all the speed of which he was capable, dragging poor Garonwy over the rocky ground and stunted brushwood. Whether the sufferings of the hunter were protracted, or he was dashed against some friendly rock at the commencement of this horrible race, was never known; but the wild animal, frenzied and blinded by terror, rushed over a beetling cliff, at a considerable distance, overhanging the seashore, and the hunter and the horse were found at the bottom, a mis-shapen semblance of what they had been when living.

There was evidently a good trade for wild-bred ponies, and Daniel Defoe in his *Tour through England and Wales*, written in 1722, spoke of 'colts, bred in great numbers on the moors, and sold into the northern counties where the horse copers, as they are called in Staffordshire and Leicestershire, buy them again and sell them for London for cart horses and coach horses . . .' As moorland vegetation would not have supported animals of much size, Defoe is probably misinformed of their ultimate line of work, and it is more likely that they ended their days pulling costers' barrows or tradesman's carts or working in mines.

New Forest ponies were no easier to catch than their Welsh counterparts, as a writer in 1868 noted. 'The catching of these ponies is as great a trial of skill as the hunting of the wild horse on the Pampas of South America, and a greater one of patience.' The ponies of Dartmoor were similar as Captain Colgrove of Dartmoor Prison found out when he employed a group of men to capture a particular pony he had selected as being superior to its peers. Having separated it from the herd

> they drove it on some rocks by the side of a tor . . . a man followed on horseback, while the captain stood below watching the chase. The little animal, being driven into a corner, leaped completely over the man and horse, and escaped.

CHAPTER FIVE

Breakers of the New World

It is one thing to be a bronco buster and another a horseman, and the
mixture of the two is rare to find.

Tschiffely's ride
A. F. Tschiffely

THE INTRODUCTION OF THE HORSE TO AMERICA

The horse was once indigenous to America but for some inexplicable
reason died out 8,000 years before the Spanish reintroduced it in the
late fifteenth century. Having expelled the Moors from Spain in
1492, they had skilled military horseman seeking fresh challenges,
and that same year Christopher Columbus, searching for new lands
and wealth on behalf of the Spanish monarchy who sponsored his
expeditions, set sail and ultimately and unexpectedly discovered the
New World. He had with him on that first voyage a number of
horses, some of which he landed on the island of Hispaniola, now
Haiti, and on his three subsequent voyages to the Americas he also
carried horses, importing around one hundred altogether, the majority being trained riding horses and stallions, as the Moorish prejudice
against gelding still prevailed.

Transporting horses by sea was a costly business, and as much as
50 per cent of the live cargo was regularly lost on the 4,000 nautical
mile journey. The horses were suspended in hammock slings
between the beams and the underdeck, or on smaller craft they stood
on the deck, hobbled and held either in a sling or in a travers-type
framework. In rough weather they were tied down but many were
swept overboard and others died of illness. If the ship was becalmed
near the equator and fresh water supplies ran low, some of the unfortunate horses were thrown overboard. Recognising the need for
breeding stock to be established in the New World, Columbus wrote
to the Spanish king in 1494 suggesting that 'each time there is sent
here any type of boat there should be included some brood mares'.

On his second journey Columbus had brought over twenty stallions and five brood mares, and other conquistadors when entering into an agreement with the king, Charles V, or his son Philip II, were bound to bring to America both stallions and mares, so a regular trade was established. Described as short-backed, short-legged, surefooted and strong, some of these horses came from the Cordoba region where a number of studs had been set up by the Moors in earlier years using Barb horses imported from North Africa. They were not only North African in blood, but their training and the style in which they were ridden was Moorish in origin, and the breaking method known and used by these invaders on the youngstock eventually bred in the New World owed much to its North African roots.

The importance of the horse in a military sense was indisputable. Columbus' first significant victory was on Hispaniola in 1495 when he attacked a large band of Indians with two hundred foot soldiers, twenty horses and a few dogs. According to Herrera, the Spanish historian, it was the horses the Indians fled from as they believed the strange animals would eat them. As further Spanish victories seemed likely to be dependent on a supply of trained military mounts, the breeding of horses became a matter of great importance. Fortunately, horses bred prolifically in the West Indies so that the nucleus of around seventy horses once recorded on Hispaniola increased until regular shipments of locally bred horses could be sent to the mainland. The first horses were reputedly taken from the islands to the isthmus in 1514, and five years later Cortés took sixteen horses, five mares and eleven stallions, two of which were coloured or spotted, to Mexico and founded the great wild herds there with them. Another conquistador, Pizarro, took horses to Peru, while in 1535 his compatriot, Mendoza, founder of Buenos Aires, took one hundred horses to the Rio de la Plata.

Five years later the settlement was ransacked by local charros and a number of horses escaped into the wild where they bred freely so that by 1590 travellers wrote of seeing wild horse herds of up to 50,000 animals on the South American pampas. One observer, writing in 1600, said there were simply too many horses to count, and four hundred years after the first Spanish horses were landed on Hispaniola there were over twenty-five million horses in America. Not only were the numbers of horses proliferating in the sixteenth and seventeenth centuries, the quality of the stock was being maintained. Writing in 1590, José de Acosta said that horses 'multiplied in the Indies and became most excellent, in some places being even as good as the best in Spain'. It was from this foundation stock that the horse herds of America developed.

THE NATIVE INDIAN AND THE HORSE

Nowhere was the horse to have a greater impact on people and change their lifestyle in so short a time as on the plains of North America. The Indians got their first horses from Spanish settlements, and it is likely that these animals were old, injured, unsound or footsore horses turned loose by the Spanish, although it is possible that some were stolen. As ranching in its early days spread north into northern Mexico and the territory that would become Texas and New Mexico, native labour was press-ganged for menial work on the ranches and, although regulations forbade Indians from riding horses, there was little enforcement of the rules. Some of the Jesuit Missions, set up in the wake of the Spanish invasion, kept cattle and horses and used the labour of Indians converted to Christianity to do the work. Some missions even disregarded the rules and mounted the Indians on trained horses to create a body of native vaqueros, thereby giving them the opportunity to learn the basics of horsemanship which they disseminated to other Indians.

As early as 1579 there were herds of wild horses in northern Mexico, and the Pueblo Indians were owning and riding horses by 1582. In 1680 this same tribe declared war on their Spanish oppressors in New Mexico, killing or driving them out, and seizing large numbers of horses which they distributed northwards through inter-tribal trading and theft. There is evidence to suggest that the Kiowa and Missouri Indians had horses by 1682, the Pawnee by 1700, the Comanches by 1714, the Plains Cree and Arikara by 1738, and the Crow, Mandan, Snake and Teton tribes by 1742. Forty years later horses were distributed right across the western plains.

The first Indian horses
According to Indian legend and folklore, the Comanches got horses first by raiding Spanish settlement in what is now New Mexico in 1705, and they passed some on to their kinsmen, the Shoshoni, and ultimately on to the Nez Perce and Flathead tribes. Although the

Comanches were not the first to own horses, they quickly became the most skilled in horsemanship, earning the respect of their peers and probably giving rise to the legend. While the dates may be doubtful, the source of the Comanche horse stock was not in dispute. George Catlin, the artist and traveller, wrote that the Comanche horses were small but powerful and 'undoubtedly sprung from a stock introduced by the Spaniards at the time of the invasion of Mexico'. Comanche warriors were adept horse thieves, and in the sign language of the plains a wriggling forefinger mimicking the silent stealth of a snake was the sign used to mean a Comanche tribesman.

James Teit, who in 1930 recorded the oral traditions and tribal folklore of the plains Indians, had a tale from the Katispel people concerning the first appearance of the horse. 'Some people saw the horse's tracks where it had passed over some sand. They called other people and discussed what kind of animal had made the tracks, which were strange to them all.' Later they saw a man mounted on a horse and 'gathered around they examined the animal with much curiosity'. Evidently these first horses acquired by the plains Indians were broken and quiet, for Teit also recorded the problems faced by Okanagan people in initially riding horses as they were very fearful of falling off. 'The first horse obtained was very gentle. The first person who mounted it rode with two long sticks, one in each hand, to steady himself. Another man led the horse slowly, and the rider shifted the sticks (as one does with walking sticks) as they went along.'

While the Indians of South America were terrified of horses, a fact the Spanish used to their advantage in warfare, the North American Indians neither feared the horse nor held it in awe. When James Adair, an Indian trader, wrote in 1775 of the tribes 'almost everyone hath horses', he might also have said that most were also very competent horsemen. By the mid-1600s horses were being imported from England and Ireland into Puritan settlements in Massachusetts, although only in small numbers, and in 1609 six mares and two stallions comprised the first horses imported into Virginia. Edicts forbade the Indians in both New England and Virginia from riding but such laws were impossible to enforce and the local tribes were soon proficient at riding and horse management. With incredible speed Indians right across the continent adopted the horse, turning themselves in the process into the last great horse culture of the world.

Up until they acquired the horse, the only livestock Indians had kept were dogs which they used for hunting and also for draught in a scaled-down form of travois. Many Indians even believed the horse was a form of large dog. The Assiniboin called it the Great Dog while the Blackfoot name for horse was Elk-dog, and the Sioux gave it spiritual significance with the title Medicine-dog.

Learning the skills of horsemanship

Most Indian horse skills were learnt rather than taught but, unlike many horse cultures in their infancy, the North American Indians had the advantage of access to at least some broken and trained horses in most cases. This accelerated their speed of learning and enabled them to begin catching and successfully handling wild horses at an early stage. In many respects their self-taught practices paralleled those of the Scythian culture thousands of years earlier, and the tack they devised was very similar except that the Indians soon adopted the stirrup. There were also clear traces of Spanish influence in the horsemanship of some tribes who mounted from the off side like the Spaniards or even copied Spanish armour by fashioning protective devices from hardened buffalo hide. Their breaking and initial handling techniques showed more diversity as the Spanish dealt with horses either bred in captivity and handled from birth or kept in at least semi-domesticated herds whereas the Indians needed to catch, tame and break animals from the increasingly large herds roaming wild. The Indians were very skilled stalkers and hunters, and they utilised these skills in the catching of wild horses. Prior to getting their first horses around 1650 Apaches had even stalked and killed buffalo on foot which says much for their stealth, patience and courage. An essential piece of equipment the Indians used was the lasso which they probably copied from the Spanish who used it in roping cattle in ranching. Made from plaited rawhide or fibre, it had to be very strong and also heavy enough to throw successfully.

Adapting hunting skills to equestrianism

The favoured Indian method of catching horses from the wild herds was to drive a large group of horses into a ravine or closed-off pass where they were pressed close together to make their main defence of flight difficult. Selected animals were then roped by one or more men, securing the running loop of the lasso just behind the jowl to cut the horse's breath off and 'choke it down'. Sometimes the catchers used fast and agile hunting ponies to pursue and rope their quarry from horseback on the open plain.

Thomas James, who was adopted as the *moneta* or brother of a Comanche chief, observed the capture of wild horses in 1832 and wrote of how mounted beaters drove the herd to a place where around one hundred Indians waited in hiding in a deep ravine.

> As soon as the wild drove was sufficiently near, these last rushed among them and every Indian secured his horse with his lasso, or noosed rope, which he threw around the neck of the animal, and by a sudden turn brought him to the ground and there tied his heels together. This was the work of a few minutes during which both horses and men were intermingled together in apparently inextricable confusion . . .

Some tribes preferred the technique of lassoing and throwing wild horses, tying their front and hind legs together, then releasing the lasso before the captive strangled, the whole operation taking little more than a few minutes. The Shoshoni were said to be the first to use the lasso, and they were experts at 'casting the cord'. Before long the use of the lasso became so widespread among the tribes that in Sioux pictograph writing the image of a lasso meant a wild horse. Some tribes used a flexible willow loop on a pole, similar to an Asian *uraga*, but whatever type was used their skill in wielding it was amazing. Captain Randolph B. Mercy in his book, *Thirty years of army life on the border*, recorded watching two young Comanche women chasing antelope on horseback with lassos, and roping two with their first throws. These skills were the result of much practice.

George Catlin who, with thirty Indian guides, a war party of ninety Comanches, and a troop of cavalry crossed the country between the Washita and Red River around 1838 commented on the wild horses and said 'Whilst on our march, we met with many droves of these beautiful animals, and several times had the opportunity of seeing the Indians pursue them, and take them with the lasso.' Among the Comanches both men and women rode, and their skill was such that Catlin was unequivocal in describing them as 'the most extraordinary horsemen that I have yet seen in all my travels', concluding 'I doubt very much whether any people in the world can surpass them.' His

Bronc riding as a competitive rodeo sport. (Photograph: DeVere Halfrich/National Cowboy Hall of Fame and Western Heritage Centre, Oklahoma City)

statement is the more remarkable considering their horse skills were not traditional but learnt over little more than a few generations. 'When starting for the capture of a wild horse' he wrote,

the Indian mounts the fleetest steed he can get and, coiling the lasso under his arm, starts off at full speed until he enter the band, when he soon throws the lasso over the neck of one of the number. He then instantly dismounts, leaving his own horse, and runs as fast as he can, letting the lasso pass out gradually and carefully through his hands until the horse falls half suffocated, and lies helpless on the ground. The Indian now advances slowly towards the horse's head, keeping the lasso tight upon his neck until he has fastened a pair of hobbles upon his forefeet; he now loosens the lasso, and adroitly casts it in a noose around the lower jaw, the animal, meanwhile, rearing and plunging. Advancing warily, hand over hand, the man at length places his hand over the animal's eyes, and on its nose, and then breathes into its nostrils, on which the horse becomes so docile and thoroughly conquered that his captor has little else to do but to remove the hobbles from his feet, and ride or lead it into camp.

To the Indian who counted his wealth in horses and derived his status from the increased mobility and power horse ownership gave him, riding became a way of life. Randolph Marcy wrote 'He is in the saddle from boyhood to old age, and his favourite horse is his constant companion.'

Developing systems of horse breaking

Like the nomadic tribesman of Asia, the North American Indians developed specialised and unique ways of breaking horses which produced animals suited to their needs. Thomas James who observed Indians breaking horses in the 1820s was amazed at their skill in handling and taming wild-caught animals. He wrote 'In twenty-four hours after their capture these horses became tamed and ready for use . . . I could perceive little difference between them and our farm horses.' Generally, Indians were firm but not brutal in their methods, and demonstrated great patience and tenacity.

Although there were inevitable tribal differences, a customary method of breaking was for several men to rope the selected horse and hold it securely by one or more slip ropes around the neck. It was allowed to pull and plunge for a little while to realise it could not escape, then one man worked his way gradually up the rope, moving slowly as not to frighten the horse, and continually talking to it. Great emphasis was placed on the sound the approaching man made. Chief Long Lance said horse talk was a low grunting sound from deep in the chest, rather like 'huh, huh', and curiously similar to the command 'whoa'. The man who approached the horse then retreated back, repeating the process time and again until the horse got used to him and to what he smelt like, as the smell of man was something most wild horses were very wary of. The man would then wave a blanket or sometimes a buffalo robe (skin) over and about the horse. If the horse leapt about, the other men held it firmly and the breaker just continued with his work. The most difficult part was actually to touch the horse and this was done with quietness and great care. It was said that not until the horse accepted the smell of man could the

breaker touch the horse gently on the nose. This led to slipping a halter on the horse's head. The halter was made of rawhide, no thicker
than a bootlace but very strong, and it was looped over the nose,
around the poll, and through the loop again. It gave the handler great
power, as the slightest pull brought great pressure to bear on the
nerves of the nose and upper neck, and the thinness of the rawhide
concentrated this pressure.

Once the horse was haltered, the other men could be dispensed
with. The breaker touched the horse, running his hand over the head,
neck, shoulder, back and flanks which might cause the horse to jump
but the man continued undeterred. All the time he communicated
verbally with the animal but now it was a hissing sound, similar to
that made by old-fashioned grooms who said it kept the dust out of
their mouths when brushing a horse although it has been suggested
that the sound pitch had a soothing effect on the horse. After the
pupil was touched on both sides, it was gently hit all over with the
loose end of the rawhide rope then its legs were touched, which was
considered one of the most difficult parts of the whole procedure.
Once the man could touch all parts of the horse, it was considered
nearly broken with the final stages of mounting and riding deemed
least difficult. The breaker moved to the side of the horse, pressed
lightly on its back, then harder, then placing his elbows on its back
drew himself up to lean right over. If at any stage the horse jumped,
a sharp jerk on the halter would check it. Gradually the horse was
then mounted, and it was reported that few animals broken in this
way bucked or resisted at all. Most stood perfectly still then, in the
words of Robert Denhardt 'after a few moments of urging would trot
off at an aimless and awkward gait'.

Once broken, the horse's ears would be notched in various patterns to denote ownership and also to facilitate recognition by feel in
the dark. Some tribes also slit the nostrils of their horses in the belief
that this increased their intake of air and made them faster. Peter
Pond, writing in 1745, said 'In order to have thare horseis long
winded' the Dakota Sioux 'slit thair noses up to the grissel of thare
head which make them breathe verey freely'. Some Indians, especially near white settlements, used Spanish-style tack including
bridles, bits and sadddles for breaking and general riding, but most
rode with only a halter or a simple jaw bridle and no saddle or just an
animal skin girthed in place.

Riding the newly broken horse

It was common practice to ride with the loose end of the single halter rope or neck rope dragging along behind on the ground so that if the rider was unseated he could grab it and regain control of the horse. Some tribes tied the head of the newly broken horse to that of an experienced and quiet schoolmaster for initial riding, and this method was sometimes used for the actual breaking itself. The same system was used by Boers in South Africa during the last century, but the drawback was that the animal never learned to go on its own, and teaching the basic aids for control was difficult. Noting the sub-duing effects of a noose around the throat when catching a horse, some Indian breakers kept a slip rope on their mount during early riding and tightened it if the horse played up.

Indians were also very skilled at using the lasso from the back of another horse to catch their prey, and this dramatic method was well documented by nineteenth-century travellers. The breaker pursued the wild herd at full speed and threw the noose of his lasso, which was between ten and fifteen yards in length and made of twisted or plaited rawhide, over the neck of the selected animal. The Indian rarely had a saddle to tie the rope to as cowboys did although some tried but discontinued tying the end of the lasso around the tame horse's neck. Having roped a wild horse, he therefore dismounted and, leaving his own horse, pulled back on the lasso until the horse was 'choked down' and fell to the ground for want of breath. Keeping the lasso on its neck, he hobbled the front legs, then loosened the noose a little to let the animal breathe while he fixed a jaw noose on its lower jaw which gave him considerable control. If the animal plunged, the hobbles held it, and the man advanced up the rope again to place his hand on its nose. If necessary he may have to throw the horse several times until it was subdued enough for him to breathe into its nostrils thereby accustoming it to the scent of man. Fatigued and conquered, the hobbles were loosened or even removed and the animal taken home to camp. This system exhausted its strength while impressing upon it the power of man.

Specific tribes adopted individual systems for handling wild horses. Canadian Blackfoot Indians employed four men on ropes to hold the horse while another used the blanket method on it, and they also used jaw noose bridles and leg ropes for hobbling. Osage Indians tied the wild horse to a tame horse for a whole week, night and day, and even rode it in this fashion, but other tribes were harsher in their methods including the Navaho who used a lasso to cut the horse's breath off then hobbled and repeatedly threw it until it was exhausted when it was mounted and ridden. According to a booklet produced by the American Horse Training Institute of Columbus, Kansas, 'among the methods used by Indians in times past have been starving the pony and denying him water until the pony was so weak that he could not resist. Then the Indian mounted and rode him.'

The Indian as a herdsman

As the Indian horse culture flourished, many tribes began to acquire large herds of semi-domesticated horses. Crow Indians added around 10,000 captured wild horses to their vast herds, and at the Great Peace of 1844 the Kiowa presented the Cheyenne with so many horses they did not have enough halters to lead them home. At the Little Big Horn in June 1876, five thousand of the Sioux and Cheyenne charging Custer were mounted on wild-bred mustangs caught and broken by their riders.

The breaking of horses from tame tribal herds was a different matter. Tending the herds was the responsibility of boys who, according to observers, began learning the skills of herding as infants by playing rounding up beetles. They learned to ride at a very early age, and later tended the herds which helped get the horses used to the smell and sight of man before they were broken. Generally, breaking was done in the Spring when the horses were three-year-olds. They practised a system which resembled 'gentling' to quieten the horse prior to actually mounting.

The Sioux along the Missouri River would lead the unbroken horses from a quiet horse into a river and, according to Frank Dobie, 'there stroked the wildish colts, unable to get away, gentling them as they grew up'. Other tribes followed similar procedures. Blackfoot boys would mount double on a quiet horse and lead the unbroken horse into water where one would mount the wild one. If the water came up to the horse's shoulders, the effect of the water plus the boy's weight restricted its movements. It was then let loose and the tame horse ridden out of the water leaving the wild horse marooned in the water to get accustomed to a rider. The process was repeated many times until the wild horse could be ridden out too. As Indians seldom rode alone, the herd instinct of surrounding a newly broken horse with other horses gave it confidence. The tribe the French called Gros Ventre, although the name was later used by English speakers too, also broke their horses in water but as swimming wild horses was for them a common practice, and as they spent so much time with their horses, basic handling to riding was a gradual process.

Horses were also broken for draught in order to pull the travois, and this was done by teaching the horse to drag a buffalo hide behind it by means of two ropes around his neck. The animal was led, and later two or more boys sat on the hide as the pupil pulled them over smooth, grassy ground. Spills were frequent.

Horse medicine cults
For teenage Indian boys, it was a great honour to be invited to take an active part in the breaking and riding of young horses as it had a rites of passage importance to it, and was part of the social structure within the tribe. Any exceptional young horseman might be invited to join the horse medicine cults, a very great honour, and the cults' spiritual power and influence was itself a part of the breaking ritual. Catlin wrote that Indians took great care 'not to subdue the spirit of the animal' when breaking horses. They developed a great relationship with individual horses, and those reserved for war or buffalo hunts were highly prized and treated with great affection. Geronimo, the famous chief, claimed to have a special relationship with his war pony and said 'My horse was trained to come at call, and as soon as I reached a safe place, if not too closely pursued, I would call him to me.' As Geronimo was known to be a compulsive liar, his claim was probably grossly exaggerated.

MUSTANGS AND THEIR CAPTURE

The Indians were not the only ones interested in the vast herds of wild mustangs. As ranching crept north from Mexico and settlers moved west from the cities, the catching, taming and breaking of mustangs became big business. The name was Spanish in origin and came from *mestengo* meaning an animal which strays on its way to pasture, and *mostrenco* meaning homeless. The term mustang came to represent feralised horses which escaped from the range controlled by a grazier, and the *mestenero* or mustanger was the man who caught them. Some were professionals, others worked on ranches and caught horses for ranch use only or to sell or as a paying sport.

Catching mustangs was a very dangerous occupation, as Judge J. W. Moses wrote in the *San Antonio Express* in 1888, when he described how he had been the captain of a party of fourteen mustangers who, thirty-eight years earlier, had caught around one hundred horses on one trip. He wrote 'Apart from casualties of the chase, the falls and possibilities of getting hurt, sometimes crippled, and the danger of sunstroke and exposure to all kinds of weather, there were roving bands of Comanches and other Indians who not only had an inordinate love for horse flesh but a decided perchant for scalps.' Thomas A. Dwyer, writing around 1872, said 'To see these mustangers in full chase was to behold one of the most exciting scenes presented by the wild sports and occupations of Texas frontier life.'

A common method of catching was to construct a circular corral of posts lashed together with rawhide, with wings of up to half a mile in length and made of brushwood, posts or branches. The corral was constructed to be strong but flexible and therefore less likely to break under the pressure of milling horses, and it was circular so that the horses could not get into any corners hurting themselves or breaking through the fence. The horses were driven in by mounted mustangers who, a contemporary observer wrote, tightened their girths, shortened their stirrups for grip, or sometimes even rode bareback for the job. Once in the corral, a bar was put across the entrance with a flapping blanket thrown over it to keep the horses off. Selected horses were roped from the outside and dragged out through the entrance or by removing a few posts from the fence. Sometimes a quiet horse was ridden into the corral and the lassoed captor roped to it or to a quiet burro and dragged out. Some mustangers fastened heavy wooden clogs above the fetlock of the front legs to restrict the mustang's movement, and some were sidelined with a rope fastening the front legs to the back legs. Other mustangers would drive the newly caught horses off in a herd of tame and quiet horses as mustangs were always much more amenable once off their familiar range. Injuries were common, but any damaged horses were just turned loose again, while minor injuries healed quickly. Unhandled, they sold as they stood for around two and a half dollars each, although some were broken in first and sold for more.

Walking down wild horses

G. C. Robinson, writing in the *Dallas Morning Star* in September 1928, described the system of 'walking mustangs down'. One or more riders would quietly follow the herd for days on end until the horses became accustomed to their presence. The mustangers never changed their clothes or their mounts or allowed other people near during this time, and they 'drifted' the horses into their corral quietly so fewer injuries resulted. The skilful Indians also used this method but they even did it on foot. It was said that some 'walkers' kept the horses from water and prevented them sleeping or resting. Working in relays, it took eight to ten days to walk the mustangs down until they could be lassoed. Sometimes the animals were allowed to drink when very thirsty, as when full of water they could be caught more easily. Those involved in catching horses by this method all agreed that Spring was the best time for mustanging when the animals were weak after the winter.

Nicking or creasing

Another method of catching was more barbaric and was known as nicking or creasing. An illustrated article in *Harpers Weekly* in November 1868 described the practice, which consisted of shooting the mustang through the top of the neck just in front of the shoulders which, being a nerve centre close to the spinal column, stunned the animal unconscious for a few minutes during which time it could be roped and hobbled. Early creasers using balls instead of bullets sometimes favoured wounding the animal closer to the poll, but it needed a steady hand and a skilful shot. It was a system learned through experience by hunters of buffalo and, although it was successful, it also meant animals were blemished and sometimes even died later through infection, while others were left with impaired neck action. An inaccurate shot could kill the horse although with so many on the plain that was not seen as a problem.

S. H. Ellis, who as a boy used to accompany his father, a noted mustanger, on mustanging trips in Texas, recalled one such expedition. His father used to bring the animal down with his large bore rifle and his son used to dash in and rope the horse down. For days they followed a very fine blue roan mustang which they desperately sought to own but it was wild and elusive and their attempts at getting a shot at it at the various water holes its herd drank at were unsuccessful. Eventually they got close enough and his father care-fully took aim and pulled the trigger and the horse fell, but the shot had broken its neck and it lay dead. Ellis recalled 'Dumb with agonis-ing disappointment and regret, I stood looking down upon the dead mustang, a moment before the wildest and most graceful and beauti-ful I had ever seen.' Other mustangers told similar tales of disappointment. Two men who attempted to crease a fine iron-grey mustang with only fowling pieces which they knew did not have the accuracy of a rifle succeeded only in stampeding the herd out of sight leaving their intended quarry dead with a broken neck.

Breaking mustangs

If the catching was hazardous, the breaking of mustangs was more so. Driving the wild horses, even as part of a tame herd, could be fraught with danger before the ranch corrals were reached. One group of mustangers driving horses through San Antonio in the late 1880s had their herd bolt into a narrow alley and through the open door of a house at the end killing several people, injuring others, and

Dennis Magner's method of handling a wild mustang.

wrecking the house. Fallen riders were sometimes trampled to death if the herd panicked.

Horse breakers were poorly paid for their dangerous work, usually around two and a half dollars, the same price as the value of a wild mustang before it was broken. The short stirrup style of riding copied from the Spanish was adapted to a style with longer stirrups as it was difficult to mount a horse with a short stirrup, and long stirrups caused less leg ache when riding all day as these horsemen did. Their breaking methods varied. Some simply rode the saddled wild horse until it gave in, some strapped one foreleg up, or fastened a sack of pebbles to the saddle, and some tied the pupil to a burro or wild donkey and left the pair loose in a high-sided corral to pull until they had exhausted each other. A female burrow was always selected for this method as jack burros could be vicious. Other breakers used a scotch hobble to tie one back leg up for as long as half a day, sometimes while the horse was snubbed to a post, or tied a blanket to the surcingle-like cinch and turned the horse loose in a pen to get used to the flapping blanket. Some breakers even spun their horses around on a rope or tied their heads to their tails so that they could only go in circles to make them dizzy before riding them.

MEXICAN HORSE BREAKING

The Mexicans were skilled breakers, and the *domador* or breaker was a knowledgeable and resourceful man who literally lived by his wits every time he rode an unbroken horse or *potro*. José Maria Cisneros, who broke horses until at eighty years of age a horse kicked and killed him, said no two horses were the same to break. The Mexican/Texan method of breaking was standardised over many years. The horse was caught by penning the *menada* or bunch of horses in which the pupil ran, then roping it around the neck and driving the others out of the pen. Usually horses were not broken until they were five years old as if they were younger they were not strong enough, and if older they could be too set in their ways and difficult. While the horse was held on a thirty-feet long lasso, the domador approached, hand over hand, up the rope and fitted a blindfold called a *tapojo* over its eyes so that the animal was in total darkness. The tapojo could be a piece of blanket or a bandana or neckerchief, or a strip of soft leather with lace ties to keep it in place, or

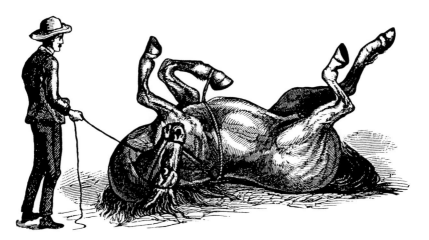

Sometimes the mustang would throw itself during taming.

just a piece of rough canvas. The domador was then handed a hackamore by his assistant which he slipped on the horse. The hackamores used were rawhide nosebands, softened with tallow, not the mechanical leverage type now often sold by the same name, and they acted on the sensitive nose of the horse.

Breakers always used the same hackamore, as they reckoned the 'hang and drop' of the rawhide noseband came from years of use, and a new hackamore took more breaking in than a herd of horses. A strong rope was attached to the back of the noseband, the tapojo was raised from the horse's eyes, and the domador gave the horse enough slack on the rope to let him career through the open gate and into the open where he was encouraged to fight for his freedom. The domador held him on the hackamore by digging the narrow, forward-sloping heels of his boots into the ground. With the help of the assistant the horse was chased, cajoled or encouraged to follow a quiet horse to a nearby tree where he was securely fastened to learn the essential lesson of being tied up. Some breakers tied the horse direct to the trunk of the tree, others tied the potro to a strong bough which kept the rope out of harm's way and allowed a little flexibility and give. While the horse was thus tied, the breaker would turn his attention to others at various stages of breaking, for as many as twenty horses may be broken at once.

The next day the horse would be tied to the tree again, and might even be left fastened up all night if it was particularly obstreperous.

One method used to cure horses which pulled back when tied up.

The system was a variation on the snubbing post theme with its Moorish roots. The potro was blindfolded again, the saddle blanket and saddle were girthed in place, the blind was raised and the horse left to get used to the feel and creaking sound of the saddle and girth. Sometimes a leg was strapped up while the horse was saddled. Experienced domadors related how some horses stood still and were sullen, while some stood a while and then exploded, and others even lay down. After some time had lapsed and the horse was resigned to its situation, the blindfold was again pulled down, and the rope was looped round into a pair of reins with the long loose end coiled and tied to the saddle horn. Some held the coil in their hand and used it to hit the horse if necessary, knowing that if they were thrown they could hold the horse with it. This practice dated from the riding of mustangs on the open range in early days when the saddle might be worth fifty dollars but the horse only two and a half so the loss of a saddle was very serious if the horse escaped.

Some domadors did the riding themselves, but others used the services of a young bronco-buster called a *jinete* who did little else. These professional rough riders adopted riding styles of their own, some wearing spurs and using them to help them stay in the saddle, and others relying on balance and sometimes extending their right arm, hat in hand, in a wide circular motion like a tightrope walker

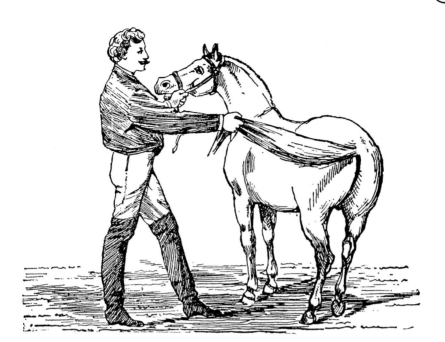

Spinning a horse by the headcollar and tail.

with a long pole to help them hold their position. Some would sit quietly, some would shout. The jinete's performance was usually watched by a crowd of enthusiastic spectators who yelled encouragement if they were being well entertained. If a rider lost his hat it was usually because he was losing his balance, and the sight of a rider 'hanging and rattling' or 'about to meet his shadow' brought shouts of disapproval from the audience. Few jinetes actually came off but if they did they mounted quickly and finished the job. Nervous riders who showed any hesitation in remounting had to endure derisive remarks from bystanders who would sarcastically advise them to take yerbanis, a herb made into an infusion and traditionally used for treating those suffering from shock.

Just as riders differed, so did the horses. Some plunged and bucked, dropped a shoulder, spun, leapt in successive bounds, or just bolted flat out in terror. A mustang's greatest enemy was the mountain lion which killed by leaping onto the back of its prey so a rider suggested the same threat and caused the horse to buck out of defence. The hackamore usually effected adequate control and the once-ridden horse, now called a *qebrantado*, was ridden twice daily, morning and afternoon, spending the rest of the day either tied to the staking tree or tethered out to a heavy log or stone to graze. On the prairie where there were no suitable trees to tie a horse to, a stake in the ground would be used. Constant handling tamed the horse. In due course the breaking hackamore was replaced with a lighter halter called a bozalillo, some artistically made of plaited hemp rope, yarn, wool or horsehair. The pupil was taught to turn and halt and, always being handled from the nearside, to turn anti-clockwise when being mounted to help swing the rider into the saddle. Later the bozalillo was replaced with a bridle and bit, although both bridle and bozalillo were sometimes used in a transitionary period with two sets of reins. After a month or so the horse would be returned to its owner broken, and a trainer called an *arrendador* brought in to continue its education. Many arrendadors were retired domadors, no longer young, and seeking lighter work.

Although most domadors were excellent and skilled men, some were not, and the latter often starved their horses before breaking to quieten them giving rise to an old saying in Mexico 'with no grass and little water results a very gentle horse'. Such men were scorned, as they broke the spirit of the animal, although many horses were broken in spirit and body anyway. Frank Dobie, writing in 1954, said 'one out of every three mustangs captured in south-west Texas was expected to die before they were tamed. The process of breaking often broke the spirits of the other two.'

Dangers of the profession
The domadors themselves were not infrequently injured and killed. The work was hard and the men aged quickly with aches and pains which led to arthritic stiffness before they were old. Many were crippled by falls or lamed, and they worked out their days in livery stables or doing menial jobs on ranches or drifting from place to place. Felipe Pachero, an experienced domador, was employed by a ranch to break horses which he did single-handed. One day a group of horses was found with a saddled potro among them, exhausted and, from the way the girth was buried in its swollen sides, one that had been saddled for several days. A search found Felipe dead under a tree where the potro had swept him off. Another domador was dragged to his death when his spurred boot became entangled in the hackamore rope. The danger of a horse falling or throwing itself

down, flattening the stirrup and trapping the foot, was very real and as one breaker recalled 'For this, we wore six-shooters . . . to shoot the horse was the only answer.' The incompetent work of unskilled bone setters in remote settlements left many injured breakers with crooked or shortened limbs which in later days fell prey to arthritic problems. The use of patent embrocations to alleviate the aches and pains of their job was supplemented with the drinking of a special tea brewed from the inner bark of the *huisache* which was an old remedy for knocks and injuries. Bad falls caused some to lose their nerve, and the cowboy saying 'A man is as good as his nerves' referred to breaking horses.

OTHER AMERICAN STYLES OF HORSE BREAKING

There were regional differences in the breaking of wild horses. In California around 1820 the system was to run the horses as a wild herd, only catching them once or maybe twice in their lives for castrating and branding. The breaker's skill with a lariot, the rope used both as a lasso and as a picketing rope, was incredible and learned from an early age. Alexander Forbes, writing a history of California in 1839, said he saw a small child with a lasso made of light twine lassoing his mother's chickens, while his elders could even lasso low-flying geese with a lariot or 'la riata' of sixty feet. The lassos were made with great care, sometimes from the tail hair of mares but never stallions as this was deemed an insult to the animal – another possible legacy of Arab horse culture.

Colts were broken at four or five years of age and, as with the Texans and Mexicans, the herd was corralled, one selected and roped, and the rest driven out, but here a second lasso was secured around the forefeet and the animal thrown. One man sat on its head to prevent it rising while another tied all four feet together. A hackamore with a long hair rope was fitted, along with a blindfold, and the ensuing stages of breaking were very similar to the Texan and Mexican method with a few distinct additions. One was the practice of fastening the young horse's ears under the headstall while it was being saddled to prevent it hearing and possibly to distract its attention from what was going on. Some riders freed the ears before getting in the saddle, or only did so when they were mounted. As an aid to staying on, many riders buckled a leather strap over the saddle with

Tying a horse head to tail.

enough room for them to slip their knees under the strap to give them extra grip and security. To release themselves, they simply straightened their legs by sliding their feet out of the stirrups. If a horse bucked persistently, a harsh method of discouraging it was to leave it with its head tied up high all night so that next morning the stiffness in its neck would make it reluctant to lower its head to buck.

The saying 'the jaquima makes the horse' referred to the use of the jaquima, or hackamore, the Americanised form of the original Spanish word, for early riding as it protected the young horse's mouth and also because a horse was less likely to rear and fall backwards in a hackamore than a bridle with a curb bit. Only when the horse was riding on quietly was it introduced to a bit, and this often caused them to regress into bucking and resisting again. The reason was because of the severity of the curb bits which, although they often had copper mouthpieces to encourage salivation, were also fitted with spades, little wheels called crickets, and other devices to further increase their severity.

Across most of America, horses were 'broke and busted' in a traditional endurance test between man and beast which evolved from the great availability of horses and the need to break them quickly and cheaply. In Louisiana in the early 1800s, particularly difficult horses were turned loose in a high-sided corral with a dry, crackling cow hide tied to their tails and left to 'frighten themselves quiet'. Considering a decent broken horse was only worth between twenty and thirty-five dollars at the end of the last century, the breakers justifiably argued that they could not afford to spend a lot of time breaking a horse.

London Brown, a veteran of the plains, produced a pamphlet around 1892 entitled 'An old time cowboy' in which he gave advice on how to ride a difficult horse for the first time. 'When you go to ride a bad horse' he wrote

> first get your horse by the bridle and pull his head to one side as far as you can and stick your forefingers in his eyes as deep as you can and if the horse pitches sit as limber as you can and twist your toes around in your saddle stirrup and you will find that it will be much easier on you and always handle stubborn horses rough . . .

His startling advice was probably intended to distract the horse's attention, in the same way as would fastening the ears under the headstall. On some ranches, especially those where better quality horses were bred specifically, the breaking was done more carefully in a specially constructed circular pen with high sloping-out sides to protect the rider's knees from injury. Like the gyrus of Roman times, the high sides helped focus the animal's concentration, and the circular track encouraged forward movement. A dummy rider in the form of a 50 lb bag of chaff was sometimes used to accustom the horse to a weight on its back before it was mounted, and the whole breaking process was spread over a much longer period of time. Some more enlightened breakers disliked the system of roping a horse to a post or tree until lack of breath caused it to fall flat, as they felt this could damage the ligaments and muscles of the neck, causing the horse to carry its head low in later life.

Hog-tying all four feet together and some forms of hobbling could cause bad rope burns to horses, while the practice of fore-footing was dangerous, as if the breaker missed lassoing both front legs a broken or dislocated leg could result. Even so, many breakers working on their own still favoured forefooting. The use of twisted rawhide bosals, some with spiked inner surfaces, could cause injury to the sensitive area just above the soft part of the nose, and some ruthless breakers used bosals covered in twisted or even barbed wire. The bosal was usually kept in place by a leather strap fastened to each side

'A sulky, vicious colt will usually kick when touched.'

of the bosal and passing around the poll called a latigo, and some had a rope from the back of the bosal and around the neck to prevent the bosal from possibly slipping off. A thin cord called a fiador or theodore which crossed the face helped keep the bosal in the correct position.

Further training after the horse was 'bucked out' was often as brutal as the actual breaking. Neck-reining was sometimes taught by throwing the horse and bruising one side of its neck with a rock or hammer, then the unfortunate animal was rolled over and the process repeated on the other side so that next day when the neck was swollen and sore the horse would be more responsive to learning. The skill of holding cattle on a rope was occasionally taught by roping a strong, wild steer to the saddle horn after which the cowboy dismounted and left the two animals to fight it out. At the end of the day, exponents of the system claimed, the horse was either good at roping or crippled. If they were hard on their horses, life was hard for the cowboys themselves and once they could no longer ride they were obsolete and obliged to eke out a living as best they could. Some turned their hand to making and selling the equipment the cowboys and breakers used including ropes of cotton, manilla, plaited rawhide, and even the fibre of maguey, bromelia, agave and other plants which they combed out and plaited. Ixtle, as the plant fibre was known, was also used to make horse brushes. They also made hackamore bosals of plaited horse hair of different colours, lassos, lariots and plaited hide riding whips called quirts.

LADY HORSE BREAKERS

Although horse breaking was essentially a male dominated occupation, there were a few lady breakers too, most of whom owned ranches and broke horses for their own use. Agnes Morley of Magdalene, New Mexico, learned ranching quickly following the death of her father and her mother's remarriage to a scoundrel who ran off leaving them to run a large ranch although neither had any experience. Stuck on a horse at the age of ten, she later wrote 'we learned to ride by the simple process of riding', but she learnt so well that seven years later her skill in riding broncs was recognised by the *Mine and Lariot* magazine who reported 'Miss Agnes and Three-fingered Pete are the best riders in the county.'

The work of breaking horses was hard and dirty but as Margaret Duncan Brown, a lady rancher and bronc buster, confessed, 'cleanliness is undoubtedly next to godliness, but there are times when I am too ungodly tired to care about either cleanliness or godliness'. If horsewomen had to suffer derision from their male peers, the immigrants and visitors who introduced the traditions of European horse breaking to the east coast of America suffered more. Evolved to produce horses for quite different purposes than the cattle herding of further west, the eastern methods and the 'pancake' English hunting saddles they used were a source of ridicule for the cowboys.

THE BIRTH OF THE RODEO

The skills of the cowboy in handling and riding wild horses gave rise to the American rodeo which developed from the day-to-day ranch work skills and wagers and challenges made between hands from different ranches. The Mexican rodeo probably owed its origin in part to Spanish influence traced back to European tournaments and combin-

If tied head to tail too short, the horse is liable to throw itself on the ground.

ing pageantry with riding skills in the form of a fiesta-type event. The word rodeo literally meant a roundup. The 101 ranch in Winfield, Kansas, claimed to have staged the first rodeo in 1882 as the town was having a fair and George W. Miller, owner of the 101 ranch, was asked to provide an unusual attraction. He had some Texas cowboys on his ranch at the time who had come up the Chisholm Trail driving cattle, and they put on a display of bronco busting. Twenty-two years later the ranch began its own famous displays of western riding skills.

At Guthrie, Oklahoma, in 1905, a huge pasture was fenced off and a mile long procession led by a cavalry band and Chief Geronimo, brought specially from Fort Sill for the occasion, opened a show which included wild-horse riding which was very popular as it was both spectacular and dangerous. It was soon copied elsewhere, and Buffalo Bill's much travelled Wild West Show even became famous in Europe where royalty and heads of state flocked to see it. At the early rodeos where the skills of horse breaking were first adapted into a competitive sport, the event was judged on how long the rider could remain in the saddle. At a rodeo in western Canada around 1920, one particular bronc threw everyone who got on it including

The Comanche war bridle recommended by Captain Horace Hayes.

the *ranahan* or top hand of the local ranch, who was injured as a result. The best bronco buster of the region was an Indian called Tom Three-Persons who was in jail at the time, but the sheriff agreed to release him with a police escort so that he could ride the horse. When he arrived, the horse was roped and thrown, the Indian mounted it on the ground and the horse allowed to leap to its feet. For ten minutes Tom Three-Persons rode the plunging horse to a great ovation from the crowd, after which the police seized him and returned him to his cell. Nowadays in both saddle bronc and bareback bronc riding, the rider is judged on style rather than the length of time he remains on the horse.

A. F. Tschiffely, writing in 1933, recalled attending a *jaripo* or Mexican rodeo at which a *charro* or horseman in a display of supreme confidence 'tied his rope, ending in a running noose, around his neck, and, when thus tied, roped and threw a wild horse. The slightest mistake in judgement would probably have been fatal.' At another Mexican rodeo, a charro

> chased a wild mare and, when he had the chance, jumped onto her back. When she had successfully tried every vicious trick in her repertoire to shake him off, the charro spurred her into a gallop, and then called his tame and splendidly trained saddle horse, which immediately came alongside the racing mare, whereupon the man jumped gracefully back into the saddle.

The trick was called the death pass, and included some of the many skills of the professional breaker.

Spinning a horse while it is tied head to tail.

From the very beginning, South American Indians had a tremendous fear of horses, and this played no small part in permitting the Spanish to establish military supremacy over them. Tabasquenos Indians called horses *tequares,* meaning monsters, and believed the horse and rider were actually one being. As wild horses prospered in South America, the Indians began to overcome their fears and to catch, break and ride horses. Some tribes ate horseflesh, drank melted horse fat, and even washed their hair in horse blood in the belief that it might imbue them with some of the qualities of the horse, including speed and stamina. Patagonian Indians were riding horses by 1585, while ten years later there were so many horses in Paraguay it was decreed that they belonged to whoever could catch them.

The vast grassy pampas of South America stretching from southern Brazil through Paraguay, Uraguay and Argentina was a great horse breeding area with huge wild herds. Cattle breeding ranches were established to exploit the natural vegetation, and Indians were employed to work on these ranches, learning horse skills in the process. The South American method of breaking was directly derived from the European method of Iberian descent and involved the roping down of the horse, hobbling, hitching to a snubbing post,

A South American gaucho quietly approaches a colt after it has been lassoed by a mounted assistant. (Photograph: Tom Ryder)

saddling and riding out. Horses were not given names until they were broken in, and the name was usually related to the colour or markings.

In Paraguay the breaking was brutal and the horse was given little rest between being roped and snubbed at the beginning and finally ridden to exhaustion with a severe curb bit and spurs. As with this type of breaking elsewhere, any injured animals were just turned loose again until sound and another roped in their place. One piece of equipment used in South America and rarely employed elsewhere was the *bolas*, a device originally used by Indians to entangle the legs of their enemies in battle. Don Felix de Araza, writing in 1837 about the catching of wild horses, said that when the catchers were close enough to the horses they

> throw their bolas, or balls, at them: these balls are three stones, about the size of a man's fist, rolled up in leather, and tied to a common centre with strong leather cords, more than a yard in length. They take hold of one, which is rather smaller, and, after flourishing or whirling the other two several times round their head, they discharge the whole three, and entangle them in the horse's legs in such a manner that it cannot run, affording an opportunity to throw the lasso. This lasso is a piece of cow's leather, of the thickness of a man's thumb, very strong, with an iron bolt at the end to make it easily cast, from twenty to thirty yards long, which they throw with admirable skill on the neck of the horse.

At this time the South American cowboy or *vaquero* not only rode with toe ring stirrups for his bare feet, a practice with close similarities to Arab horsemanship, but some still carried a short spear, reminiscent of Spanish influence, and used it along with a lasso for controlling cattle.

GAUCHOS

The gauchos as a sociological group developed in the 1600s when these itinerant horsemen lived by hunting wild cattle and horses and, to a lesser extent, by doing casual work on ranches in later times, plus a little rustling. Most were part or even pure Indian and, although many became legitimate vaqueros in time, their breaking style still remained the same. Charles Darwin, who observed their work first hand, wrote

> One evening a domidor (subduer of horses) came for the purpose of breaking in some colts . . . A troop of wild young horses is driven into the corral or large enclosure of stakes, and the door is shut . . . The gaucho picks out a full grown colt; and, as the beast rushes round the circus, he throws his lasso so as to catch both the front legs. Instantly, the horse rolls over with a heavy shock, and whilst struggling on the ground the

The gaucho gently touches the colt prior to slipping a strong rawhide halter on its head. (Photograph: Tom Ryder)

gaucho holding the lasso tight makes a circle so as to catch one of the hind legs just beneath the fetlock, and draws it close to the front two. He then hitches the lasso so that the three legs are bound together, then sitting on the horse's neck, he fixes a strong bridle, without a bit, to the lower jaw. This he does by passing a narrow thong through the eyeholes at the end of the reins, and several times round both jaw and tongue. The two front legs are now tied closely together with a strong leather thong fastened by a slip knot; the lasso which bound the three together being then loosened, the horse rises with difficulty. The gaucho, now holding fast the bridle fixed to the lower jaw, leads the horse outside the corral. If a second man is present, he holds the animal's head, whilst the first puts on the horse cloths and saddle and girths the whole together. During this operation, the horse from dread and astonishment at being thus bound around the waist, throws himself over and over again on the ground, and till beaten is unwilling to rise. At last, when the saddling is finished, the poor animal can hardly breathe from fear, and is white with foam and sweat. The man now prepares to mount by pressing heavily on the stirrup, so that the horse may not lose its balance; and at the moment he throws his leg over the animal's back he pulls the slip knot and the beast is free. The horse, wild with dread, gives a few most violent bounds, and then starts off at full gallop. When quite exhausted, the man by patience brings him back to the corral, where, reeking hot and scarcely alive, the poor beast is let free. Those animals which will not gallop away, but obstinately throw themselves on the ground, are by far the most troublesome.

The gaucho halters the colt for the first time. (Photograph: Tom Ryder)

Slight variations on the same method were practised throughout South America. Miers in his book, *Travels in Chili* [sic], written around 1860, said

> When the gauchos wish to have a grand breaking-in, they drive a whole herd of wild horses into the corral. The capitar (chief gaucho), mounted on a strong steady horse, rode into the corral and threw his lasso over the back of a young horse, and dragged him to the gate. For some time he was very unwilling to leave his comrades; but the moment he was forced out of the corral his first idea was to gallop away: however, a timely jerk of the lasso checked him in the most effectual way. The peons (labourers) now ran after him on foot, and threw a lasso over his forelegs, just above the fetlock, and twitching it, they pulled his legs from under him so suddenly that I really thought the fall he got had killed him. In an instant a gaucho was seated on his head, and with his long knife, and in a few seconds, cut off the whole of the horse's mane, while another cut the hair from the end of his tail. This they told me was a mark that the horse had once been mounted. They then put a piece of hide into his mouth, to serve for a bit, and a strong hide halter on his head. The gaucho who was to mount arranged his spurs, which were unusually long and sharp, and while two men held the horse by his ears he put on the saddle which he girthed extremely tight. He then caught hold of the horse's ear, and in an instant vaulted into the saddle; upon which the man who held the horse by the halter threw the end to the rider, and from that moment no one seemed to take any further notice of him. The horse instantly began to jump in a manner which made it very difficult for the rider to keep his seat, and quite different from the kick or plunge of an English horse; however, the gaucho's spurs soon set him going, and off he galloped, doing everything in his power to throw his rider.

Another horse was immediately roped and given the same treatment so that within an hour about twelve horses were mounted. Some squealed with rage, others lay down, some stood stock still but, as the writer went on, 'I could not help thinking that I would not have mounted one of those for any reward that could be offered me, for they were invariably the most difficult to subdue.'

When catching and breaking wild horses on the open pampas without the benefit of a corral, the gauchos used a slightly different method. Mounted on a steady horse, the gaucho would pursue a selected wild horse armed with only a forty-feet lasso made of plaited rawhide, well greased for suppleness, and with an iron bolt in the end for weight. One end was tied firmly to the saddle girth with the rest held coiled in the left hand and leaving about twelve feet of

The colt is tied securely to a snubbing post. (Photograph: Tom Ryder)

Securing gear in the form of a long rawhide strap is put on the colt to act as a form of hobble. (Photograph: Tom Ryder)

Once the securing gear is in place, the gaucho can handle the colt and lift its feet in safety. (Photograph: Tom Ryder)

the lasso, including the noose, in the right hand ready to throw. When close enough, the gaucho would throw the lasso around the hind legs of the wild horse then, drawing slightly to one side, would jerk the rope to throw his prey on the ground. Before it had a chance to get up, he was dismounted and upon it and, snatching the poncho from his shoulders, wrapped it around the animal's head like a blindfold. Using the lasso to keep the horse immobilised, he put on the saddle and bridle, bestrode the horse, then loosened both the poncho and the lasso, at which the horse leapt up and tried in vain to dislodge him. It is likely that the process of roping, throwing and tying a young horse put it into a state of shock, and Sir Francis B. Head in his book, *The horse and his rider*, comments on the method of roping a horse down then cracking a whip all around the horse which, bombarded with what it fears, eventually gives in and accepts its surroundings and treatment. While the methods of the gauchos may have left much to be desired in terms of a philosophical and compassionate approach to horse training, it accurately defined the true meaning of breaking in the equestrian sense.

CHAPTER SIX

Tamers and gentlers

'Mongst all the wonders known of late, is Rarey's rising fame, How he
subdues the vicious horse, and can the wildest tame.

Rarey the equine king
Hamilton McCarthy

THE WORLD'S MOST FAMOUS HORSE BREAKER

On 26 November 1857, a thirty-year-old American who was destined to become the most famous horse breaker in the world sailed
quietly into Liverpool docks. Born in the village of Groveport, Ohio,
in 1827, John Solomon Rarey was the youngest survivor of a family
of eleven, his father being a successful farmer and tavern keeper.
From an early age, Rarey appeared to have an affinity with animals,
especially horses, although his early attempts at taming and breaking
at around the age of twelve resulted in the family physician being
called out three times to deal with Rarey's fractured or dislocated
bones. By his early twenties, Rarey had progressed to practising his
rough-riding skills on wild horses corralled as a result of wild horse
roundups in Texas, and he even trained a pair of elk to go in harness
so that he could drive them to country fairs where he peddled a little
booklet entitled *The modern art of taming wild horses*. He travelled
extensively giving demonstrations of horse taming and breaking,
perfecting his technique continually.

Although supremely self-confident and possessed of unique skills,
it was not until Rarey met a Toronto general dealer and businessman
on a visit to Canada in 1857 that his career took off. R.A.
Goodenough, a New Englander by birth and a shrewd businessman,
recognised the financial potential of Rarey's skills and the two
became partners. Goodenough arranged for Rarey to give a
demonstration to General Sir William Eyre, commander of the
British forces in Canada, who was greatly impressed by what he
saw and, encouraged by the ubiquitous Goodenough, issued letters

John Solomon Rarey.

of introduction and testimonials to military colleagues back in Britain. In a letter to the Horse Guards, Sir William said Rarey's system 'was new to him and valuable for military purposes'. With the scene thus set, Rarey, accompanied by Goodenough, sailed for England in search of the success and recognition that had eluded him in America.

Rarey's success in Europe was dependent on finding sufficient wild or vicious horses as subjects for his demonstrations, and he initially based his activities at the Piccadilly dealing premises of Joseph Anderson and his assistant, George Rice, who found the ideal candidate, a black horse sold to Sir Matthew White Ridley then returned as being completely unmanageable. None of the yard staff could control it. Rarey was given a week to tame the animal, at the end of which a large crowd of horsemen, sceptics and journalists turned up at Anderson's yard to judge for themselves. Those who had not seen the tamer before were surprised to find that, instead of the hard-riding, rough nagsman they expected, a man of 'about five feet nine inches in height, delicately made, decidedly prepossessing, light haired, light complexioned, with intelligent grey eyes and an open countenance'. In action he was athletic and light on his feet but calm and patient, and he was said to be a brilliant talker 'in the colloquial style'. His mastery of the horse was more surprising for, as a corre-spondent for the Sporting Magazine observed of the black horse after the Rarey treatment.

> His nature was changed and the devil fairly gone out of him ... Mr Rarey proceeded to mount him and with the rein loose on his neck the horse moved and turned just as the rider moved his hands. There seemed no effort on Mr Rarey's part and there was nothing anxious or nervous in the look of the horse. In fact he was so calm, his eye so steady and so much at ease, that it was difficult to imagine he could have been the obsti-nate brute too many could speak of..

One spectator, smoking a cigar, was so confident in Rarey's trans-formation of the horse that he mounted and then dismounted by sliding off over the animal's tail, something the owners said would have been impossible a week earlier. Although the spectators wit-nessed the results of Rarey's work, few if any had any understanding of the philosophy behind the system or why it worked. Rarey merely said his method was founded on kindness towards the animal, and he had come as an educator not a gladiator.

Rarey's royal patronage

Rarey's success came to the attention of Colonel Alexander Hood, later Viscount Bridport, an ex-Scots Guard, who was groom in wait-ing to Queen Victoria as well as Prince Albert's equerry. His wife, Lady Mary, had a personal interest in the handling of difficult horses for her brother, William, had been killed in 1844 as a result of a fall from a horse. Rarey was invited to give a demonstration at the Royal Stables at Windsor which Hood was in charge of. Hood, his wife, and the other spectators were so impressed that they made sure that Queen Victoria and her consort, Prince Albert, were made aware of the phenomenal American. Intrigued, they asked to see Rarey at work, and in January 1858 a demonstration was arranged at Windsor

Castle. There, before a rapt audience, he tamed a number of horses including a colt of Prince Albert's deemed too dangerous to use. The horse was shut in a loosebox with Rarey for quarter of an hour after which the Royal guests were invited to enter. As Rarey explained in a letter to his sister, Margaret, dated 17 January 1858, 'When Queen Victoria and Prince Albert entered, they found the animal lying down, and I lying beside him, with one of his hind feet under my head and the other over my chest. This so astonished them that they laughed . . .' He went on to crawl all over the prostrate animal, sitting on it, and even knocking its hind hooves together. The other guests were summoned and at the Queen's request Rarey ordered the animal to rise, which it did, and he jumped onto its back. For a finale, he put up an umbrella which he waved around the horse's head, and even beat a drum on its back. This so impressed the queen that she allowed him a grand tour of the castle 'from kitchen to cellar, the state rooms and the queen's private rooms' as he confided to his sister in a letter, and he was invited to dine at the castle and was presented with a money order to the value of $125. Moreover, he was asked to give a second demonstration for the crowned heads of Europe and other dignitaries who were assembling in London for the forthcoming marriage of Princess Victoria and Prince Frederick William of Prussia.

Rarey wrote to his sister that the audience would include 'more royalty perhaps than has ever been brought together on any previous occasion', and the demonstration in the magnificent riding school at Buckingham Palace took place on 24 January, the day before the wedding. Before such a distinguished audience, Rarey put on a memorable performance. One of his subjects was a livery stable horse well known for its vicious nature. After being 'Rareyfied' as people called it, the horse would canter up and down the arena at Rarey's whistle, follow the horse tamer like a dog and, on command, lie on its side. As the audience roared with laughter, Lord Alfred Paget, son of the first Marquis of Anglesey and equerry and clerk-marshal of the royal household, ran a wheelbarrow up and down a plank placed against the side of the once-vicious horse. Queen Victoria, who had laughed as much as anyone, sent a message to Rarey later advising him that a place would be reserved for him in the chapel of St James's Palace so that he could witness the marriage of her eldest daughter.

John S. Rarey in the process of throwing a difficult horse.

Tattersalls and the subscription list

Goodenough arranged for Rarey to meet Richard and Edmund tattersall, owners of one of the most important horse repositories in London where large numbers of hunters, hacks and carriage horses were regularly sold from their Hyde Park premises. Aware of the fact that Rarey had only been in England a matter of months and was already something of a celebrity, they hurried to set up a Rarey Horse Taming Subscription List. The subscribers each had to pay ten guineas in advance and sign a written declaration undertaking not to reveal Rarey's system under penalty of a £500 fine. As soon as the subscription list reached five hundred, Rarey promised to divulge the secrets of his success. As his fame grew and he enjoyed the patronage of London society, he won over many influential allies including

Mark Lemon, one of the founders of *Punch* and a writer noted for his anti-American sentiments who became a devotee of Rarey. Other influential pupils who in March 1858 signed a testimonial to the effectiveness of the American's methods included the prime minister, Lord Palmerston, the Marquis of Stafford, the Duke of Abercorn, Lord Dufferin, Vice Admiral Rouse, a leading light of the jockey Club, and the second Duke of Wellington, son of Napoleon's conqueror. Rarey hunted with Gladstone, then Chancellor of the Exchequer, and dined at the Garrick Club with Charles Dickens and William Thackeray. While Rarey was a good conversationalist and a gentleman in all ways, his partner, Goodenough, was snubbed by society as he smacked of 'trade' and was too financially orientated.

Cruiser, the fiend incarnate

One of Rarey's sceptics was the racing correspondent of the Morning Post who challenged Rarey to 'go down some morning to Murrell's Green with a few of his aristocratic friends, and try Cruiser, and if he can ride him as a hack, I guarantee him immortality, and an amount of ready money to make a British bank director's mouth water'. Murrell's Green, near Ascot, was home to Lord Dorchester's stallion, Cruiser, stated to be 'the most vicious stallion in England'. As a two-year-old he was reckoned to be the fastest horse in England, but the vicious nature he displayed as a foal had developed until he was, in Dorchester's own words, 'a fiend incarnate'. Foaled in 1852, and a Derby favourite in 1855, he turned killer and had mauled two grooms to death. On one occasion he bit through a one-inch iron bar in his stable, another time he bit through a man's arm, and Dorchester admitted seeing the horse lean against the wall of his loosebox and scream and kick for ten minutes at a time. At one stage the Rawcliffe Stud Company had bought a half share in the horse and they employed a groom to lead him to their establishment in Yorkshire. Against orders not to stop on the way, the groom did so and stabled the horse at a country inn. In order to get the stallion out of the building, it had been necessary to remove the roof and rig up a derrick. After two years in Yorkshire, the Rawcliffe Stud had had enough and returned Cruiser to Ascot where his viciousness had led Dorchester to consider having the animal blinded for the safety of his grooms. Dorchester had told Rarey that the mere approach of a human was enough to send the horse into a rage. Naively, Rarey asked Cruiser's owner to send the horse up to London but Dorchester explained that this was impossible and Rarey would have to come down to Ascot.

Cruiser was believed by many to be the ultimate challenge for Rarey. 'The right horse in the right place for Mr Rarey' a writer in *The Morning Post* of 2 March 1858 announced. On arrival in Ascot, Rarey was shown the brick stable with its heavy oak door down a narrow lane. Feed and water were apparently slipped into the stable through the half-door, and to lead Cruiser out twenty-foot chains were clipped to his headstall by the grooms, who advised Rarey that the horse had not been ridden for three years. Cruiser reputedly wore an 8 lb steel and leather muzzle at all times with an iron bar across the front of his mouth and he fed by licking his corn up as best he could. When Rarey opened the top door of the stable, Cruiser flew at him bellowing. The tamer stood out of reach then, choosing his moment, grabbed the headstall and tied the horse to the hayrack. For fifteen minutes Cruiser screamed and bellowed like a fiend. So much so, that Dorchester begged Rarey to give up on him. Rarey waited until he felt the time was right then went into the loosebox. Three hours later Rarey and Lord Dorchester took turns to ride the reformed Cruiser up and down the lane. Rarey, with Dorchester's agreement, took Cruiser back to London to continue his education and did so by tying him behind his dogcart, to the astonishment of the staff at Anderson's Piccadilly yard when they arrived. The news of Cruiser's taming and the promise that Cruiser would be exhibited at the lessons gave a fillip to the subscription list which was only half-filled at the time.

Rarey and the zebra

Eager for new challenges, Rarey tamed a zebra from London Zoo. There is no evidence of what kind of zebra it was but, judging from the engraving in Rarey's booklet, it was probably a mountain zebra, reputedly the most difficult of the zebra sub-species to tame. Said to be less flighty than his relatives on the open plain, the mountain zebra was alleged to be more determined and uncooperative. The animal was delivered to Rarey, according to *Household Words*, a magazine edited by Charles Dickens, in a crate which 'looked strong enough to confine three lions'. His keepers at the Zoological Gardens

John S. Rarey throwing a horse using his strapped-up foreleg method.

had lassoed him in his cage and dragged him up to the bars to get a thick wooden bit in his mouth before he was manhandled into the crate. The bit was probably Rarey's suggestion, as he favoured the use of a one-and-a-half-inch thick straight-mouthed wooden bit for vicous horses which might bite. The first taming lesson took four hours and was a great struggle. By the second lesson the zebra was quieter but not tamed. According to the melodramatic press of the time the zebra, before its meetings with Rarey, would kick out in all directions at once, stand on its hind legs and tear at the wooden rafters of its cage, leap up and swing on the rafters by its teeth while kicking out, or even grab the hayrack in its teeth and hang suspended. During lessons with Rarey, it could do four or five rapid somersaults in rapid succession.

'So artistically' was this done, Charles Dickens reported, that the zebra 'is the only animal that ever made Mr Rarey laugh'. A more sceptical reporter referred to the zebra as 'the striped, sleepy-looking animal called the 'wild zebra of the African dessert' and went to see it after taming at the Zoological Gardens in Regents Park in 1860.

The animal was kept in an eight-foot square pen, and its keeper sadistically poked the animal with a barbed seven-foot pole, to the delight of the audience, but the animal remained docile despite 'the treatment to which he was subjected in my presence'. By the end of May it would lie down and turn over at command for Rarey, but the wooden gag bit remained in its mouth and prevented it from seizing a man's arm or leg. Rarey intended driving it through Hyde Park although there is no evidence that he ever did. Some sceptics believed the zebra was really a pony disguised with painted-on stripes to look like the wild animal but a group of critics including the Duke and Duchess of Bedford were among those who verified it was what it was said to be.

Emperor Napoleon III's Stafford

Rarey's reputation abroad was enhanced by the taming of another vicious horse, a brown stallion called Stafford, owned by the Emperor Napoleon III. Described as having 'an affectation of the brain', the six-year-old French coaching stallion had killed three men and had been shut up in a building for two years. Stafford was brought into the ring for Rarey blindfolded and rearing and plunging between two ropes. The drama was heightened when a third man rushed in and hacked at the ropes with a knife until the horse was free. After half an hour alone with Stafford, Rarey rode him into the ring, controlled by only a snaffle bridle. To the astonishment of his large audience, Rarey pulled the bridle off and, guiding him with only the slightest movements of hand and leg, put him into a gallop, then stopped him with a word. He fired a six-chambered revolver from his back and, although Stafford had never been in harness before, drove him alongside a mare through the streets of Paris. The *Paris Illustrated Journal* reported 'Mr Rarey concluded his first exhibition by beating a drum on Stafford's back and passing a hand over his head and mouth. Stafford was afterwards ridden by a groom, and showed the same docility in his hands as in those of Mr Rarey. The Emperor led the praise of the remarkable American.

Other notable conquests, among hundreds, included a horse called King of Oude who before taming was so vicious that at the demonstration one spectator 'got to the back of the boxes and confessed that his knees knocked together'. Another horse, a grey four-year-old Thoroughbred, 'seemed at times to be about to jump into the spectator's boxes', while another, a Suffolk carthorse said to be the largest and most powerful horse Rarey met with, terrified the audience who 'moved to the backseats and started calculating the quickest way out'. The press was full of tales of man-eating horses and, as Rarey tamed them all, the list of potential pupils was soon over-subscribed with other subscription lists set up in Liverpool, Manchester, Yorkshire, Dublin and Paris.

Rarey abroad

Rarey travelled extensively, visiting Sweden where the king, following an exhibition in Stockholm, presented him with a medal giving him entrance to all the royal palaces and arsenals. He travelled on to Lapland, then Germany, where he gave a demonstration at the Royal Riding School followed by a formal dinner at which one of the guests was the prominent German scientist, Baron Alexander Von Humbold who, at nearly ninety, expressed the hope that he would live long enough to meet the famous American, which he did. Rarey went to Russia where he gave an exhibition before Czar Alexander at St Petersburg, which included the taming of a horse said to be the wildest that could be found on the steppes. The peasant who brought it in said he had never been able to touch the animal, yet he watched while Rarey went up to him and passed his hand over the horse's neck and up to its ears. After returning to England in 1859, Rarey visited the Middle East early in 1860 where he watched Arabs gentling their horses. His travels took him on to Cairo, crossing the desert to the Red Sea, sailing from Alexandria to Jaffa, then on to Jerusalem, the Dead Sea, Beirut, Rhodes and Constantinople where as the guest of the Sultan he was reported to have smoked a pipe with an amber mouthpiece set with diamonds.

Rarey returned to England an even greater celebrity with honours heaped on him and the press at his feet. The Royal Society for the Prevention of Cruelty to Animals awarded him a gold medal in 1860 for giving a free lecture to the London cabmen and omnibus drivers. Victorians danced to the Rarey Waltz composed in his honour by a grateful pupil, Matilda Langen, while Hamilton McCarthy penned a poem, 'Rarey the equine king', as a tribute to the great man. Even the Staffordshire potteries who were producing figurines of well-known personalities of the day included a likeness of Rarey and Cruiser.

John S. Rarey and a horse subdued by his unique taming method.

Rarey's last exhibition in England

Rarey's last exhibition was at the Crystal Palace on 27 October 1860 in front of eight thousand people, and soon after he sailed from Liverpool with a Thoroughbred mare, four Shetland ponies, and Cruiser, having bought the Rawcliffe Stud's half share and been given Dorchester's share. Back in America where the Civil War was raging, Rarey was hailed as a hero. He gave performances in Boston, Chicago, Philadelphia and Cincinnati, and he even offered a prize for the most vicious horse that could be found to test his skills. As the star attraction at Niblo's Gardens in New York City alongside Edwin Forrest, the great tragedian, Rarey had turned horse taming into a theatrical entertainment. In September 1862 he gave a demonstration in aid of the Soldier's Aid Society in Columbus, Ohio, and in December of that year he was invited to inspect the horses and mules of the Army of the Potomac. By this time he had accumulated some considerable wealth. In Europe where his private lessons cost £25, the equivalent today of over £500, his earnings up to July 1858 were estimated at around £20,000, and he ultimately used some of his wealth to build a mansion in his home town of Groveport where he lived with his widowed mother. In December 1865 he suffered a stroke from which he never really recovered, and on 4 October 1866 he died quietly and was buried at Groveport.

Over his short life – he was only thirty-eight when he died – Rarey's impact on the breaking and handling of horses was immense. Colonel Thomas Seymour wrote of him 'If he could find a way of training the Cruisers of mankind, Christianity would assign him a place among the Apostles.' The editor of *Punch* magazine praised him saying his system might be effective on 'obnoxious politicians', while *Harpers* magazine thought it may work on wayward husbands. Ralph Waldo Emerson asserted that Rarey's system had 'turned a new leaf in civilisation', and William Lloyd Garrison, the abolitionist, hailed Rarey for substituting 'the laws of love for the spirit of brutality'. In a plethora of tributes the *Illustrated London News* called him 'a missionary of civilisation and mercy among all too-long ill-treated horses', and concluded 'the American deliverer sweeps away all the cruel traditions of horse-breaking . . . and proceeds upon the theory of gentleness and mutual confidence'.

The secret of the system

Rarey had been in no hurry to reveal his system. People often assumed it was trickery, and one reporter believed 'that the horse was prostrated by the means of a powerful drug'. Since his first public demonstration, critics, spectators, challengers and disbelievers had regularly announced that they knew his secret and, in many cases, were prepared to sell it. So much so that on 23 April 1858 Rarey had authorised Tattersalls to pay £1,000 to anyone who could satisfy them that they could teach the system without having learnt it from the American himself. Among the contenders to the well-publicised challenge was a Mr Norman Macree who advertised to reveal Rarey's system to anyone for five shillings and said that Rarey starved his horses to weaken them and then blew up their noses. Others said Rarey exhausted them with hard work before the demonstrations, or purged them, and one man even said

> It is no more nor less than the use of magnifying spectacles, placed over the eyes of the animal so as to terrify him with the apparent immensity of objects. I have been led to this belief from the fact of my often having

seen horses in the Crimea brought to a sudden halt and exhibit great symptoms of terror at the sight of a camel.

Rarey had studied horses at considerable length. He believed they had intelligence, contrary to the view of other breakers, and could understand and respond if they knew what was required of them. The three fundamental principles of his system were:

(a) That the horse is so constituted by nature that he will not offer resistance to any demand made of him which he fully comprehends, if made in a way consistent with the laws of his nature.
(b) That he has no consciousness of his strength beyond his experience, and can be handled according to our will without force.
(c) That we can, in compliance with the laws of his nature by which he examines all things new to him, take any object, however frightful, around, over, or on him, that does not inflict pain – without causing him to fear.

Rarey's careful gestures, body language, and well-modulated voice were matched by his great courage, sublime self-confidence and great patience. A reporter from the *Sporting Magazine* wrote that one of Rarey's equine pupils once kicked 'so close to his chest, that we thought there was an end to Mr Rarey, but he stood without changing colour, and just got an inch out of its range'. Although he gave several performances a week, no two were the same. Bad-handling, fear and misunderstanding were the causes of most problem horses, Rarey believed, and his method was basically to establish contact and then power over the horse as quickly as possible. In his own words, having got to the horse he tied up the near foreleg, 'There is something in this operation of taking up one foot that conquers a horse quicker and better than anything else you can do to him, and without any possible danger of him hurting himself or you either, for you can tie up his foot and sit down and look at him until he gives up.' He added ' . . . by conquering one member, you conquer to a great extent the whole horse'. By drawing up the other foreleg so that the horse was brought to its knees, it could be made to lie down. Rarey would fasten the end of a long strap around the off fore pastern then through a ring or loop on a strong surcingle buckled on the horse when it had one leg up and could not kick or buck. Rarey went on

Keep the strap tight in your hand, so that he cannot straighten his leg if he rises up. Hold him in this position, and turn his head towards you; bear against his side with your shoulder, not hard, but with a steady equal pressure, and in about ten minutes he will lie down. As soon as he lies down he will be completely conquered, and you can handle him as you please. Take off the straps and straighten out his legs; rub him lightly about the face and neck with your hand the way the hair lies; handle all his legs, and after he has lain ten or twenty minutes, let him get up again. After resting him a short time, make him lie down as before. Repeat the operation three or four times, which will be sufficient for one lesson. Give him two lessons a day, and when you have given him four lessons he will lie down by taking hold of one foot.

A horse's main defence is flight, so when he is immobilised he is more inclined to give in. Horse breakers had known and used this to their advantage for centuries, but Rarey progressed it one stage further to incorporate something the others had neither understood nor practised. Mr S. Sidney, a noted horseman, pupil of Rarey's, and hunting correspondent of the *Illustrated London News*, said the next stage was to 'Smooth his ears, rub his legs, scrape the sweat off him gently with a scraper, rub him down with a wisp or brush, give him a drink of water, then go over him again as if you were a shampooer at a Turkish bath . . . rubbing his head, breathing in his nostrils.' Sidney went on 'One of the curious results of the Rareyfying or strapping up and laying down is, that after being duly shampooed or being mesmerised, the moment he rises he seems to have contracted a personal affection for the operator.'

The effect was astonishing, horses would follow Rarey and do as he commanded. Casting the horse brought it under Rarey's influence in the shortest time possible, and once he had mastered the horse he made friends with it. 'As long as you are calm' Rarey said 'and keep down the excitement of the horse, there are ten chances to have him understand you, where there would not be one under harsh treatment.' Audiences who attended Rarey's demonstrations with the expectation of a spectacular fight between man and beast saw something quite different but they were still entranced. Rarey had great patience and, on occasions, would keep his audience waiting while, according to the press, 'the cool American, resting his hands on his hips, proceeded to talk . . .' Spectators said Rarey was inclined to be long-winded, especially in his pre-demonstration introduction. At one demonstration an audience in Liverpool did get bored and restless when Rarey took two hours to get a halter on a young colt. Despite the fact that people kept calling out or dropping things to distract or startle the colt, Rarey never lost his composure or patience. He understood the significance of not only immobilising the horse but of immediately flooding it with the close proximity, sight, sound and smell of man in such a way that the horse responded favourably. It was said that his actions mimicked the positive social stimuli of the herd in the wild. Although so many people saw him at work, very few fully understood why his system worked, and none seemed to be able to emulate him with anything like the same degree of success. Some lacked his personal qualities, most just did not understand.

The origins of the Rarey system

Rarey always insisted that he had thought out and devised the system he used himself. He said it was 'the result of many experiments, and a thorough investigation and trial of the different methods of horsemanship now in use'. He claimed to have studied the psychology of the horse, watched the reactions of horses to less enlightened breakers, made comparisons and formed theories. He said he knew a horse's every thought and could predict its reactions, anticipate its movements.

Household Words magazine reported 'Long practice enabled him at such critical moments to tell from the sudden tension of the muscles how the horse is inclined to act, and just to get out of the range of a kick ...' Rarey described his method as gentling. Years later Captain Hayes, a very successful horse breaker, defined gentling as 'the act of handling him in a soothing, though firm manner, while he is under such restraint that he will be unable to resist our friendly advances'. The *New York Coach-Builders Magazine* of October 1858 claimed that Rarey's success with Cruiser was nothing 'but a more noised-abroad practice, under the patronage of Royalty, of the Macedonian success', suggesting that Alexander The Great had tamed Bucephalus using the gentling technique.

Charles Dickens, a great friend and supporter of Rarey, had searched with the help of researchers from *Household Words*, the magazine he edited, to find evidence of Rarey's system or anything like it in equestrian publications, veterinary journals or cavalry manuals, and found nothing from the time of Gervase Markham to Nimrod, the sporting writer. He could not have searched very hard.

Willis J. Powell, an American tamer known to and quoted by Rarey, wrote 'In the year 1811 whilst residing in Georgia, I read an account of a man who lived more than a hundred years ago who would take any wild horse and shut himself up with him in a small yard or stable and, at the end of a few hours, come out with the horse perfectly gentle.' Similar references to quick taming practitioners in America are not difficult to find. Some commentators said that a comparative study of the Arab method of gentling horses against the rough-riding method of American breakers helped Rarey formulate his system. Rarey wrote that the horse was

> to those who govern him by brute force, and know nothing of the beauty and delight to be gained from the cultivation of his finer nature, a fretful, vicious and often dangerous servant; whilst to the Arab, whose horse is the pride of his life, and who governs him by the law of kindness, we find him to be quite a different animal.

However, as Rarey did not observe Arabs handling their horses until 1860 when he was already very successful himself, the likelihood of the Arabs contributing to the development of his system seems remote.

Denten Offutt and the study of phenology

Although Rarey always denied it, many believed that he learned his system from a horse tamer called Denton Offutt from Georgetown, Kentucky, and Rarey was certainly a pupil of Offutt's at Georgetown for a time. Another of Offutt's pupils, Mr K. Richards, a racehorse breeder in later years, described Offutt as 'uneducated but full of originality', and Richards was in no doubt that Offutt was the originator of the system expounded by Rarey. So much so that Offutt sued Rarey in later years and although Offutt got judgement in his favour, the judgement was reversed at a higher court. Carl Sandburg in his biography of Abraham Lincoln, whose first employer was Offutt, described Offutt as 'a liar and a cheat' and, although he was skilled in the use of leg straps, he seemed unaware of the wide implications of the process, commenting that it was useful for getting a horse to lie down when being shipped by water. Offutt did seem aware of the importance of touching a horse as verified by extracts from his system published in *Turf, Field and Farm* commencing in January 1878. It took the form of a dialogue between the horse and the man:

MAN   I wish to put my hand all over you

HORSE   This you may do by commencing at the face. Commence rubbing on the face, and repeat it; then pass on down the neck, first as slight as possible, and as I become used to it, rub the harder. Remember to rub the way the hair lies smooth. My tail is, when I play, to be held up high: as my pride and beauty, you must be careful in handling it. But after you raise it, be sure to repeat it, and raise it and put it down several times, until it goes up quietly.

MAN   Then the more I rub you, and repeat it, the quieter you get?

HORSE   It is so in all beasts.

Offutt also believed in phrenology, assessing the mental faculties of a horse by studying the shape of the skull, and he claimed to be able to ascertain the nature and character of an animal by merely looking at its head. Another past pupil of Offutt's was a man called O. H. P. Faucher, said to be the most successful 'thrower' of horses, and reputedly the man who taught Rarey this particular skill. Faucher, who like Rarey came from Ohio, had lived among the Comanches at one point and probably learnt some of their skills by observation, and he was apparently well practised in the art of throwing prior to 1844.

JAMES TELFER, THE NORTHUMBRIAN HORSE BREAKER

It is possible that Rarey learnt at least part of his system from a man called Robson from Northumberland, England, who had emigrated to Canada around 1838. Robson had worked as an assistant for the Northumbrian horse breaker, James Telfer, before emigrating, and Telfer in later years was to become Rarey's greatest challenger. Conflicting evidence says that Robson lived in the same village in Canada as Rarey at one time, or moved to Ohio and met Rarey there, or that Robson told Goodenough his secret and it was passed via him to Rarey. If there was any secret, it was not Robson's but his teacher's, James Telfer's, and in commenting on Rarey's work William Youatt wrote 'another person, a farmer in Northumberland, states that he has practised the system with entire success for several years'. Fred Taylor, an ex-pupil of Telfer, was adamant that Rarey was capitalising on Telfer's method and claimed to have verified this when in 1858 he was invited to have breakfast with Rarey at his rooms at 35 Pall Mall. Rarey had learnt that Taylor had tamed a horse using a method very similar to his own and had got six photographic negatives taken by a firm of Bond Street photographers on behalf of the London Stereoscopic Company who wished to use them to illustrate the 'whole art of horse taming as exhibited by Mr Rarey'. Captain Piper of Shepherd's Bush placed his stud of horses at Taylor's disposal, and a powerful grey carriage horse was selected as the subject. As Taylor wrote 'I tackled my subject, and after a few abortive struggles, he lay helpless at my feet.' The photographs were duly taken. Because of the slow shutter speed of early cameras, a quiet horse which would remain still for the required time was essential, which is why photographs of nineteenth-century horse tamers and breakers are rare, and most of those artificially staged. On meeting Rarey, Taylor was asked if he had seen Rarey before, which he denied. 'How did you get hold of this method of taming horses?' pursued Rarey, opening a portfolio and producing six carefully mounted photographic prints, reproduced from Taylor's negatives and taken the day but one previous. Taylor agreed to tell him provided Rarey would answer one question. Taylor asked 'Now, Mr Rarey, on our honour as a man, do you know one Mr James Robson, a horse trainer, residing and carrying on business in the district where you came from?'

'I do' Rarey replied.

'Did you ever see him practise the system as illustrated in these photographs?'

'I have – something like it.'

'Is it not *your* so-called system?'

'Well, something like it', Rarey answered.

Taylor went on, 'Now, I will tell you how I got hold of the great secret as you call it. Of course you know that Mr Robson is an Englishman?'

'I do.'

'Well then, the same man who taught Robson to apply the method, before he emigrated to Canada, has also taught me.'

Telfer's challenge

James Telfer was a Northumberland farmer who gave horse taming exhibitions in a small way. He was active before Rarey came on the scene, and he claimed to use the same system. When an engraving of

Rarey taming a horse appeared in the *Illustrated London News* in January 1858, Telfer's supporters encouraged him to challenge Rarey's claims that it was a new system. Telfer was championed by his ex-pupil, Fred Taylor who, having run away from home at the age of seventeen to join Her Majesty's 8th Royal Irish Hussars, with whom he served for a number of years, became a reporter for *The Review* under the pseudonym, Ballinasloe. Rarey was thirty, Telfer in his fifties, and Taylor tried to win support for Telfer by decrying Rarey as a teacher of old maids and the upper classes while Telfer was 'an honest, hard-working fellow' who depended on 'his own sterling ability'.

A Liverpool paper took up the class cry and said that Telfer, unlike Rarey, being a 'real honest Englishman' practised his art openly and in front of everyone, which was not entirely true. Both men demanded some degree of privacy when working, both used a thick one-and-a-half-inch wooden bit, and both tied up a front leg and threw the horse. The Northumbrian's methods certainly bore many similarities to the American's and in his book, *Telfer's system of horse taming*, actually 'ghosted' for him by Fred Taylor, he advised strapping up a foreleg and throwing the horse, adding 'Repeat the

Many breakers strapped up a horse's foreleg at some point in the early stages of breaking.

treatment two or three times a day for a week, and the savage is then thoroughly tamed.' In April 1857, Telfer tackled an unhandled stallion and within an hour had haltered, tamed and harnessed him, and driven him through the streets of Liverpool. However, *The Field* of March 1858 carried a report by someone who had seen Telfer at work but it had not been successful and it was said that he could only cast horses of average temper. The same March demonstration by Telfer had also been witnessed by a reporter from the *Illustrated London News* who said it 'had only very partial success'.

EARLY EXPONENTS OF SIMILAR SYSTEMS

Even Telfer could not claim to have invented the system, for other breakers had used the theme of tying a leg up and throwing the horse but without continuing the process to win the respect and affection of the animal as Rarey did. William Browne, who described himself as 'an old northern man', born around 1554, included in his book, published in 1624, an illustration of lungeing a horse around a turning post with its near foreleg strapped up. W. J. Miles, writing in 1868, claimed that Grisone performed in the style of Rarey in the late 1500s, which seems unlikely, although he may have strapped a foreleg up. Dick Christian, a horse breaker specialising in racehorses and active from around 1780, who lived at Melton Mowbray in Leicestershire, strapped a foreleg up then rode the horse. Described as 'that great professor of rough-riding' by *The Druid*, Christian was said to be plucky and patient with immense strength, although he was only five feet six inches in height. He could apparently lift the fore-end of a horse. Among his rough-riding feats he rode a bull bareback and was thrown off but was 'on him again . . . whiles he was so blown he couldn't run no longer'. Married before he was twenty, he sired twenty-one children. He rode up to twenty unbroken horses a week using his strapped foreleg method. Although Christian was uneducated 'having no taste for reading', he was described as 'a genius in his way'. He often pulled the other foreleg up, throwing the horse, so the mechanics of his method came close to Rarey's in some ways.

Another Englishman called Bull from Stanton-le-Vale, Lincolnshire, also practised a similar method. A reporter for *Bell's*

Life, a London publication, who gave Bull one guinea to learn the system described it as

> First, buckle a surcingle around the body; second, tie up the foreleg by buckling a strap tightly around the foot and forearm; next, attach a strap to the off-fore foot, bring it over the horse's back, and grasp it firmly with the right hand. With the left, catch the near rein of the bridle, and pull the head around towards you. When the horse is made to stop, pull the foot from under him, bringing him on his knees, when in a short time he will lie down; this was the whole secret.

Like Rarey, Bull could make a horse lie down and get up at command, sometimes several horses at once.

Jumper the Yorkshireman

Around 1800 another exponent of the same system was a Yorkshireman called Jumper. He kept his system a secret but it was virtually the same as the rest. James Castley, veterinary surgeon to the 17th Lancers and a regular contributor to *The Veterinarian*, once bought a horse cheaply in Yorkshire as it was unmanageable and unridable. 'When made to move forward with even nothing more than a saddle on, he instantly threw himself down upon his side with great violence, and would then endeavour to roll upon his back', Castley wrote.

> There was at that time in Yorkshire a famous colt breaker called Jumper who was almost as celebrated in that country for taming vicious horses into submission as the famed whisperer in Ireland. We put this animal into Jumper's hands, who took him away, and in about ten days brought him home again, certainly not looking worse in condition, but perfectly subdued, and almost as obedient as a dog; for he would lie down at this man's bidding, and only rise again at his command – carry double or anything. I took to riding him myself and may say I never was better carried for six or eight months during which time he never showed the least vice whatever.

Castley then sold him to a Lincolnshire farmer who rested him for the summer, after which he was as bad as ever again, and he ended his days pulling a coach.

Among the thousands of horse breakers operating in Britain, there were plenty of examples of other men who used methods similar to Rarey's including Sanger, Cook and Calthrop but none enjoyed the American's unique success. Some breakers, like Bartley, the bootmaker, who was practising around 1830, purported to work in the Rarey style although this was not the case. A Thoroughbred horse that had defied the efforts of all the Household Cavalry's rough-riders was sent to Bartley, who broke it using a regime of starvation, purging with physic, depriving the animal of sleep, violent lunge-ings, whip and spur.

Rarey's failures and critics

Rarey was not without his failures. Dennis Magner, a very capable horse tamer and breaker in his own right, discovered that in his early career Rarey 'travelled alone, town to town, with but very indifferent success', and this was verified by Magner's further research around Groveport, Rarey's birthplace, where Magner 'could obtain no facts showing that he possessed any unusual aptitudes or ability in the control of horses during his early career'. What is more, at some of Rarey's demonstrations 'there was failure to give the satisfactory results claimed and expected'. Emperor Napoleon III's stallion, Stafford, took advantage of an error of judgement on Rarey's part when the two first met in private in Paris. The stallion grabbed Rarey's shoulder in its teeth and, had it not been for Goodenough armed with a pitchfork, Rarey could have been seriously injured or even killed. As a showman, which in many ways he was, Rarey was not above sensationalising things, and the muzzle reputedly worn by Cruiser was a piece of fiction. A muzzle and halter were exhibited at Rarey's shows and even modelled by the reformed Cruiser as the *Illustrated London News* revealed when it wrote '. . . it was touching to see Cruiser look at his old muzzle, which was placed on him to show what he had been – his glance was almost reproachful'.

Goodenough, whose partnership with Rarey was short-lived and who was not necessarily to be trusted, was interviewed by Magner in New York in 1877 and he admitted that the muzzle was 'all advertising deception. I had nothing to do with that. There was no muzzle at all on him.' Eight years later Goodenough signed a written statement saying how Cruiser, Stafford and the zebra were really tamed. He claimed that he and Rarey had left the horses tied up overnight to subdue them, and that at Murrell's Green, Cruiser had been ridden with one foreleg tied up but that he became so excited when taken out that he was returned to his stable where he was thrown, both forelegs tied, a collar put on and his hind legs tied to that. Trussed up like a chicken, the horse was left thus overnight. Even after Cruiser had been led to London behind the dogcart, he was tied up that night, and thereafter Rarey trained him every day for two weeks so that the tamer could stand in the ring and call Cruiser from his stall. Stafford was tied up and left trussed for ten nights, and the zebra for two weeks. Goodenough admitted that the 'leg-up and cast treatment' had not tamed Cruiser. He said

> We did not subdue him by that treatment. We tried it thoroughly upon him, and failed. I then advised Rarey to tie him down. We did so and let him lie all night and the night following, when we could handle him as we pleased. This was the only alternative that suggested itself in the emergency, and we employed it.

According to Goodenough, Cruiser was not caught by Rarey in his loosebox at Murrell's Green as described above. A wagon loaded with hay was backed up to the loosebox with Goodenough standing on the wagon to get a rope on the horse while Rarey under the wagon slipped the leg straps on through the wheel spokes. Goodenough immodestly reckoned it was he who broke Stafford in really, and gave the impression that he was largely instrumental in Rarey's success. This was unlikely as, despite his association with Rarey, Goodenough never proved his competence with horses. At one exhibition, Rarey was ill but battled on and tamed a very vicious young colt but was then too weak to get on and ride it. According to an observer 'the boasting Mr Goodenough tried his hand, and was beaten pale and trembling out of the ring by that equine tiger . . .' The gift seemed to be Rarey's alone.

One of Rarey's many critics, an American tamer called Robert Jennings, wrote 'The Rarey system is one purely of subjugation and exhaustion; the spirit of the animal is thus often broken.' This view was shared by Galvayne, the Australian breaker, who used the exhaustion technique himself to control horses. Other critics said that Rarey really only broke three or four bad horses and 'exhibited them around the country as reformed characters for lack of new subjects', and that his method did not last. The ringmaster of an American circus once borrowed Cruiser, who was a great crowd puller, for an exhibition. The ringmaster bungled tying up Cruiser's front leg and, getting impatient, at the fourth attempt touched Cruiser with the whip. The horse plunged forward, attacked the ringmaster with its teeth causing him to flee, and careered around the ring terrifying the panicking crowd. Fortunately, Rarey was in the audience and he brought Cruiser to heel by just calling his name. It is possible that Cruiser respected one person only, the man who had tamed him. Telfer's book advised that if you tamed a horse it 'will obey *you*, but (for the present) *you alone* in everything', but warned 'if he change hands, and be again ill-used, and challenged, as it were, to fight, it will again revive his old hatred to mankind, and he will relapse, and be as bad or worse than ever'.

Many people, including the equestrian writer, William Youatt, believed that Cruiser was never really cured and had to be 'tamed' by a specially trained breaker whenever he was required for exhibition. Cruiser was taken back to Groveport where, outliving his tamer by nine years, he was left to Rarey's brother, Joseph, with the stipulation that he was to be well cared for. He ended his days in the paddock at Groveport where he died on 6 July 1875 at the age of twenty-three. Rumours abounded, however, that Cruiser really died on the voyage to America and that the animal Dennis Magner went to see at Groveport and which he described as showing 'great sensitivity and courage' was an imposter.

J. H. Walch, who saw Rarey perform, believed he was a good tamer but not a good breaker, adding 'we need not, therefore, be surprised that he has overlooked the importance of acquiring a fine mouth'. It was something Rarey never mentioned. As well as not mouthing, he never lunged or apparently long reined, both accepted breaking practices of the time.

Rarey as an instructor

Rarey's exhibitions were aimed at the more affluent who could afford his fees, but most breaking was undertaken by people of working class and limited means for whom Rarey was too exclusive. It could be that Rarey knew that his system in the wrong hands could cause great harm and therefore restricted his demonstrations to the more sensitive and learned classes by charging highly to attend. Some American tamers prefixed their name with the term 'professor' to give themselves an element of academic and social exclusiveness, and most dressed, like Rarey, in top hats, frock coats and other apparel which a horse breaker traditionally would not have worn.

The unexpected publication of his early pamphlet on breaking horses, unknown to Rarey and probably initiated by Goodenough for mere financial gain, may have brought Rarey to the working man in the street but it caused outrage among his ten-guinea paying clients who now felt they could have got the same knowledge for the six pence the pamphlet cost. Rarey's pamphlet, dismissed as a 'meagre and imperfect description' of his method, was long-winded and vague and disclosed little, but Rarey was obliged to write to *The Times* explaining that it had been circulated without his knowledge or consent, and he 'at once and entirely' released his subscribers from their pledge of secrecy. The secretary to the subscription list wrote 'It is quite absurd to assert that the little pamphlet teaches the art of horsemanship now practised by Mr Rarey.'

Rarey did plan to write a book explaining in full the philosophy behind his method and how it should be followed, but ill-health prevented him from making a start on it. Under the auspices of Rarey, some people appeared to have acquired his skill like Lord Rivers who, after one lesson in the Duke of Wellington's private school, successfully saddled 'a wild and biting colt'. Those who tried to teach the Rarey system, even if they had been pupils of the American, seemed incapable of explaining it or even understanding it fully themselves, and they dwelt on the 'leg up and cast' element and not the philosophy that under-pinned it. Twenty years after his death, his old pupil, S. Sidney, wrote 'Rarey's reputation has suffered from the inevitable reaction after an extraordinary season of sensation, and it is often sneered at by writers who are ignorant of, or incapable of comprehending, the principles of horse breaking which he illustrated in his lectures.'

As Omnibus of *Sporting Magazine* said, the age soon tired of him and by 1866 Rarey's system had died with him. His name and reputation had been commercialised into the sale of Cruiser gag-bits, zebra hobbles, Rarey straps, and the like, much of it marketed by Stokeys, the firm who originally supplied Rarey with customised equipment, and his system was to be imitated, often with disastrous results, across many parts of the world. Even in Groveport he was regarded as a prophet in his own country, and a present-day member of the Rarey family recalled 'My grandparents seemed more concerned about his reputation with the ladies than his fame. Poor man, his travels were a little too much for the conservative town of

Groveport.' Although Rarey lies in Groveport cemetery, there are no vestiges of his fame left now other than that the football team of the Groveport-Madison High School built on the site of the Rarey mansion are called The Cruisers.

WILLIS J. POWELL, THE HORSE TAMER

While Rarey was the most famous and successful of the so-called tamers, there were many others, especially in America, some of whose methods bordered on the absurd. Willis J. Powell, an American, who once wrote of his secret 'I was always jealous of having the honour of being the first that ever made it known to the world', was, before becoming a tamer, a teacher of Latin, Greek and modern languages. He described one method in common use in the early part of the last century whereby the horse was turned loose into a yard or large loosebox with the tamer who flogged him harshly with a whip. When the horse, seeing it could not escape, came towards the man, the tamer dropped his whip and handled him kindly. If the horse got uneasy or showed signs of hesitation, he was flogged again until he came back to the man. Powell watched someone tame a horse in this way then saddle him, mount him, and ride off. As Powell noted 'I observed, that the horse frequently trembled, when he went to get on him, notwithstanding he rode him off perfectly well.' He added such horses rarely remained gentle. 'Whip breaking', whereby the horse was rewarded through the cessation of pain when it approached man, was practised by many travelling horsemen, and Professor Jesse Beery of Ohio, a well-known breaker working around the turn of the twentieth century, refined the idea into a more humane practice which he called the 'confidence lesson', although the principle remained the same. At a demonstration in Fort Wayne, Indiana, Beery and his assistant gave two colts this confidence lesson after which they went through an unrehearsed drill, side by side, turning off and crossing each other's paths with each colt following the man who taught it.

Another system Powell knew of was to 'stop up the horse's ears so that he cannot hear at all, and you can very soon handle him as if he were a gentle horse . . . but when you unstop his ears, he will become

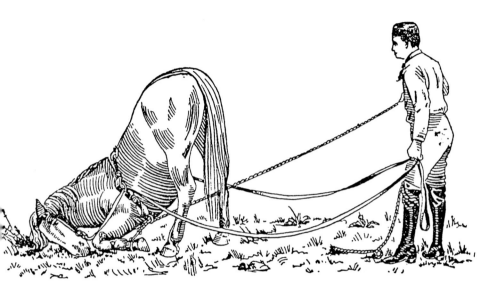

Using the double safety rope to bring a horse to its knees.

as wild as ever.' Repeated, the method was no more successful. It was reminiscent of the cruel, and often fatal, system of putting lead shot in a horse's ears which temporarily distracted the animal making it 'easier' to handle until the more serious consequences of the system manifested themselves.

Powell was no stranger to cruelty. He studied the learning capacity of different animals by, amongst other things, copying the method used in the East Indies to teach camels to dance on a hot floor by heating tin plates and placing dogs on them while he struck a triangle. He admitted it was a failure 'having most miserably burned two or three dog's feet in the experiments', although he did teach turkeys to dance. However, he devised a system of handling wild horses, allegedly copied and used by Rarey, and based on patience and the natural curiosity of the horse. In 1825, Powell used the system to tame a wild boar. He enjoyed some success and included in his testimonials one from the Governor of San Louis Potosi in Mexico whose wild horse he tamed so successfully in sixteen hours that five or six people could ride it at once! An astonished Englishman called Humstead, who had watched the whole business, offered $1,000 for the horse there and then at a time when a good broken horse cost $30 to $40.

PROFESSOR NORTON B. SMITH,
THE CANADIAN TAMER

Professor Norton B. Smith, a Canadian who promoted himself as 'the emperor of all horse educators', began his horse taming career in his home country, progressing, to touring the mid-west with great success then, with his manager, Nat Behrens, recruited in 1891 and who had been associated with Buffalo Bill's Wild West Show, came to England. He invented a system called the double safety rope or W-running rope which was very successful. It consisted of two fetlock straps and a twenty-foot rope and was used in conjunction with a surcingle. Norton Smith marketed all his equipment through his

Professor Norton Smith, the Canadian trainer, at work at one of his taming exhibitions. (The Strand Magazine, 1898)

1 *The tin pan cure*

2 *'A liberal acquaintance with the press'*

3 *'Round goes the roller and up goes the horse'*

4 *The paper cure*

5 *After the wrestling*

6 *The umbrella cure*

7 *'Whirling him round'*

manager, the surcingle costing £1. It was eight feet long and four inches wide with four two-inch rings, one each side, one on top and one underneath. The method used, according to its inventor, was to 'take a rope twenty foot long, snapping to strap on near fore limb, place through ring in surcingle underneath his body, draw through ring on off front limb, and back through ring in surcingle'. The system gave considerable control, both in long reins and when driving in harness, and with skilful use could throw a horse onto its knees, which was also dramatic for exhibitions. Around 1900 an Irish horse tamer called One-Eye was using, or abusing, the double safety rope to control horses while he shouted and berated them into quietness.

Many tamers, indeed most, cast their horses, although they used diverse methods. R. P. Hamilton was described as 'a very unique character who was engaged in the horse taming business. He was a natural showman, and combined with his performances tricks of legerdemain. Though very successful at the time, his modes of treatment were extremely limited.' He claimed to have originated the idea of throwing but his methods were said to be crude. They must have been for he was reported to have killed two horses and seriously injured several others while demonstrating in New York alone.

Professor Norton Smith's training bridle.

The double safety rope on a harness horse with one foreleg immobilised.

DR BUNTING'S BREAK

Around 1860, an inventor called Dr Bunting caused a minor sensation in the London horse world when he began demonstrating his unusual equestrian invention to the city dealers and jobmasters. Advertised to accustom even the wildest and most unruly horses to go quietly in harness in the shortest possible time, the contraption known as Dr Bunting's break received considerable attention and made Dr Bunting something of a short-lived celebrity. The break comprised a heavy pivoting post secured in a firm base with two strong twenty-foot poles radiating horizontally out from the post and supported at their extremities by stout cartwheels set about twelve feet apart so that the horse could travel between the poles without any risk of touching either. Two shafts, one on each side of the horse, connected the poles. The inner shaft was fixed but the outer shaft was removable so that the horse could be put to or taken out or turned around to work on the opposite rein. Two heavy leather straps, one over the withers, one over the croup, were buckled to the shafts like kicking straps and prevented the horse rearing, plunging or kicking. Two similar straps fastened under the horse's body made it impossible for him to throw himself down or get under the shafts. The fully harnessed horse was put to the break and his traces attached to the rear pole. His lead rope was tied to a light wooden bar

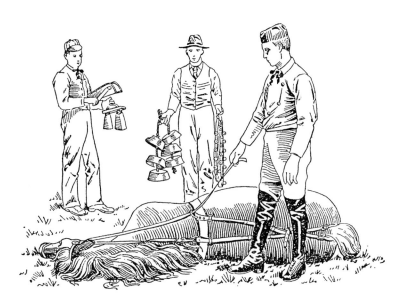

Throwing a horse and bombarding it with the sounds it was afraid of.

projecting from the front pole and this prevented the horse getting his head under the pole and possibly injuring himself. Thus harnessed, the horse could only go forwards or backwards in a circle around a centre post, and a man on foot or perched on a little seat on or behind the rear pole kept him moving forward.

Dr Bunting insisted that his invention quickly accustomed horses to going in harness with no danger of blemishing the animal through accidents, and effected a tremendous saving in terms of man hours and possibly broken vehicles and harness. Furthermore, the break was inexpensive to purchase, it took up little room and, being constructed from seasoned ash, was durable and needed little maintenance. With a large enough model, up to six or seven horses could be worked at one time by one or two men, and, by adjusting the height of the horizontal poles and the size of the wheels, the break could be used for any size of horse or pony. Joshua East, a dealer and one of the biggest London jobmasters with around 1,000 horses in his stables at any one time, was especially intrigued, and Dr Bunting was invited to demonstrate his invention at East's Mayfair premises. J. H. Walch, the writer and a spectator at the demonstration, wrote enthusiastically of Bunting's apparatus, commenting

Controlling a horse with the double safety rope while accustoming it to the sound of pan lids tied to its tail.

the horse operated on being certainly the most unruly brute I ever saw. At each step, he kicked so strongly as to lift the wheel attached to the pole behind him off the ground; but nevertheless, he was perfectly powerless, and soon submitted to being driven quietly by Dr Bunting

THE IRISHMAN, DENNIS MAGNER

On the other side of the Atlantic, Dennis Magner, a skilled and astute horse tamer, was using a very similar contraption to break carriage horses in the late 1860s. Magner was an Irishman who, at the age of fourteen, emigrated to America, where he initially worked as an apprentice to a carriage builder in New York. Later he entered into business with a partner in Myersville, Pennysylvania, and there he first began to establish his reputation as a horse tamer by employing his skills on difficult horses taken in part-exchange for vehicles. Magner's knowledge of both vehicle construction and horse breaking may have led him coincidentally to invent a breaking device uncannily similar to Dr Bunting's. Conversely, it might be that Magner either saw or heard about the doctor's invention and simply copied the idea. Claiming to have invented the Magner Breaking Rig as he called it, he went as far as patenting it in the United States on 6 July 1880.

In a booklet on Joshua East, the author, W. J. Gordon, wrote

Dennis Magner.

Some thirty years or more, J. S. Rarey came across the Atlantic to teach Englishmen horse-taming; associated with him came Dr Bunting, who soon transferred his services to Messrs East, and while with them invented this American Brake [sic] they now have which is the only one in the country.

Gordon's statement is ambiguous for there is no evidence to suggest that Bunting had any connection with Rarey or that he was employed by Joshua East, and there were certainly many of Bunting's breaks in the ownership of dealers, jobmasters and private individuals. Sir Walter Gilbey had one at his premises, Elsenham Hall, and he described it in a little article he wrote on horse breaking.

Magner, described by the *Maine Farmer* of 24 February 1864 as 'a modest, unassuming young man', summed up his own method as 'the art of direct subjugation'. He began his demonstrations in small towns in New York State, and at one of the first someone brought a vicious biting mare who attacked Magner, forcing him to dive out of the ring, although he did later halter and tame her. He achieved this

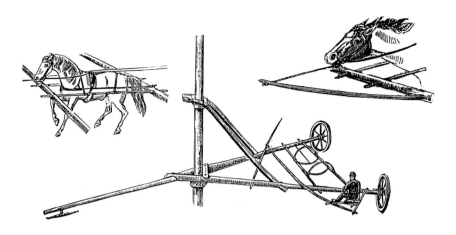

Magner's patent breaking rig.

by a method used by other tamers whereby they took hold of the headcollar in one hand and the tail in the other and spun the horse around five or six times in either direction. Less skilled tamers using the spinning method met dismal failure; one in an exhibition could not move the horse at all, and another got so dizzy he let go of the horse which flew off while he fell to the ground, to the delight of the audience. Magner followed up spinning with throwing and the use of his 'war bridle', a form of halter which brought pressure to bear on the sensitive area behind the ears.

In 1877 Magner published his book, *The art of taming and educating the horse*, believed by most to be the best of the many books written by breakers and tamers. *Turf, Field and Farm* said of Magner 'At last we have one man who professes horse taming, and who at the same time rises above the vulgar tricks of the charlatan,' while the *New York Sunday Democrat* went one step further and, making the inevitable comparison with Rarey, announced 'Rarey taught us our ABC, but Magner teaches us how to put the letters together.'

Magner was certainly effective, and on his first visit to Maine in 1863 advertised to 'take any colt that had never been haltered and, within twenty minutes, make him perfectly gentle to lead, ride and handle'. *Frank Leslie's Weekly* reported that 'a notoriously vicious horse was brought into the ring, and in less than thirty minutes was trotting in harness ... and this, too, without throwing or harsh treatment'. Another of his converts was the Mount Vernon horse,

Dennis Magner's method of dealing with a confirmed kicker.

'one of the most dangerous and difficult horses ever bred in that country', and on another occasion he broke the Buffalo Omnibus Company's horse which had bitten and crushed a man's arm nearly killing him. After taming, Mr M. Ford, the Company's agent described the reformed animal as now 'one of our best horses, as docile as a lamb, and all the drivers like him'.

The Michigan Gazette included in its pages a report of

the Allegan man-eater, the Cruiser of America, who had previously killed one man, and crippled several for life. When brought into the ring his eyes became bloodshot and gleamed like balls of fire, he sprang at his trainer like a wild beast, biting, striking and kicking in the most determined manner, breaking the ropes and stakes, springing upon the seats and throwing them down, tearing pieces from the centre pole with his teeth, lunging at any person who met his eye, actually screaming with rage when foiled in his attempts to seize his intended victims. Nearly every person was driven from the tent, some in their haste tearing holes in the canvas and escaping through the roof.

Three hours later the animal was tamed, and the next day could be driven by strangers in the street. At one exhibition, Magner stood on the axle of a pair of wheels and, holding onto the tail of a newly

Magner's distinctive method of proving a 'horse's entire submission in harness' following breaking.

Dennis Magner tames the notorious Hettrick horse.

tamed horse, was pulled around the arena to the astonishment of his audience. Another horse was subdued to quiet obedience so effectively that when one day in the street a passing street car struck and demolished the rear wheels of the buggy it was harnessed to with a splintering crash, the horse was not alarmed and stood patiently as the wrecked buggy was moved. Robert Bonner, a publisher and owner of trotting horses, said Magner was 'the most scientific and successful educator or tamer of vicious horses that I have met'.

SHOWMEN AND CHARLATANS

Some tamers were more like showmen including A. H. Rockwell of Broome County, New York, who advertised his skills by, among other things, driving three horses abreast without reins, controlling them only with verbal commands and flicks of the whip. A pupil of Rockwell's called C. H. C. Williams performed, like his mentor, in the style of Rarey although he denied emphatically that Rockwell had taught him and announced 'When a man from jealousy or malice

McKenney's patent horse controller with the single rein working through a pulley on the pad.

Professor Oscar Gleason used the double safety rope to restrain horses while accustoming them to frightening sights and sounds.

becomes thus reckless of truth and honour, he relinquishes his man-hood and becomes an object of mere disgust and detestion.' At one of Professor Williams's demonstrations in Vermont, a young man called Oscar R. Gleason was 'struck with wonder and amazement to see what power man did possess over the dumb brute'. He duly became a tamer himself and at one of his exhibitions in Washington in 1886 attracted the attention of members of congress. Representative Wise even introduced a bill in the house under which Gleason would be requested to write a book on his methods to be purchased by congress and published for government use. The bill was never passed but his book was duly published by a Philadelphia firm.

Some tamers were true charlatans. One was a man called O. S. Pratt from Batavia, New York, who bought trained trick horses from Dennis Magner after a week-long intensive course to show him how to handle them. Soon afterwards he was advertising himself as 'The greatest horse tamer in the world', and he even wrote a book describing his new system. In Magner's words he resorted to the 'boldest

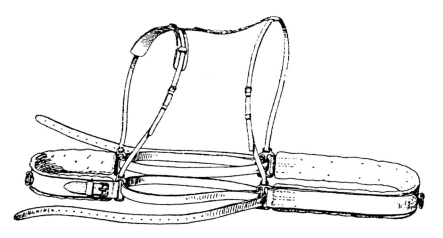

A strait-jacket for a horse.

methods of charlatanism, such as buying articles and arranging to have them presented to him as if voluntary gifts from his classes'.

Not all tamers were as flamboyant, some preferred to keep a low profile and avoid the limelight. One such person was Konstantin von Balassa, a major in the Austro-Hungarian cavalry who, aside from writing a book in 1835 entitled *Taming the horse*, worked quietly in his military environment transforming wild horses into troop horses using a throwing and gentling technique.

HORSE TAMING MACHINES AND INVENTIONS

While some tamers like Robert Jennings, who only took up taming after a career as an errand boy, print office assistant, confectioner, coppersmith, and surgical instrument manufacturer, needed only 'a common rope halter, a three or four-ply cotton cord about twelve-feet long and a piece of line webbing' for his work, others used complex equipment. A Mr Mitchell, described as 'an excellent breaker', got good results with kicking horses by attaching two stout seven-foot poles in front of the chest and behind the quarters, then let them kick it out. Mr Litchwark, a New Zealand breaker, invented a device to make a horse stand still to be mounted which consisted of a hobble on the off-fore pastern with a ring on the side. A rope with a fixed loop which went around the neck was threaded through the pastern ring so that the leg could be pulled up and secured to the

The strait-jacket on the horse.

neck loop until the rider had mounted, when it could be released. An equine strait-jacket called the hippolasso was invented by Raabe and Lunel and intended for restraining horses for veterinary purposes, but the tamers soon began using variations of it for controlling horses during breaking.

The most unusual device of all was the invention of a flamboyant American tamer called Professor Silas Sample who arrived in England in 1885 after a successful tour of Australia. Self-indulgent and arrogant, he decreed that a breaker should be able to make an animal ridable and drivable before it was ridden and driven. His first demonstration was a fiasco because the wild horses ordered never turned up but undeterred, he battled on, despite the irksome news that one of his ex-pupils, Sydney Osborne, was touring the country under the name Professor Galvayne and demonstrating Sample's system as Galvayne's system. Galvayne was not a great horseman, although he later earned fame for his work on equine dentition and his system of telling a horse's age from its teeth. Sample had devised a new breaking system based on the spinning theory whereby he tied the horse's head to its tail so that the animal spun itself in circles while Sample gentled it with a long pole. He claimed to have intro-duced the method into Australia and England, although it was well known in America, and he said it worked because the horse found

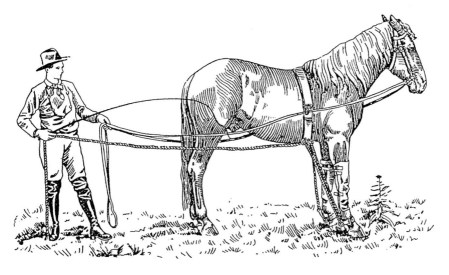

Professor Jesse Beery's method of using the double safety rope while long reining a horse.

revolving more irksome than being touched. It did not, he warned, work with horses of a sulky nature. The idea was to tie the head and tail together loosely enough at first to make the animal turn and not go forward, then gradually tighten the cord to increase the control but not so much that the horse become giddy and fell down. A whip was then cracked all around the horse, he was touched all over with the pole, and finally he was accustomed to rattling cans and waving banners. Only when he accepted everything calmly were the head and tail cords removed.

Sample then thought up his bizarre invention, a horse-taming machine, probably suggested by his experience and success with the spinning method. The machine comprised a narrow box, like a cattle crush, set on a platform which revolved, causing the horse to get so dizzy that when released it could be handled with ease. The machine could be revolved by steam or by hand, but a dearth of wild horses and problems with the machine itself meant it was a dismal failure. At one exhibition, the steam engine had to be abandoned and Sample's helper, an ex-sailor called Joe, had to try and turn it by hand. He moved it so slowly and laboriously that the audience shrieked with laughter. Captain Hayes, who appeared to find Sample an engaging and entertaining character despite his arrogance, impe-

Professor Jesse Beery advised using the double safety rope as a control device while the horse was accustomed to flags, newspapers and umbrellas.

cunity and dire failures, surprisingly wrote of his machine 'I feel certain that it would be a valuable means of saving labour in rendering quiet freshly caught horses which have been brought up under uncivilised conditions.' Hayes even tried to persuade Dr Fleming, the principal veterinary surgeon of the army, that Sample's machine might be worth investing in, but Fleming only gave Sample a kind testimonial. Like Leighwort, Hyland, and many other tamers, Sample subdued horses effectively but neither tamed nor taught them, and he spent endless time wrangling with a succession of ex-pupils who copied his method with consistent failure. One, an Australian rough rider called Frank, set up in opposition to Sample at one stage, while another, an ex-printer's clerk called Franklin, rigged himself out in cowboy boots and a sombrero and masqueraded as Leon, the Celebrated Mexican Horse Tamer.

One of the last American horse tamers was Professor Jesse Beery, a skilled and sound horseman, who in the early years of this century promulgated his knowledge through a correspondence course in horsemanship, including breaking. His instructional booklets were full of good advice such as 'accomplish just one thing and no more, or you will confuse your horse', and 'it is not profitable to begin with a colt under eighteen months or two years of age'. He practised his skills on western-bred broncos shipped to the east of the States, completely wild and unhandled, commenting 'they are splendid advertising subjects and never fail to draw a large crowd'. He devised a system to get horses used to firing guns, umbrellas and newspapers, which involved holding the horse on a pulley form of a war bridle while brandishing the object. Once, having successfully trained a horse fearful of umbrellas, the lesson completed, Beery removed the pulley bridle when a 'hard gust of wind hit the tent broadside, which pulled all the stakes out of the one side, and instantly the tent fell over on top of us'. The horse, his lesson learnt, stood stock still.

The last word on tamers lies with Captain Hayes whose observations were generally rational and unbiased. He said 'The art of mere horse taming is of little practical use; for the need of its application is of but rare occurrence, especially in countries where horses have been brought up under civilised conditions.' Changing methods of horse rearing and management, a decline in the number of wild and vicious horses, and ultimately the advent of the motor vehicle, brought about the demise of the horse tamers, and by the turn of the twentieth century they had virtually all gone.

CHAPTER SEVEN

Folklore and magic

Some – there are losses in every trade – will break their
hearts ere bitted and made,
Will fight like fiends as the rope cuts hard, and die dumb-mad
in the breaking-yard.

Thrown away
Rudyard Kipling

Since man's first encounters with the horse, he has accorded it a type
of mystique not reserved for other animals. Perhaps because the
horse was the most difficult and consequently the last of the now-
domesticated animals to tame and control, he held it in awe and
attributed to it qualities that went far beyond its speed, beauty and
the high intelligence he assumed it possessed. Ever since and across
the world, horses have figured largely in folklore and mythology.
When people first saw riders on horseback, they fled in terror,
assuming horse and rider to be one, and the power of the centaur
image, rooted in early history and embellished into legend, was to
underpin man's attitude and relationship to the horse for centuries
to come. Many horse-owning cultures believed the horse had
spiritual powers, and examples abound of man's attempts in both
real-life and mythological events to use this power to human advantage. Priests among early Germanic tribes kept special sacred
horses in wooded groves and, according to Tacitus, interpreted omens
from their movements and neighing, while horse sacrifice was
prevalent among many cultures as the most valuable and worthy
offering that could be made. From Pegasus, the winged horse of
Greek mythology, to the Buraq with the head of a woman and the
tail of a peacock on which Mohammed rode to the Seventh
Heaven, the magical aspect of the horse in man's service has been a
recurring theme and, not surprisingly, the man who had the skill to
tame and break such a revered animal was believed to have special
powers himself which elevated him, both figuratively and literally,
above his peers.

Folklore, mythology and legend are full of references to horse breaking from the taming of Pegasus to the traditional tale from the Russian Kirghizanian culture which relates how the Polar Star was a post around which the horse moved, changing the seasons. The tying of a horse to a post was fundamental to many styles of breaking, and the parallels with some form of lungeing and the seasonal breaking of horses are significant elements.

AMULETS AND TALISMEN

Since the earliest days of horse ownership, horsemen have believed in the power of certain amulets, charms, substances or artefacts to endow the bearer with special skills. In Roman times, it was thought that success with horses could be achieved through the possession of what Gaius Plinius Secundus called the hippomane or 'horse frenzy'. Known as Pliny the Elder, to differentiate him from his nephew, he wrote his *Natural history* in the fifth decade AD and, although some of his statements are questionable and some quite misinformed, his work is nevertheless of great interest. He said the hippomane was 'found in the forehead of horses at birth, the size of a dried fig, black in colour, which a brood mare as soon as she has dropped her foal eats up, or else she refuses to suckle the foal'. He added that anyone taking it before she gets it is driven into a madness by the love-poison, but in Pliny's day and for centuries after it was thought to confer special powers. It has been speculated that the hippomane was the name given to the flat piece of gristle kept in the foal's mouth for most of its unborn life and spat out at birth, so a horseman would need to be present at the moment of parturition to try to collect such a prize. Some believed that a horse would follow the man who possessed its own hippomane, and others saw it as a charm to ward off evil. To a horse tamer and breaker, such a talisman was seen as invaluable.

SHAMANS AND MEDICINE MEN

The shamans of Asian nomadic tribes sometimes carried little leather bags in which they kept herbs, amulets and objects imbued with spiritual or healing potency, some of which gave them power over horses, and this power could be temporarily transferred to other tribesmen at times of need such as when going on wild-horse hunts or when breaking horses in. As people invested with special powers to communicate with the spirits, heal illnesses and read omens, shamans held a position of great importance. Scythian shamans would prophecy when it was a good time to break horses in by sticking willow wands in the ground, and they could cure lameness with simple operations and sickness with herbal remedies. The shamanistic approach to taming and controlling horses, and healing them of ailments, was based on an empathy with the animals which stemmed from careful observation of their natural instincts and behaviour, studying individual animals, constant practice on a trial and error basis, and questioning accepted tradition. Under the guise of magical or spiritual power, it was a scientific system often passed down from father to son as shamanism was frequently a hereditary calling. The unique relationship shamans were observed to have with horses was seen as magical, and in later-tribal warfare on the steppes shamans were spared death from the hands of other tribes who feared spiritual retribution.

According to Hungarian folklore, Magyar shamans supposedly owned horses which were lame and had extra teeth, and the discovery of shamans graves dating back to the eleventh century and containing horses with pathological lesions which would have caused lameness, as well as extra incisors, would substantiate the legend. Aspiring horsemen could ask the shamans for help or advice, and they might be given talismen or herbs to enpower them. For horse breakers, the shaman's gift might be an oil or vegetable substance which calmed the horse, or it might be an object, the possession of which gave the man confidence because of his belief in it, which consequently made him more effective.

Although North American Indians were not animal herders, they had a shamanistic tradition curiously similar to that of the Ural-Altaic people of the Siberian steppes. Indian medicine men cured illness, interpreted dreams, and provided protective amulets and medicine pipe bundles. A horse medicine bundle belonging to the Blackfoot Indian medicine man, Wallace Night Gun, included two pouches containing secret potions for curing sick horses and another containing a substance to be used when catching wild mustangs. Navaho medicine men could quieten horses with their power or make others unridable. Most plains Indians included in their culture

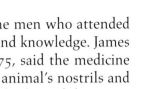

a horse medicine cult which comprised medicine men who attended special cult ceremonies and exchanged secrets and knowledge. James Adair, a trader with the Indians, writing in 1775, said the medicine men blew smoke from herbs and roots into the animal's nostrils and dosed it 'with concoctions compounded by the leaders of the secret cults who preserved the mysteries of horse medicine'. Upon request and through the offering of suitable gifts, medicine power could be transferred from one person to another, enabling less skilled men to tame, handle and break horses with success.

THE INDIAN BLANKET ACT

Observers credited the Indian medicine men with magical power over horses as they were able to take a completely wild adult horse and have it broken to ride within an hour. The secret was neither magic nor the use of substances which acted as sedatives, but was based on the study and understanding of equine behaviour. These North American shamans had noticed that wild horses rounded up into a corral would show great alarm at the sight of a buffalo robe or cured skin either laid on the ground or thrown over the rails of the corral. At first the Indians made use of this knowledge by hanging a buffalo robe over the single flimsy pole across the corral entrance to keep the horses in. However, after much snorting and wheeling around, the horses would approach the robe gradually, although this might take some time. Once they had smelled it and touched it, they lost their fear of it and paid no further attention to the robe. The principle was that if a horse was allowed in his own time and space to examine an object he is frightened of, he loses his fear of it and remains so.

The Indians developed what they saw and understood into a breaking system whereby a man replaced the buffalo robe or coloured blanket as the object of fear and suspicion. A horse would be driven into a high-sided corral large enough to allow it to move about freely and yet small enough to compel it to be aware of the buffalo robe or blanket. Respect for the horse's personal space was an essential element in the system. A man would enter the corral with a buffalo robe or blanket and gently moving it to and fro would hold the horse's attention without either frightening it or advancing towards it which would have impinged on the horse's flight distance

The horse tamed and broken in less than an hour using the Indian Blanket Act method being ridden through the streets at the Indian Pow-wow and parade at Okanagan, Washington State, in 1922. The outriders were a safety precaution. (Photograph: George Dawson)

or the space between it and the threatening object at which it feels it must fight or flee. The Indian had to keep the horse's attention and eventually the horse, having got used to the sight and smell of both the robe and the man, would advance to sniff and touch them. Once the horse had accepted the Indian and had no fear of him, the remaining aspects of breaking were apparently easily and quickly accomplished. Although it was said that this method worked in a very short time, those who have tried it say that it could take up to several hours before the horse would approach the man but it eventually always did.

One of the last times this breaking method, known as the Indian Blanket Act, was performed was at the Indian Pow-Wow and Parade at Okanagan, Washington in 1922. The wildest horse they could find was rounded up and corralled, then an Indian medicine man went in. Half an hour later he led the unbridled horse out into the street, controlling it with only one hand on its nose. The pair returned to the corral, where the Indian worked in private so that the horse had no distractions, and half an hour later reappeared with the horse bridled and the Indian riding him bareback.

Dr George Dawson, who witnessed the event, recalled that both the horse and the medicine man 'were blanketed in brilliant scarlet, giving the appearance or thought that they were blended together, more or less, a unity of all life'. The horse appeared quiet and calm and was ridden in the parade later that day without incident although there were outriders as a precautionary measure. Dr Dawson, to further his study of equine psychology, tried the method himself some years later and reported 'the horse soon advances to the performer and stands quietly, totally without emotional expression of any kind, excepting possibly an unusual feeling of attachment for the performer'. On one occasion Dr Dawson corralled a three-year-old stallion and a few mares in a barbed wire enclosure. The stallion was completely wild and, if roped, would probably have ended up cut by the wire so Dr Dawson tried a variation of the Indian Blanket Act.

> After from two to three hours of facing this horse, at from 120 to about twenty feet, with him never looking away from me, he finally slumped into relaxation; soon thereafter, he advanced steadily but slowly towards me, nuzzled me around the chest, the face, and extended his nose over my left shoulder. I put a rope and half-hitch on him but he knew nothing of a rope. I pulled on the rope and he reared, but I slackened off while he was in the air. He settled down and within three minutes was back with his head over my shoulder and his neck again tightly against my shoulder.

Jeff Edwards, one-time director of the Wild Horse Research Farm in California, also had experience of the Indian Blanket Act. A wild two-year-old colt was corralled then, he explained, 'by moving in and out and using his handkerchief, my son approached the horse until the horse made the last advance of three feet. Guy then petted and rubbed the horse . . . then turned and walked to the halter (on the fence) and the horse followed and allowed him to put the halter on. It was just that easy and natural.' Perhaps because this system of taming produced dramatic results quickly and calmly, people thought some form of magic or spiritual power was involved.

The Indians who rounded up the wild horse for taming and breaking at the Indian Pow-wow and parade, Okanagan, Washington State, in 1922. (Photograph: George Dawson)

Around the 1820s, Willis Powell, the American horse tamer, used a taming method which he claimed worked very successfully on particularly fearful horses. It consisted of taking a handkerchief and moving it gently before the horse, tossing it up, waving it and generally moving it about the horse's body. Then 'take one or two yards of thick stuff, such as cotton bagging or the like, throw it down at a distance two or three times, then make him smell it'. From this point Powell's method consisted of bombarding the horse with those things that were likely to frighten him and that included 'sacking out' the horse by throwing the cotton bagging over his back and all around him, tying a mat around his neck and a dry ox-hide to his tail, and even tying a rope in a slip knot around the horse's belly and pulling on it. After a heavy Spanish saddle with wooden stirrups had been placed on the horse's back and secured with a tight girth and cord crupper, then removed and replaced several times, and the horse forcibly accustomed to being slapped vigorously and generally handled, he was deemed to be broken. 'You may get upon him with all safety' Powell assured his readers 'and ride him through the most populous city in America without him being frightened at any of the objects he meets in it'. The idea of saturating the horse with things that frighten him until he becomes oblivious to them was common to many styles of breaking. The Indian Blanket Act allowed the horse to learn in his own time whereas Powell's method, which was not dissimilar in the early stages, accustomed the horse to fearful things but in the tamer's time with the horse being taught rather than learning for itself.

HORSEMEN'S SOCIETIES, A BRITISH SHAMANISTIC TRADITION

In East Anglia and parts of Scotland in the late seventeenth and early eighteenth centuries, a type of shamanistic brotherhood with strong similarities to animal cults in other parts of the word developed. Although the roots of these Horsemen's Societies probably went back to very early times, they gained momentum as the horse's role in agriculture became more important, and they prospered between the 1820s and the 1930s. The individual branches were scattered up the eastern coast of Britain and their purpose was to form a brotherhood for horsemen who would share their knowledge and experience and, most importantly, their power over horses. In essence they represented a type of shamanism for working men coupled with many of the benefits of an early Trade Union. Horsemen's societies were highly secretive, male-only organisations which met under cover of darkness at isolated venues. Nominees for membership were young men, not more than thirty, who had demonstrated their skill as horsemen and been recommended for consideration. Membership could not be applied for by the individual. In many cases boys started work on the land at the age of fourteen and within two years were handling a pair of horses and a plough with competence. A year later the young ploughman would find an envelope under his pillow with a single horsehair inside. This was his notification that he had been summoned.

The ceremony of initiation was generally conducted at Martinmass and varied in form according to the wishes of the senior horseman of the area but included the reciting and acceptance of an oath. The wording for the oath of an East Anglian Society began 'I of my own free will and accord do hereby most solemnly vow and swear before God and all these witnesses that I will always heal, conceal and never reveal any art or part of this secret of horsemanry which is to be revealed to me at this time or any other time hereafter.' It went on to bind the initiate not to reveal the secret to anyone at all except a 'blacksmith or a farrier or a worker of horses', and then it was not to be 'given to anyone after the sun sets on Saturday night nor before he rises on Monday morning . . .' The format for the ceremony which was conducted in secrecy at night had a strongly religious but non-Christian feel to its liturgy. The oath concluded 'Furthermore I vow and swear that I will always be at a brother's call within the bounds of three miles except I can give a lawful excuse', these being wife in childbirth, mare foaling, bad health, or the master's employment.

In a Scottish version of the initiation ceremony, the inductee had to bring with him a loaf of bread, whisky and a candle, and before a make-shift altar of sheafs of corn and the elders of the society he had to kneel and answer a series of standard questions, one of which was what did he wish for, to which he had to respond 'more knowledge'. At the end of the ceremony the 'secret' was revealed to the young horseman. It took the form of a password or short phrase, the most common being 'both in one' or 'eno', which was simply the word 'one' backwards, signifying man and horse as equal partners. As such there was really no secret at all but the guaranteed help, advice and support of other more experienced horsemen in the locality. This support, and the self-confidence it engendered in the newly sworn-in horseman, made him able to break and handle difficult horses with ease. The accumulated knowledge of the societies to which all members had access included dealing with problem horses and gaining mastery over them, cures for diseases and injuries, and secret potions for 'drawing' or attracting horses as well as binding or 'jading' animals to make them refuse to move as if paralysed.

Shaking hands with the Devil
Sometimes the ceremonies of initiation had a more sinister feel to them. One ritual intended to frighten the young initiate into safeguarding the secrecy of the Society was known as 'shaking hands with the Devil', and involved taking the young man at night to an isolated barn where, blindfolded, he was forced to shake hands with the cloven foreleg of a calf. Sometimes the oath included

a final clause whereby the young horseman asked to be cut into four pieces with a horseman's knife or dragged apart by wild horses if he ever revealed any part of the secret. Another ritual included sending the initiate at night to a graveyard to retrieve a horseman's whip from the darkness of an open grave. As the young man reached into the grave a hand would grab him and pull him in; then a reassuring voice would say 'Brother, brother, it is only your brother' as the unseen presence revealed himself to be one of the brotherhood. 'You will remember this night' the older man would explain, 'you will remember what it is like to be alone, to lose your footing, to be forced to a task you have no taste for. You will remember what it is like to be a horse and you will remember what it takes to be a horseman.'

Secrecy and knowledge

William Orr, who was born in 1899 and started work in farm service at the age of fourteen and a half, worked for many years travelling stallions. Like all Horseman's Society members, he respected the secrecy of the cult and when questioned said 'Oh, they wouldn't tell you anything. I was going to join but couldn't make up my mind.' Asked how Society members might have tamed or subdued unruly horses, he said 'They reckoned the first job they do they roped them up and pulled them down, you know, put them on the bottom, then keep them down, sit on them there. That's the start, but what else they do I don't know. But they reckon that was the start.' It was said that if a sworn-in horseman could not tame a horse, no one could.

Another stallion traveller, Bob Jack, was employed by McNeils of Crieff in Perthshire to travel their Clydesdale stallion, Lord Dundurran. On the day of the local stallion parade the stallion went mad but Jack tamed him, although he modestly said 'I've done nothing to him. I just whispered in his ear this morning to be a good fellow.' Jack could let the horse loose in a yard then William Orr, who knew him, said 'he made him lie down, and he sat on him, then telled [sic] him to get up and get back into the box . . . but he was a sworn-in horseman, he was clever'.

Members of the brotherhood were required to share any new-found knowledge within the Society, and most were open-minded to new ideas or inventions. William Orr saw an advertisement for Professor Jesse Beery's correspondence course in horse breaking and wrote off for details as well as buying one of the Professor's horse-taming bridles. Orr recalled 'Why it worked was a little pulley that just catched [sic] the horse at the back of the ear, here, and down into the mouth and then the rope came down through the mouth up into this little pulley at the back of the ear, and then you pulled on it – you could have held the Titanic with it.'

Calling on Satanic powers

For those with the courage to do so, there was another way in which horsemen could enpower themselves to handle horses but this involved invoking the help of the Devil through a strange rite known in Cambridgeshire and East Anglia as the Waters of the Moon. It necessitated catching a frog or toad, killing it, and either burying it in an ant-hill or hanging it on a thornbush until only its skeleton remained. Then one night when the moon was full, the horseman had to go to a stream alone and throw the whole skeleton in the water. As it was swept downstream, one bone would separate itself from the rest and float upstream against the current. This bone was a small forked bone like a tiny wishbone and similar in shape to the frog in a horse's hoof. While it was in the water the horseman had to concentrate and not allow his attention to be distracted despite the strange noises and movements all around him as if there was a hurricane or earthquake. If concentration was lost, so was the magic. Lifted from the water and taken home, the bone gave the horseman power over horses but at a price, for the satanic power of the bone resulted in many horseman going mad or dying in strange circumstances. To say of a horseman 'he had been to the river', meant he had practised this strange rite.

Taming oils and potions

In perpetuating the tradition of compounding secret oils and potions to facilitate the taming, breaking and general handling of horses, members of the Horsemen's Societies were following a practice of great antiquity. It was already centuries old when in Roman times it was customary to give a horse a purgative before it was broken in to make it quieter. Common ingredients were mustard, ground pannax root, oil, honey, wine, gall nuts and juice of coriander. By medieval times, the pre-breaking drench was formulated also to work as a physic to cleanse the system at the end of the winter when breaking was undertaken. The gypsies used to boil a plug of tobacco in a gallon of ale until the strength was extracted, then they dosed the horse with enough to make it so sick it was amenable to any kind of handling.

Denton Offutt, the American horse tamer, claimed 'a strong decoction of tobacco will subdue his viciousness. One quart will make a horse very sick. Others of a bilious nature require a gallon.' Dennis Magner once sent out for two ounces of Tincture of Lobelia which he gave to a particularly difficult horse at one of his taming demonstrations. Half an hour later the horse 'became so sick that he could not resist', and he remained quiet thereafter although Magner admitted he was liable to colic attacks. Specialist suppliers marketed a whole range of feed additives, horse spices, conditioning powders and patent drenches, many of the ingredients of which were traditionally used by horsemen to calm, quieten, tame or attract horses. A sixteenth-century herbalist from Kent sold aniseed, fenugreek, parsley, tumeric, bay-berries, rue, linseed and licorice as additives to be put into a horse's feed to preserve it from illness or disease, and two centuries later a London merchant, John Rowley, 'having fix'd up two large mills which I work with horses', was advertising many of the same ingredients. Curiously, many of these herbs or plant extracts were essential components of the secret potions used by members of the Horseman's Societies. A mixture of molasses and aniseed smeared on the fingers was commonly employed by farm horsemen when approaching a strange horse, and a little henbane in a horse's mash was known to quieten the animal after which a tonic of ash tree buds might be given.

Willis J. Powell, the American horse tamer, led people to believe he tamed horses through the use of secret oils and substances although he later admitted 'I now declare to the world that I had heard of some of them . . . but found them without the least effect.' A great experimenter, Powell studied the effect of a whole range of substances on horses. Knowing that some people used hollow horse bits into which opium, tobacco and laudenum were inserted during breaking, he tried opium on horses, expecting to find it stupefied the horse but it had little effect. The sweat from the armpit 'has a tendency to make a horse sleepy' he declared, and mare's milk, oil of cumin and asafoetida, an ill-smelling gum resin substance, were also ineffective.

Spectators at Dennis Magner's demonstrations used to sniff him to see if they could detect any unusual scents though none were used. Some more unscrupulous tamers used the successful throwing method but led people to believe they used magic taming potions which they sold at the end of the performance.

Faucher, the American author of *The Arabian secret of taming horses*, sold bottles of taming oil for up to fifty dollars a bottle, the contents being two parts of oil of rhodium and one part each of oils of cumin and anise. Faucher claimed that if the oil was rubbed on the hands and the horse approached from the windward side and touched on the nose, it would follow the bearer anywhere. Strangely, a nineteenth-century horseman advocated something very similar and advised 'the oil of rhodium possesses peculiar properties: all animals cherish a fondness for it and it exercises a subduing influence over them. Oil of cumin: the horse has an instinctive passion for it. Both are natives of Arabia.' He added 'with this knowledge, horse taming becomes easy, and when the horse scents the odour he is drawn towards it'.

Farm horsemen and drawing oils

Farm horsemen made considerable use of drawing or attractive oils. A little of a mixture of oil of origanum, oil of rosemary, oil of cinnamon and oil of fennel about a horseman's body was said to be a great help in catching difficult or wild horses if the bearer stood upwind so the horse could smell him as he approached. In warm weather, a few drops on the forehead would be enough, or a few drops in an oat cake fed to the horse would be enough to render it amenable. A horseman's stick, such as the type carried by stallion men, sometimes had a plug of wool impregnated with drawing oil in the end, or the oil could be smeared on his clothing. A Norfolk man, almost certainly a sworn-in horseman, applied for a job travelling a stallion in Essex but, since the previous leader had died suddenly, the horse would tolerate no one else and had aggressively driven them from the stable. Feed and water had to be lowered into the stall from the loft above. The man threw his cap, evidently with drawing oil on it, into the stable, saying 'if that's welcome, so am I'. The horse was immediately quiet, and was duly bridled and taken to the smithy to be shod. The drawing oil recipe of a Caithness horseman was 'Tincture of opium, ten drops; oil of aniseed, fifteen drops; and then ten drops each of oils of thyme, cinnamon, rosemary and nutmeg. Mix with orris powder, two grams, and apply a little to the palm of your hand and rub across his nose, then you can do with him what you like.'

Denton Offutt, Rarey's alleged teacher, wrote

> To catch a horse, mule or cow, take oil of rhodium, oil of anise, oil of cinnamon, three equal parts, mix them together, and let them smell it by putting it on your finger ends, and rubbing it on or in the nose, and in ten or twenty minutes they are ready to receive your kindness and your plan of teaching, etc. It has an astonishing effect on the animals of the world.

Another of Offutt's recipes was a cake of oatmeal and honey which was baked, after which he wrote 'Put the cake into your bosum, and keep it there until it sweats, and when the horse has fasted 12 or 24 hours, give it to him to eat. Then use him kindly and gently.' Mare's milk, mixed with salt, and given to the horse to lick from the horseman's hand three or four times a day was another of Offutt's secrets which he referred to as the Spanish method.

Other horsemen had their own favourites. Fred Taylor fed his horses pieces of carrot soaked in aniseed while Dick Christian preferred the use of oil of rhodium and stallion wart or the powdered chestnut from the leg of a stallion. Chestnuts are found on the inner foreleg of all equines and on the hind legs of all but donkeys and zebras. Known from very early times as the spur, leg wart, ostlet or castor, it was dried, finely ground, and kept in a small airtight box or bottle until required. It was believed to be the remnant of a once functional gland or organ. 'Important evidence of this view' according to an early publication of the British Museum Department of Zoology 'is the fact that when cut the callosities yield a fluid which will attract other horses . . . such a fluid is almost certainly derived from an ancestral scent gland'. Denton Offutt was a great believer in the power of ground chestnut and suggested that by 'putting it into a goose quill that will hold a dose for each nostril, it will serve to sicken or stupefy him'.

Rarey claimed he used nothing but the 'oil of experience' and he was scathing of the preparations used and marketed by other breakers. 'Recipes of strong-smelling oils are got up to tame horses, all of which, so far as a scent goes, have no effect whatsoever . . .' he said.

THE HORSE'S SENSE OF SMELL

However, no one could dispute that a horse has a keen sense of smell and is influenced by certain scents. Most horses react strongly to the smell of pigs. Ancient nomadic tribesmen knew something of the power of scent when they hunted wild horses and reputedly rubbed themselves with horse urine before setting out. Nineteenth-century mustangers in America never washed or changed their clothes during a hunt which might last several weeks as it was important that they always smelt the same and the horses could get used to that smell. Fortunately, not washing or changing came naturally to many mustangers. Bob Lemmons, a successful mustanger, insisted that the scent he carried had to be acceptable to the horses or he could not manipulate the herd. Early American settlers often owed their lives to their horses, who could smell Indians waiting hidden and in ambush, and Apaches, who ate horseflesh, emitted an unpleasant odour which horses could detect and react to, just as others would be wary of trappers carrying the odour of dangerous animals such as mountain lions or bears.

Jading oils

Jading or binding oils, which were repugnant and offensive to horses, worked on this principle, and sworn-in horsemen used them extensively to demonstrate their power. The practice was very old; it is recorded that Clovis, the sixth-century Frankish king, had to make an offering of one hundred pieces of gold to St Martin of Tours, whose monks had 'bound' his horse so that it would not move from the stable. The ransom had to be doubled before the un-Christian monks would lift the jinx.

Jading could be used to help control horses or it could be used to cause problems for others, and was achieved by means of strong-smelling substances smeared on the horse's muzzle, bridle, cart shaft, manger, or even on the ground in front of the horse, making it unwilling to move. Often the jading substance was smeared around the stable door so that the horses would not come out, or on field gate-posts so they would not enter. Although the recipes for jading potions were very secret, a main ingredient was a red gummy resin obtained from a kind of palm fruit and known to the horsemen as 'dragon's blood'. Other components included ground stoat liver, a

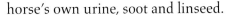

horse's own urine, soot and linseed.

One farm horseman, confined to his bed through illness and concerned that the second horseman was overworking his horses, made up a jading solution by asking different members of the family to fetch ingredients so no one knew the full recipe. The solution was then daubed on the field gate-posts jading the horses from passing through. The practice was apparently sometimes used on equipment too and in September 1756 a man called Peter Pairmy was accused of jading a plough. The jading solution could be removed or neutralised by washing it off with water or milk and vinegar. A Suffolk horseman in the brotherhood came to the rescue of a younger member whose horses had been jaded. He said 'I just went a-front there with my milk and vinegar; rubbed it in my palm and fingers; and then I rubbed it inside the horses' noses and inside their nostrils.' Another horse was bound when a jading powder was surreptitiously scattered around it, but freed when an experienced horseman grabbed the horse's bridle, turned its head sharply then backed the horse out of the affected area. Rubbing the edge of the manger with a moleskin would jade a horse from eating.

WITCHCRAFT AND SORCERY

Horses could also be adversely influenced by witchcraft, sorcery and curses, according to the superstitious beliefs of the time, causing them to be wild, vicious or unmanageable. It provided a simple and acceptable explanation for equine behavioural problems which people could not understand or solve. In Roman times, curse tablets made of lead were frequently used to bring misfortune or illness on other people's horses, the inscription on one tablet reading 'I adjure you, demon, whoever you are, and I demand of you from this hour, from this day, from this moment, that you torment and kill the horses of . . .' An appropriate offering to the gods might lift such a curse, but incompetent professional horse breakers faced with horses they could not handle could claim the animal was under a curse, making it untrainable.

In medieval times, young horses brought into a stable or barn to be broken which did not settle and were found sweated up and tired in the morning were assumed to have been ridden by witches overnight. A foal's cowl, the thin membrane covering its head at birth, hung up in the stable was believed to keep witches at bay, or a holed piece of flint called a hag-stone could be hung over the horse's back in its stable to prevent the witch from mounting.

Robert Herrick in the sixteenth century put his cure for this problem into verse and wrote 'Hang up hooks, and sheers to scare, hence the hag, that rides the mare, till they be all over wet, with the mire and the sweat: this observ'd, the manes will be, of your horses, all knot-free.'

A horse-shoe hung up in the stable also scared off both the witches and the devil, the former because being metal and man-made it was repulsive to witches, and the latter because according to legend St Dunstan, blacksmith and saint, was once asked by the Devil to shoe him. Having trussed the Devil up, St Dunstan made such a painful job of shoeing his cloven hooves that he vowed never again to enter a building where he saw a horse-shoe hung up. The tradition goes back many centuries, as Pliny the Elder recommended a horse-shoe hung up to catch good luck and ward off troubles, and Lord Nelson sailed into battle with a horse-shoe nailed to the mast of the Victory. Even American Indians used the horse-shoe symbol to signify good luck and success although they did not have a tradition of shoeing horses in their culture. If talismans and hagstones did not safeguard the horse from witches and demons, the 'possessed' animal may be exorcised or shut in a stable with a black cat which, having absorbed the evil from the horse, could be killed. In severe cases in thirteenth-century Europe, the unfortunate horse might even be tried, convicted and executed.

Another reason superstitious people believed difficult horses may be possessed was the assumption that horses could see and hear things humans could not, a characteristic often also attributed to witches. Pausanias, writing in his *Itinerary of Greece* in the middle of the second century, speaks of places at the hippodrome haunted by an equine ghost at which horses shied, causing accidents. The brutality of breaking such animals was often more to do with the suppression of the evil possessing it than teaching it to be of service.

Witches were also believed to have the power to 'overlook' a horse causing it to behave out of character for no apparent reason. A cure for the evil eye was something bright and shiny to distract the unwelcome onlooker, and metal amulets were often hung in the stable or attached to the horse itself to ward off evil. In the last century

Turks hung 'something like a jewel about their necks, and a broad ribbon which was full of amulets against poison, which they are most afraid of', Miles wrote in 1868, adding 'the "evil eye" is as rife among the Arabs of the present day as with the highlanders of two centuries or three centuries ago. In dread of this, many tribes are loth to show their horses – but more especially their mares – to strangers; and never omit to fortify the animal against it by a prayer to 'Mashallah'. If a horse falls ill after such a visit, they immediately call in a sort of wizard, who, uttering some cabalistical words, breaks an egg on the frontal bone of the patient who, never-the-less, generally dies.' As early as the seventh century, Arabs hung amulets on their young foals to offer them protection and keep them tractable. Horse brasses, usually in the shape of a symbol of good fortune, were used on agricultural horses in Britain up into the twentieth century.

EYE CONTACT AND HYPNOTISM

The use of eye contact in horse breaking has been well established for centuries and there are many examples of breakers who produced good results by mesmerising or even hypnotising horses by staring at them. When Rarey tamed the vicious horse, King of Oude, he apparently controlled it with such a fixed stare that a writer in the *Sporting Magazine* of 1859 was moved to write 'We never till that moment thought there was so much influence in a firm man's glance . . .' Another observer in New York recounted how Rarey could hold a horse's attention with 'his glittering eye'. Even Willis Powell, whose style was often more theatrical than scientific, professed to have hypnotic power over horses which enabled him to control them with eye contact only. 'Sometimes' he wrote 'I have met with an extremely wild horse which seemed to be gentled, as by enchantment, in a few minutes.' Other tamers claimed to have hypnotised their sleepy horses when they had actually drugged or purged them, one professional using a hollow mouthed bit into which he had slipped a piece of tow soaked in tincture of myrrh.

THE HUMAN VOICE

The voice was even more important in breaking and training horses, particularly in some of the 'gentling' methods where it was imperative to establish a rapport with the horse. Both the Greeks and Romans recognised the importance of speaking to a horse to reassure and inspire confidence in him, and by the sixteenth century horsemen were well aware of the effect of 'loud and terrible voices' and 'gentle cherishings' on an impressionable young horse. Many rightly understood that it was the tone of the voice which calmed the horse, and Willis Powell, active at the beginning of the nineteenth century, ratified this, advising 'Talk to the horse in Latin, Greek, French, English or Spanish, or any other language you please; but let him hear the sound of your voice.' Rarey used his voice considerably when dealing with difficult horses but always in a calm, soothing way. 'One harsh word' he warned 'will so excite a nervous horse as to increase his pulse ten beats in a minute.' However, some breakers, like the Irishman known as One-Eye who was working around the turn of the century, used the power of the voice to brow-beat their horses into submission, and footmen and grooms at one time were selected for their 'terrible voices and cruel looks' which were thought essential for berating horses into obedience.

Many people were ready to believe it was the actual words spoken when handling a horse that really tamed it. For centuries gypsies had claimed to tame horses with the use of secret words whispered in their ears, the words being derived from the ancient Sanskrit language. As a style of horse breaking it was rooted in ancient times but evident in differing forms in many parts of the world. North American Indians appeared to use a similar method although it was closely allied to the practice of chewing special herbs and plants and blowing into the animal's nose and ears to pacify it. Gauchos also used to chew tobacco then spit it into the animal's mouth to calm it, and onlookers interpreted this as whispering to the horse, giving rise to the term 'horse whisperer'. Some breakers would stand on the horse's near side and, with one hand on its muzzle and another on its shoulder, whisper into its ear. By smearing an ether-based solution on the left hand, the animal could be partially anaesthetised while 'whispering' distracted the attention of the audience. One showman horse breaker in Atkins, Arkansas, successfully tamed a horse using this system then inadvertently wiped his nose on the back of his hand and passed out to the hysterical laughter of the audience who immediately saw through his guise.

SULLIVAN, THE HORSE WHISPERER

The most famous whisperer of all was an Irishman called Sullivan from Mallow in County Cork who, up until his death in 1810, earned a phenomenal reputation as a tamer of horses. Described by the Reverend Townsend in his Statistical Survey of the County of Cork as 'an ignorant, awkward rustic of the lowest class', he was an illiterate alcoholic, but there is ample evidence of his amazing skills that enabled him to 'tame into the most submissive and tractable disposition any horse or mare that was notoriously vicious or obstinate'. Sullivan reputedly learned his skill from a soldier in return for a gallon of porter on condition he never revealed the secret to anyone, and Sullivan stuck to his word. He took no pupils and the secret died with him. The secret was said to be an Indian charm which led some people to assume the soldier had served in India although other sources suggest that he had served in America, in which case the secret was more probably of plains Indian origin. Youatt, writing in 1831, said Sullivan got the name of 'The Whisperer', 'from the vulgar notion of his being able to communicate to the horse what he wished by means of a whisper ... the singularity of his method seemed in some degree to justify the supposition'.

Mr James Castley, a veterinary surgeon and a regular contributor to *The Veterinarian* magazine, said of Sullivan, 'his mystical art was practised for such a length of time, and on such a variety of subjects, that there is no such thing as doubting the fact', and a spectator of Sullivan's skills, Mr George Watts of Dublin, confirmed this. 'If I had not seen it myself' he said, 'I would not believe it.' As Youatt pointed out 'Every description of horse or even mule, whether previously broken or unhandled, whatever their peculiar habits or vices might have been, submitted without show of resistance to the magical influence of his art, and in the short space of half an hour became gentle and tractable.'

Sullivan's method was to be locked up in a closed stable with the horse, sometimes for as little as half an hour, sometimes overnight, and he always insisted that he was not to be disturbed until he gave a signal when the stable doors could be opened. He would enter the building with nothing more than a rope, and while in with the horse little or no sound was audible. When the doors were opened the horse would be lying down and quiet. People said that he used no

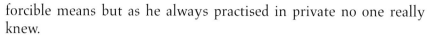

forcible means but as he always practised in private no one really knew.

An observer wrote

> After a tête-à-tête between him and the horse, during which little or no bustle was heard, the signal was made, and on opening the door the horse was found lying down, and the man by his side playing familiarly with him like a child with a puppy dog. From that time he was found perfectly willing to submit to any discipline, however repugnant to his nature before.

No one seemed to know how Sullivan achieved his remarkable results, although James Castley who saw Sullivan tame a vicious troop horse said afterwards

> I observed that the animal seemed afraid whenever Sullivan either spoke or looked at him; how this extraordinary ascendency could have been obtained it is difficult to conjecture; he seemed to possess an instinctive power of inspiring awe, the result perhaps of a natural intrepidity [sic], in which I believe a great part of the art consisted; though the circumstances of the tête-à-tête show that upon particular occasions something more must have been added to it.

Many God-fearing people were quite sure where the power came from and when the local priest could not extract the secret from him at the confessional it was assumed to be the power of the Devil. It is recorded that the parish priest, believing Sullivan to be in league with the Devil, would cross himself and move to the other side of the road when he saw Sullivan approaching. The priest of Ballyclough, according to Sullivan's son, met Sullivan one day as both rode towards Mallow and accused Sullivan of being 'a confederate of the wicked one', at which Sullivan laid the priest's horse under a spell and caused the priest such anguish that he agreed to leave Sullivan alone forever.

Sullivan at work

At the Curragh of Kildare meeting in 1804, Mr Whalley's race horse, King Pippin, was brought to run. A very vicious animal, it would attack people without provocation. It would even seize its jockey by the leg and drag him from the saddle, and a length of stick called a sword which was attached at one end to the bridle and at the other to the girth had to be worn at all times to prevent him from doing this.

A volunteer helper at the meeting who offered to put the bridle on the horse was worried like a rat in the jaws of a terrier. Sullivan was sent for and shut up with the horse all night. In the morning the horse followed Sullivan about, lay down to command, and would even open his mouth and allow any person's hand to be put in. He won a race at the meeting, stayed docile for three years, then killed a man and had to be put down.

On another occasion Sullivan bought a dragoon's horse at Mallow that was so savage it had to be fed through a hole in the stable wall, yet after taming was so quiet it worked between the shafts of a jaunting car. The results of most of Sullivan's work seemed to last too. Youatt noted 'Though more submissive to him than to others, the animals seemed to have acquired a docility unknown before.' Witnesses observed that Sullivan was fearless and that the animals he tamed were terrified of him afterwards.

The ubiquitous Willis Powell, who believed he and Sullivan shared the same secret, pointed out in criticism that Sullivan dealt with handled horses, familiar to man, 'but the horses I generally had to deal with have been running wild in the plains and woods for four, five, six and even ten years, and which, during that time, had never had a rope on them'.

Various theories were put forward for what Sullivan did, including a variation of Rareyfication under the mask of whispering, hypnosis, brainwashing the horse, making a noise in its ear like a dog whistle which only the horse could hear and which terrified it into submission, drugs, purging drenches, and demonic power.

Sullivan literally drank himself to death, leaving three sons, one of whom followed his father's trade as a horse breaker. However, as Youatt commented, the son had only a small portion of the art and 'either never learned the true secret, or was incapable of putting it into practice'. Another source confirmed this and cited the example of a troop horse called Lancer which was very difficult to shoe. When the regiment was stationed in Cork, young Sullivan was sent for but 'Lancer seemed to pay no attention whatever to his charm, and at last fairly beat him out of the forge; he was fain to make his escape from so unruly a customer.' A grandson of Sullivan's, under the patronage of the Marquis of Waterford, opened a subscription list to teach his grandfather's secret but his career was without distinction.

Imitators of Sullivan were as numerous as they were unsuccessful and their methods generally deemed cruel and ineffective. Castley reported that Sullivan received great offers to exercise his art abroad 'but hunting and attachment to his native soil were his ruling passions. He lived at home in a style most agreeable to his disposition, and nothing would induce him to leave Duhallow and the foxhounds.'

The technique behind whispering

An article in the magazine *Household Words* related how a Kent coachman called in a professed whisperer because his horses were getting beyond his mastery. After the whisperer's ministrations, the horses 'had the worst of it for two months' when their ill-humour returned. The coachman tried the system himself and darkening the stable 'held what he termed a little conversation with them' which kept them placid for another two months but he himself did not seem to approve of the system and admitted it was cruel. Some whisperers used twitches, throat nooses and other devices, and some were said to invoke satanic powers, as spectators claimed they could smell brimstone through the door.

A number of whisperers and mystical breakers who achieved fast results owed their successes to simply wearing the animal down by bombarding it with the things it feared until it became careless of them. Fatigue in the short term achieved little, for as Captain Hayes noted 'Fatigue may be used as a valuable adjunct to other means of control but should seldom be employed alone; for its effects usually are as transient as the sensation itself.' Even so, the notion of 'riding a horse quiet' was an accepted and common method of breaking horses although the results were sometimes less than successful. Gauchos were observed to ride young horses until they fell down exhausted, thereby impressing upon them the power of man, and gypsy horsemen also broke using a form of the 'saturation' method. In their case, without tiring the horse unduly they kept it by them constantly, tethering it by the campsite, tying it to the caravan or alongside the shaft horse when moving from place to place, and constantly handling it until it grew accustomed to the presence of man. As Powell wrote 'Whenever a horse that you begin to handle hangs down his head, or appears sleepy or careless, your business is half-over.'

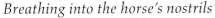

Breathing into the horse's nostrils

If the actual words did not tame the horse, many believed that by breathing into the horse's nostrils or ears some kind of empathy with the horse was established which eliminated fear and brought mutual acceptance. As Henry Hall Dixon wrote in the middle of the last century,

> The latest instantaneous system which acquired a certain degree of temporary popularity was that introduced from the western prairies by Mr Ellis of Trinity College, Cambridge, which consisted in breathing into the nostrils of a colt, or a buffalo colt, while its eyes were covered. But although on some animals this seemed to produce a soothing effect, on others it totally failed.

Breathing into a horse's nostrils possibly worked either because the tamer chewed special herbs which acted as a sedative on the horse, or because the process accustomed the horse very quickly to the smell of man which it feared. It is significant that Mr Ellis' breathing method came from the American prairies where the Indians had used it for many years. As experienced hunters they knew the smell of man could stampede the animals they stalked and for this reason they kept downwind of the herds. When they acquired horses, they inbuilt this knowledge into their taming methods by getting the animals used to the smell of man at an early stage. As a practice it also mimicked equine behaviour, as strange horses touch noses and snort on meeting. Catlin wrote that the Indian breathing method conquered a horse and made it perfectly docile.

In an article in *The Observer* in 1954, Barbara Woodhouse, who was later to make her name through dog training, wrote that she once lived in Argentina where she broke horses from the wild herd of 6,000 on the estancia where she lived. One day, she wrote,

> I met a very old Guaranee Indian, of which tribe there are very few left now. I stopped to talk to him about the very beautiful little mare he was riding, and he told me that his tribe do not have to break in their horses as we do; they just catch them with a lasso, and then stand near them, with their hands behind their backs, and blow gently down their nostrils. The horse understands this as 'How do you do?' in its own language and returns this greeting by approaching the human being and sniffing up his nose. From that moment the horse has no further fear, and the breaking in is simply a matter of showing the horse what you want.

Mrs Woodhouse later tried this method on a mare which had killed three men and which she bought for fifteen shillings. 'She stopped trembling and came slowly up to me as I blew down my nostrils, while standing quite still in the corral where she had been penned for me. She raised her head until her nose touched mine. I blew gently up her nose and then put my hand out to caress her. She never moved.' She was saddled and ridden away and was never any trouble, even being shipped to England when Mrs Woodhouse moved back to Britain.

THE POWER OF TOUCH

Touch is an important aspect of breaking and taming, and horsemen were quick to recognise the immediate effect of getting a hand on a horse and touching those parts of its body most receptive to the taming touch. The system became known under the broad heading of 'gentling' and was based on assuring the animal by touch that it was in no danger from man. Rarey believed that of the four senses the horse used that 'the sense of feeling is, perhaps, the most important . . . he makes use of his nose, or muzzle, as we would of our hands', and observers noted the way Rarey stroked, caressed and fondled his horses, rubbing their ears through his hands, and gently touching their temples – an action now understood to be stress relieving. Rarey said 'As soon as he touches you with his nose, caress him . . . always using a very light soft hand . . . always rubbing the way the hair lies . . .' Other horsemen suggested grasping the loose skin on the shoulder very gently, as this could distract and calm a horse, and scratching a horse on the withers was usually accepted as a friendly gesture which many horses would try to reciprocate as two horses would when standing head to tail in a field.

Twitches, barnacles and other devices
While for centuries many people had been aware of the sensitivity of the muzzle and the ears, few seem to have questioned why this should be. A twitch, a short piece of wood with a cord loop in one end which was placed around the horse's upper lip or ear and twisted to exert pressure, was a tool used since early times to control difficult horses for shoeing or veterinary treatment, and horse breakers also made use of it to control restive horses. The general belief was that a

Using a twitch on a horse's muzzle to subdue it for shoeing.
(Photograph: C. Richardson)

twitch simply distracted the horse from whatever was happening to it while also anchoring the horse, who soon learnt that by moving it caused itself more pain. Following scientific research there is now evidence to suggest that the nose, a traditional acupuncture point, is the juncture of many nerve endings which when stimulated produce a feeling of calm because of the release of endorphins, opiate-like substances produced by the brain and pituitary gland with pain-killing properties.

Various kinds of patent twitches were once marketed by veterinary suppliers.

Youatt described 'barnacles' which were special pinchers which nipped the nose to produce a similar effect to a twitch, and in the wake of Rarey's demonstrations 'magic horse-taming nose pinchers' were sold in London and elsewhere. The ear had similar sensitivity to that of the nose and it is surprising how many taming secrets centred around it, from the bizarre practice of sewing a horse's ears together to stuffing them with tow to make the horse deaf. An old farmer related how his head horseman calmed a farm horse, one of a working pair, which would not settle to its work, by sticking a dress-maker's pin through the tip of one of its ears. With the pin in place, the horse worked quietly and steadily all day. Rarey said he 'once saw a plan given in a newspaper to make a bad horse stand to be shod, which was to fasten down one ear . . . I tried it several times, and thought that it had a good effect.'

Another horseman cured a draught horse which lay down in the road and refused to move by slipping a little lead shot, which he kept in a small tin in his waistcoat pocket, into one of the horse's ears. He reckoned that as the horse shook its head to dislodge the shot, the tiny lead pellets must have sounded like thunder, causing the horse to leap up and move on. In many cases this barbaric practice caused serious problems or even fatalities.

Charles Gardner, a native of Diss in Norfolk, said his father used an unusual device to bring recalcitrant horses to heel. It comprised a metal ring which went over the horse's ear and a waxed thread with a bead on the end which dangled inside the ear. Repeatedly placed on the horse, removed, and replaced again over a period of several hours it was said to make any horse quiet. When his father was in a cavalry regiment in Egypt during the First World War, he successfully subdued a difficult horse there with the ring and bead device.

The sensitivity of the area immediately behind the poll led horsemen to invent a whole range of bridles and halters which brought pressure to bear on that area. Some combined the actions of a twitch and a halter such as the device which comprised a rope passing over the poll and under the horse's upper lip, while others were variations on the Indian War Bridle which brought pressure on the poll and mouth together. An article in *The Veterinarian* of 1828 mentions the use of a form of twitch bridle by North American Indians, said to be effective on wild horses.

BLINDFOLDS FOR TAMING

Blindfolding an animal to calm it was an old trick, known in Greco-Roman times, and practised throughout the Renaissance period when a 'closed bridle' was a commonly used piece of equipment in riding schools. 'Blind headstalls' with a piece of heavy canvas filling the space between the cheekpieces, noseband and browband were popular in the last century for, as Captain Hayes commented, 'Blindfolding is an efficient means of control with the majority of horses.'

In earlier times, depriving a horse of its sight was thought to concentrate its mind on its work, and Holmeshead, writing in the 1500s, said it was advisable to blind horses intended to work in the repetitive work of mills. Horses that were proving difficult to break for harness work were sometimes 'moped' by having a shield fitted over their eyes so that they could not see forwards, others were worked

Hard work in a mill or capstan would generally subdue the most unruly horse. (Photograph: Beamish Open Air Museum)

with a blindfold on all the time, and some unfortunate animals were intentionally blinded to subdue them. At the time that Rarey came on the scene, Lord Dorchester was considering having his stallion, Cruiser, blinded to protect his grooms from the horse's viciousness and to try to bring the animal into line.

In the middle of the last century a man called King exhibited a horse he claimed to have tamed by pinching a nerve in its mouth which he called the 'nerve of susceptibility'.

WOMEN AND HORSE BREAKING

One piece of folklore that seemed to be virtually universal up until this century was the belief that horse breaking was best practised only by men. Even in cultures like the Sarmatians, where women rode as much as men, the catching, taming, handling and breaking of horses remained a male province, and it was thought that a woman's presence could taint a horse and weaken its stamina. Comanche Indians, who employed the services of a medicine man to 'empower' horses before buffalo hunts, raids on other tribes or races, by administering special potions by spitting them into the horses' mouths or ears, prohibited women from approaching a horse thus treated, and would carefully wash the 'magic' off in a creek later. In Brazil, the belief was taken a step further and not only women but people of a nervous disposition were barred from being present at the gelding of a horse, as it was thought they may adversely affect the character of the gelding. In male-dominated cultures, women were given few opportunities to learn and practice the skills of taming and breaking, and it is likely that long-held prejudices can be traced back to this fact. Those women who did break horses inevitably broke them in the harsh masculine style of the time, and still faced criticism and ridicule from their male peers.

During the Crimean War, a French lady horse breaker called Madamoiselle Isabell was brought over to England with the glowing recommendations of the French war minister to break horses for the cavalry. This was contrary to the wishes of General Griffiths, head of the Cavalry Training Department, who saw the woman's Maidstone-based sojourn in England as a prohibitive expense, more so as she apparently ruined many good horses with the use of her new type of dumb jockey and a severe spur attached to the end of a whip.

Around the same time in America, a Mrs Bunnell of Wellsboro, Pennsylvania, was training horses to go in harness and be driven without either reins or bridles, although the credit for her skill went to A. H. Rockwell, the man who bought them and in 1862 gave a demonstration driving three of them abreast in this unique fashion. Another horsewoman, Alice Hayes, who with her husband broke hundreds of horses in India, Ceylon, Egypt, China and South Africa at the end of the last century, was quite used to dealing with some

A whip spur.

very obstinate animals. A consummate rider, she showed her skill on the backs of some very wild horses, 'the most trying animals' she admitted 'being those of which I was the rough rider at my husband's horse breaking classes'.

In Britain, the prejudice against women debarred them from membership of the Horsemen's Societies, and most tamers and showmen, including Telfer, banned women from their demonstrations. Rarey was an exception, and noted 'It is a general remark how quiet some high-spirited horses will become when ridden by ladies. The cause of this is that they are more quietly handled, patted and caressed by them, and they soon become sensible of this difference of treatment from the rough whip and spur system generally adopted by men.' This comment, coupled with his belief that horses were intelligent and capable of love and affection, led critics to denounce him and his system as effeminate. As one magazine reporter pointed out, not only could horses not love, but English horses could not love an American. Following a Rarey demonstration, another less-critical writer commented, 'a young and beautiful peeress has taken off her bonnet before going to a morning fete, and in ten minutes laid a full-sized horse prostrate and helpless as a sheep in the hands of the shearer'.

Using skill rather than strength, Henry Hall Dixon said 'not only have boys of five or six stone become successful horse tamers, but ladies of high rank have in the course of ten minutes perfectly subdued and reduced to death-like calmness fiery blood-horses'. By proving that brute strength was not necessary to break a horse, Rarey helped break the prejudice against women in horse training. He was not entirely alone in his beliefs about gentle handling but like Calthrop, another famous breaker described as having 'a most patient and delicate manner', he contributed significantly towards the emancipation of horsewomen.

BLEEDING TO CALM THE UNRULY

Horses which were unruly or over-excitable were often believed to suffer from over-heating of the blood, and the old remedy of bleeding a horse to calm it was common to nearly all horse cultures. It possibly originated with Asian nomads who bled their horses to drink the blood as part of their diet and who noted the effect it had on

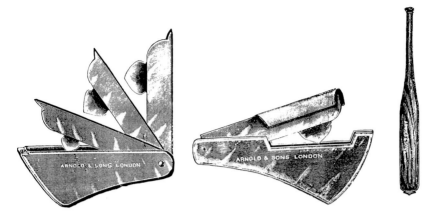

A three-bladed fleam, a single bladed fleam, and bloodstick.

some horses. In Turkestan and Persia horses were often bled on a precautionary basis to keep them manageable, and in Roman times the blood was sometimes fed back to the horse as a tonic.

Dixon, writing in 1858, said 'bleeding a vicious horse has been recommended in German books on equitation', and it came to be recommended as a cure for physical problems too. Usually the horse was bled with the aid of a fleam, most of which consisted of several blades of varying size set in a protective cover like a folding pocket knife. The chosen blade was placed against a vein in the neck, upper leg or in the roof of the mouth and struck sharply with a small lead-lined mallet called a bloodstick. Youatt advised 'making a large orifice for abstracting the blood as rapidly as possible, for the constitution will thus be the more speedily and beneficially affected', and according to reports of the time up to a gallon of blood might be taken from a horse at one time which would certainly have a subduing effect. Once the 'bad blood' had been let out, sometimes through a hollow straw, the flow was staunched and the hole sealed with a thorn and cobwebs. An ancient and bizarre variation of bleeding was to stand the horse in a farm pond or slow-moving stream and allow leeches to do the job.

Some folklore related to horse breaking had a factual base and some appeared to be groundless superstition. The magic horse ropes used by Blackfoot Indians were rubbed with plant extracts to calm the horse, but why eighteenth-century European horse breakers believed in the power of hangmen's ropes is unclear.

Florinus, writing around 1750, asserted that the ropes used to hang men, wrapped in woollen cloth and tied around the legs of refractory horses 'turned lions into lambs', and hangmen supplemented their meagre wages by selling such ropes to horse breakers. Similarly, there is no logical explanation for the strange practice among country horsemen for searching woods and marshy places in early summer for a wild plant, a type of orchid, with tiny twin bulbs the size of field beans. The bulbs were dropped into water whereupon one would sink and one would float. It was said that if the floating bulb was grated into a horse's feed the animal was irresistibly drawn towards its handler, but if the sinking bulb was used the result was the opposite. The demise of horsepower on the land and a more scientific approach to horsemanship in general has seen much of the folklore of horse breaking disappear in recent decades.

CHAPTER EIGHT

Modern breaking

His hand is the best who gets his horses to do what he wishes with
the least force, whose indications are so clear that his horse cannot
mistake them, and whose gentleness and fearlessness alike induce
obedience to them.

Lord Pembroke
Sermon to the colt breaker, 1860

MODERN PRACTICE AND TRADITION

The taming and breaking of horses in the twentieth century is
almost exclusively based on traditions learned over centuries of handling horses and passed down from one generation to the next, first
by word of mouth and then by the written word. These tried and
tested systems have been adhered to on the basis of historical success,
and the discovery and development of new approaches to taming and
breaking by horse-owning cultures was not always communicated to
others, and even when it was it was not always emulated. Thus the
use of the nosering as an unsatisfactory control device survived long
after other horsemen were using the more effective mouth bit, and
the pole and neck yoke suitable for harnessing cattle but unsuitable
for horses continued in use for nearly 3,000 years before in the third
century BC the shaft, breast collar and neck collar were invented in
China giving far more economical draught. The evolution of horse
breaking was thus a disjointed and often regressive business, light-
ened with occasional rediscoveries of good practice but stifled by the
engrained and unprogressive attitudes of generations of pragmatic
and fiercely traditional horsemen.

New systems, from the Indian Blanket Act to whip breaking, gentling to whispering, inevitably proved to have been practised
somewhere else before, and the emergence of every innovation from
the Middle Ages onwards could, with few if any exceptions, be traced
to an earlier time. Sometimes the practitioners of a supposedly new
method were more successful at it than the previous discoverers
because they brought other skills and qualities to the method,

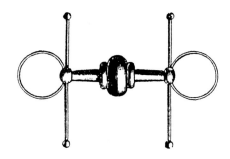

Rarey bit.

Straight mouthed breaking bit.

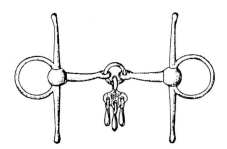

Jointed breaking bit.

perhaps an understanding of equine psychology, enabling them to understand why the system worked and thereby assisting them to develop it further. All too often, however, the new practitioners knew only the mechanical steps of the system and failed to understand the philosophy behind it as known by the original demonstrator, producing nothing more than poor imitators. Some succeeded because they had a natural affinity with horses and Percy Thorn, writing in 1922, noted that in the army some city clerks could gain the favour of horses although they had no previous equestrian experience. 'This

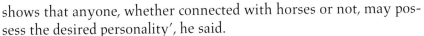

shows that anyone, whether connected with horses or not, may possess the desired personality', he said.

At the time when John S. Rarey was astounding the world with his new approach to taming and handling wild and vicious horses, not only did he have to contend with challengers claiming he had copied their system, but for decades after even the press sought to disprove his originality. A leading article in the *Evening Standard* of 30 June 1893 read

> This horse-taming business is very, very old. Mortals who have been privileged to view the glorious collection of Greco-Scythian art in St Petersburg will see it there in practice – exactly the same twenty-five hundred years ago as that with which Mr Rarey made such a prodigious sensation in the days when most of us were young. There, on a silver vase in relief, is a Scythian warrior lassoing a horse; there he is roping its foreleg up; there, again, he has it on its knees, and finally, in the last group, it stands, saddled, bridled, 'tamed'. Probably there is not one of these latest methods which could not be traced in ancient times. And still somehow we go on breaking horses in the accustomed way, and vice is as common as ever.

Irrespective of what method was employed or for what purpose, or where in the world and at what period in history, the object of breaking has always been the same. Captain Hayes succinctly defined it as being (1) To make the animal quiet, both in and out of the stable; (2) To teach him to obey the orders of his rider or driver with promptness and precision; and (3) To establish in him the habit of applying his powers to the best advantage.

MAN'S ATTITUDE TOWARDS THE HORSE

The varying styles of breaking over the ages have been largely influenced by man's attitude to the horse. For centuries after Xenophon's day, the horse was regarded in the same way as present-day motorists might regard cars; they used them until they were worn out then replaced them. The Renaissance brought the beginnings of a move towards understanding horses, knowing their learning capacities and how to train them, but there was little real affection for horses evident, as the brutal cruelty in some of their handling methods showed and, while these early European masters were elevating riding as one of the arts, horses were still being burned at the stake

Pulling the horse's forelegs from under him was recommended by many breakers as a cure for horses which bolted in harness.

for being possessed by the devil. Although the work of Rarey and other more enlightened tamers, together with the publication of Anna Sewell's *Black Beauty* in 1877, instigated a more humanitarian approach to horsemanship in general, including breaking, in both Europe and America, elsewhere the old indifference to cruelty prevailed. Charles Darwin during his travels in South America was once riding with the owner of a large estancia when his tired horse began lagging behind. The estanciero shouted to Darwin to spur the horse and when Darwin explained that the animal was tired the estanciero replied 'Never mind, spur him – it is *my* horse', being totally oblivious to Darwin's compassionate hesitation. With that underlying attitude to animal welfare, it is hardly surprising that cruelty should abound in such countries or that their breaking methods were, and still are, to European standards very harsh.

In many countries throughout Asia, South America and North Africa, daily life for the people was a struggle for survival and their animals had to share the hardships of arduous labour and long hours. Even in Britain right up to the end of the horse era, most people who broke and trained horses professionally belonged to the lower social orders and the image of 'ignorant, loutish, coarse and cruel' individuals was a theme favoured by the press as well as other institutions. *Punch*, the English humorist magazine, condemned

> those savagest of beasts, the stablemen and horse breakers . . . who, instead of using kindness to bend horses to their will, only do their best to 'break' them, bone and spirit. Unable to appeal to his superior intelligence, they know no way of winning the affections of the horse, and can only make him tractable by beating the pluck out of him . . .

The Illustrated London News joined them in commenting on 'the cruel traditions of horse-breaking, all the menaces, the blows and kicks with which equine education has hitherto been conducted'. As early as 1822, R. W. Dickson said 'The practice of breaking horses, as usually performed, is far from being proper, and shows that it is not well understood. There is a great deal too much of harshness, roughness and brutality . . .'

Colonel George Greenwood, Late Lieutenant-Colonel of the 2nd Lifeguards, ratified this in 1861, saying 'The very best lesson for a horseman, young or old, is colt-breaking; and if in the attempt the young horseman fails to do the colt justice, he will at least do him

Backing a yearling. (Photograph: Beamish Open Air Museum)

George Bowman tests to see if a young horse is ready to start lungeing/long reining by applying very gentle pressure on the bit. The horse should step back without hesitation. (Photograph: Sally Taylor)

less injury than the country colt-breaker or the generality of grooms.' In nineteenth-century England, as elsewhere, the professional horse breaker was viewed with derision and scorn.

The concept of a kinder approach to horse breaking still kept surfacing throughout the last century in Britain. Captain Lewis Edward Nolan, killed in the famous Charge of the Light Brigade in the Crimea in 1854, had introduced to the British Cavalry the novel theory of a less coercive approach to the breaking and handling of young horses, with the intention of establishing a rapport between man and horse. A few individuals in the cavalries of other European countries as well as America shared his view, but as Major R. S. Timmis pointed out in later years 'Unfortunately for the horse, many cruel horse breakers have shown apparent success in the past, and thus cruel methods have been followed by others.'

Although most horsemen agreed that a horse was not mature enough to break until it was at least two years old, preferably three, many unscrupulous horsemen broke them far younger. In fact, yearlings were raced in England from 1786 until 1876, and in other countries horses were often put to work very young and crippled through excessive labour. Writing around 1900, Captain Hayes said of Persian horses, 'The colts (which are very seldom castrated) and the fillies are put to work as soon as they can carry a rider, and it is no uncommon sight to see a ten or twelve-stone man riding a yearling in a heavy native saddle.' In India and Pakistan, the breaking of yearlings and immature two-year-olds for heavy draught work is still common but in these countries where children work in appalling factory conditions both human and equine labour is cheap and expendable.

The horse's attitude to man also had to be considered. The first horsemen were dealing with what was essentially a wild animal and it must have taken generations of domestication even to begin to breed out some of the wild instincts. Consequently, the horses of ancient Greece must have been flighty, highly couraged animals necessitating careful and sympathetic handling compared to the great horses of medieval Europe which must have been very tolerant of the treatment they received from their breakers. The nineteenth century brought innovations terrifying to the quietest of horses including trains, motorised vehicles and steam engines, and in 1860 a New York newspaper reported 'In Rochester, New York, the other day, a horse was so frightened by an engine letting off steam that it trembled and in a moment fell dead from fright.' For the horse breaker, accustoming his pupils to such terrors was a constant challenge.

THE ORIGINS OF THE TERM 'BREAKING'

The actual term 'breaking' was never questioned for what it had for centuries implied. Professor Jesse Beery declared 'I do not like to hear the word "break" applied to a horse except in the sense of breaking a habit. Many speak of "breaking" their colt and, to their shame, they have "broken" them – broken their spirit and that superb pride that makes them the most admired of all animals.' Soldiers were said to be 'broken' when demoted in rank, and the equestrian term very probably had military origins.

The changing role of the horse from a working animal to a recreational luxury in the post-war years had a great impact on the way horses were broken in those parts of the world where motorisation and mechanisation had ousted horse power. The need for quiet, well-mannered horses with good temperaments which were safe and easy

A young horse perfectly controlled and moving freely forward during long reining. (Photograph: Sally Taylor)

to handle, ride or drive, meant that a gradual breaking process had to be adopted with initial handling and breaking merging into an overall education of the horse. The old system of 'breaking an animal quickly and working it quiet' was no longer acceptable. From the moment a very young foal is first held with a stable rubber around his chest its education has begun. Few, if any, of the stages of modern breaking which the young horse will experience in its early years are new. Xenophon in the fourth century BC advised leading a horse through the streets to accustom it to new sights and sounds, the equivalent today of introducing a young horse to traffic, and the ancient Greeks were using keyed bits very similar to modern breaking bits and designed to make a horse salivate and mouth. Long reining was practised in Roman times, and lungeing was well established by the time of the Renaissance. However, our attitude to horse breaking has perceptively changed, producing consistently better results and fewer problem horses than in times past. 'The restive or vicious horse is in ninety-nine cases out of a hundred made so by illusage, and not by nature', Youatt wrote, but at a time when horses had to be broken and put to work as quickly as possible for economic reasons it is hardly surprising that vicious or unmanageable animals should commonly result.

An advertisement for Professor Henry Miller, an American horse tamer living in Ipswich around the turn of the century and claiming to be 'The greatest horse tamer since the days of Rarey', said

> Read the manner in which these vicious brutes kill their grooms. When he entered into the box stall to feed the stallion, it turned upon him, and seizing his arm with its teeth, raised the groom from his feet and gave him a vicious shaking. The human sufferer's cries summoned help, and with bale sticks endeavoured to beat the infuriated stallion. At every blow the animal reared, carrying his groom high in the air. Finally, the brute loosened its hold and the dying man fell to the ground. The stallion's teeth had penetrated deep into his elbow joint, his shoulder was dislocated, and his head badly cut. The man is now dead, and the family mourn the loss of an honest, true and loving husband and father.

Miller was quoted as saying 'I glory in meeting these destroyers of the human race . . . I will subdue these murderers.'

At the end of a long reining lesson, George Bowman asks a young horse to stand perfectly still. (Photograph: Sally Taylor)

HORSE BREAKING METHODS WORLDWIDE

In America, the sharp contrast between the European style of breaking and the traditional bronco-busting style gave way to a sort of compromise. There no longer being an endless supply of cheap horses, the rough-riding methods were gradually relegated to the rodeo specialists, and young horses haltered as foals or yearlings, sometimes lunged and long reined, sometimes 'sacked out' with a burlap sack or blanket, saddled and bridled and turned loose in a corral, often in the company of an older quiet horse, and allowed to get accustomed to the feel and smell of the saddlery before being mounted and ridden in a circular pen. Some breakers, harking back to the old Spanish style of handling, tied their pupil to a quiet 'snubbing' horse, tied the animal head to tail and left it to circle for a while, or fastened a bag of chaff or a dummy to the saddle.

Some die-hards today still use a snubbing post or tree to which to tie their young horses but incorporate an old car tyre in the fastening rope for elasticity and to reduce the risk of the young horse hurting himself when pulling back. Earlier this century on ranches where horses were bred to sell but lack of time precluded much early handling, the horses were snubbed to a post, taught to lead, sacked out, hobbled, blindfolded and ridden in a bronc pen of around forty square feet. It was said that if a horse persistently bucked it did so because of too much feed, too little work, a badly fitting saddle, a dirty saddle blanket, a cinch which irritates, bucking lineage, or the memory of a bad experience sometime in the past.

Commenting on the demise of the old western style of breaking, Professor Jesse Beery wrote in 1908 'I am glad to say that in the west the handling of their horses now is very similar to that accorded the eastern horse.' In South America the gaucho tradition did not change, and even today young horses are still lassoed with a rawhide rope and tied to the ring on the girth of a quiet 'snubbing' horse, there being no horn or tree on a gaucho saddle. Thrown, trussed tightly, saddled, then released and ridden to exhaustion, as a breaking method it may be brutal but it is not ineffective. Like similar breaking systems, it stresses and traumatises the horse, putting it into a state of shock which permits the handler to do what he wishes with the animal while it remains in this state. In the wild, an animal caught by a predator often 'freezes' into a state of shock in which it feels no pain, rather like a mouse dangling motionless in the jaws of a cat. As soon as it is dropped, the mouse springs to life but on being caught by the cat again resumes its trance-like state. A hobbled horse in a similar state of shock learns nothing but is handled easily, and it is not until he is saddled, bridled and mounted by a rider and released that he regains his full consciousness and may then learn.

Australian horse breaking was, before European-style methods infiltrated, similar in many respects to that of America. Rough-riders developed a style of riding wild horses whereby they kept their right hand on the saddle pommel, while their left hand was placed up near the horse's head to help them keep their balance. Sometimes a rolled blanket would be tied to the front of the saddle to give the rider extra security of seat, and Captain Hayes developed this idea to produce the Australian buck-jumping saddle which had 'two leather covered leaping heads in front of each thigh.' In time these became modified into knee rolls.

After the Australian Gold Rush of 1851, many horses escaped from mining settlements and these brumbies, as they became known, proliferated in the wild. An Australian horseman who, earlier this century, made a living from catching these feral horses and driving them up to a hundred miles to a railroad for loading and transportation to the abbatoirs broke selected animals by tying them head to tail, a common method but one which he called 'galvayning', no doubt after the Australian horse tamer, Sidney Galvayne. The American influence also revealed itself through the occasional use of snubbing posts and through a form of whip breaking using a sixteen foot long bull whip.

In South Africa, the Boers of the Transvaal, Cape Colony, Orange Free State and Natal developed a style of breaking which comprised fitting a strong head collar on the young horse and tying it with a short length of rope to a quiet 'schoolmaster' horse. Sometimes the two horses' tails might be tied together too. Thus secured, the young horse could not bolt, rear or buck but it got confidence from the older horse. After a few days of this regime, the young horse was saddled then mounted and ridden alongside its companion. Horsemen who practised this system said it was fast and safe but taught the young horse nothing about the aids or developing a 'mouth,' and when released to go on their own many horses were nappy and awkward.

Gypsy horsemen

One group of horsemen whose methods have changed little over the last few centuries are gypsies. Although their lifestyles are largely mechanised now, they still retain their interest in horses and break them by a gradual process of handling during which the horse is constantly in the company of man. Christina Dodwell, Britain's foremost female explorer and an accomplished horsewoman, noted that the quickest way to tame an unridable horse was to travel with it as the gypsies did. 'I have had total rejects' she said, 'and they lose all their nonsense in three days because the only constant thing in their lives is you'. One gypsy horseman summed up the Romany breaking method by likening it to getting a nervous horse used to traffic. 'Take him to the busiest road there is' he advised, 'and by the time he has shied at one car, six more will have passed. He cannot stay frightened of them forever. Breaking horses is like that.'

The breaking of farm horses

Up until mechanisation displaced horse power on the land, the breaking of agricultural horses had changed little since medieval times. Jack Megginson, a Yorkshire horseman who was breaking heavy horses earlier this century, said the practice was to teach young horses to be tied up as foals and yearlings but not to break them until the spring of their third year. They were mouthed by fitting them with a keyed breaking bit and tying them in pillar reins in their stalls

Breaking a farm horse in long reins. (Photograph: Irene Megginson)

Gypsies often break horses to drive by tying them alongside a quiet shaft horse. (Photograph: C. Richardson)

or turning them out in a small paddock, fold-yard or stack-yard. In due course they would be long reined around the farm and on the roads before being 'yoked' alongside a quiet horse and hitched to a log of wood to learn to pull a weight. Once the young horse was working quietly, harrows would be substituted for the log, and eventually the pupil would take his place in a ploughing team. J. H. Walch, writing in 1883, said 'Many farmers break their colts in by putting them to plough between two older horses', adding that it was hard work and could cause a well-bred horse to jib.

In Ireland, farm horses were broken to chains and learnt to plough alongside an older horse in the lay sod, which meant the first working of the field with the plough when the young horse was given the benefit of the firm ground and the older horse worked in the furrow. As the young horse learnt to pull into its collar, it was called 'making the collar'. Throughout the early stages of breaking, the horse was

Lungeing a horse over jumps at the Ballinasloe Horse Fair, County Galway, Eire. (Photograph: C. Richardson)

taught to respond to verbal commands, 'arve' or 'ah' meaning to turn right and 'gee' or 'gee back' to turn left. In some parts of the country, the command 'cuppy' was used for left and 'wheesh' for right. Only when the young horse was working quietly in a plough would it be considered ready for the final stages of the breaking process and hitched to a wagon alongside a quiet schoolmaster. After several weeks of working as one of a pair, it would be harnessed on its own to a two-wheeled cart with shafts, although as a safety precaution a kicking strap, buckled to the shafts and passing over its croup to prevent it kicking, would be fitted.

'The agricultural horse is sometimes wanted to ride as well as draw' Youatt pointed out, and went on to suggest a bizarre and dangerous method whereby it might be taught to carry a rider. 'Let the first lesson be given when he is in the team. Let his feeder, if possible, be first put upon him. He will be too much hampered by his harness and by the other horses to make much resistance, and, in the majority of cases, will quietly and at once submit.'

Throwing a horse using two men.

Diverse views

Horse breaking has always been a controversial subject with practitioners often holding contradictory and opposing views. Henry Wynmalen said 'Many trainers advocate a course of long-rein driving before actual backing, and although this can certainly do no harm, I have never found it either indispensible or very useful', yet Captain Hayes advised 'a few days driving in long reins would make the wildest or most vicous horse quiet to handle'. Similarly, when J. Boniface, writing about military horses in 1903, said 'Throwing a horse is a personal contest in which the horse is made to realise man's power over him, and this is most important', he was commenting on a tradition common to many forms of horse breaking and going back

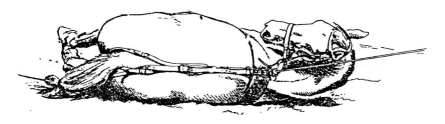

The thrown horse.

Young farm horses often learnt to work ploughing alongside a quiet schoolmaster.

many years. When Captain Hayes, also a military horseman, said of throwing, 'It is liable to injure him by causing him to fall violently on the ground', he was perhaps influenced by an incident in South Africa when Hayes broke the back of a two-year-old horse during a demonstration. Even working a horse in a circle, either on the lunge or under saddle, and now standard to much modern breaking, was at one time severely criticised. The American horse tamers never lunged a horse, and Telfer, the English breaker, was cautious of it, saying 'A clever horse breaker will never practise a horse in a circle beyond a gentle pace, for if he is urged to fast trotting, it teaches him an uneven, jogging style of going, the outer leg, having to step out longer than the inner one, sometimes appears lame.'

A young farm horse is given confidence by the presence of an older, experienced companion.

When Rarey was at the height of his fame, it was believed by many, including William Youatt, that his system would gradually replace all previously known breaking methods and become the accepted practice for the future. Yet, at a time of great change and innovation when fashions and trends came and went rapidly, the novelty of Rarey soon wore off and his system fell from popularity. Many people on both sides of the Atlantic tried to resurrect Rarey's methods in later years but, as the great tamer himself prophecied, by failing to understand the philosophy behind the system or having the patience, skill and other personal attributes to make it work they often did more harm than good.

THE SECRET OF HORSE TAMING

In a startling article published in the *New York Tribune* in 1858 and subsequently re-reprinted in *The New York Coach-maker's Magazine* later that year, the newspaper purported to reveal once and for all the secret behind all successful horse taming methods from Rarey to whispering.

> The one principle which you must establish firmly in your mind, and which is so essential in horse-taming that it is almost the corner-stone of the theory, is the law of kindness. Next to kindness you must have patience, and, next to patience, indomitable perseverance. With these qualities in us, and not possessing fear or anger, we undertake to tame horses with perfect assurance of success, if we use the proper means.

The article went on to explain that a horse must both love and fear man if it is to respect and pay attention to the breaker.

> In subjugating the horse, we must make a powerful appeal to his intelligence; this can only be done by a physical operation. It is an undisputed fact that the battles of all animals (except such as are garnished with horns) are fought by seizing each other by the throat. A dog, that has been thus held by his antagonist for a few minutes, on being released, is often so thoroughly cowed that no human artifice can induce him to again resume the unequal contest. This is the principle upon which horse taming is found . . . Choking a horse is the first process in taming, and is but the beginning of his education. By its operation a horse becomes docile, and will thereafter receive an instruction which he can be made to understand. Teaching an animal to lie down at our bidding tends to keep him permanently cured, as it is a perpetual reminder of his subdued condition . . . It requires a good deal of practice to tame a horse successfully; also a nice judgement to know when he is choked sufficiently, as there is a bare possibility that he might get more than would be good for him. We advise persons not perfectly familiar with a horse to resort rather to the strapping and throwing down process (unless he is very vicious) . . . It is the fault of most people who have owned a horse to imagine that they are experts in his management; while, on the contrary, many professional horsemen are the very worst parties to attempt his subjugation. Unless a man have a good disposition he need not attempt horse taming.

Bearing in mind the style in which Sullivan , the Irish whisperer, was reported to work, the description of the steps to be taken is of special interest.

A young horse working alongside an experienced pair in a harvest field.

Retire with the animal to be operated upon into a close stable, with plenty of litter upon the floor 'tan-bark' or sawdust is preferable). In the first place fasten up the left fore-leg with the arm strap, in such a manner that it will be permanently secured. Then take a broad strap and buckle and pass it around the neck, just back of the jaw bone.

Draw the strap as tight as possible, so tight as to almost arrest the horse's breathing. The strap must not be buckled, but held in this position to prevent slipping back. The animal will struggle for a few minutes, when he will become perfectly quiet, overpowered by a sense of suffocation: the veins in his head will swell; his eyes lose their fire; his knees totter and become weak; a slight vertigo will ensue, and growing gradually exhausted, by backing him around the stable, he will come down on his knees, in which position it is an easy matter to push him on his side, when his throat should be released. Now pat and rub him gently for about twenty minutes, when, in most cases, he will be subdued.

There is evidence to suggest that some present-day breakers in America still practise a version of this system which owes its origins to Blackfoot Indians.

RE-DISCOVERY AND RE-INTRODUCTION

In recent years there is evidence of a move towards re-evaluating and re-introducing some former elements of horse breaking such as the use of drawing oils. Those who have studied equine behaviour assert that horses can respond favourably to certain scents. Orby, winner of the 1907 Derby, was so affected by the smell of cornflowers that his jockey, Johnny Reiff, tied a bunch to his whip and believed their scent helped him to win the race, while a blacksmith who hung bunches of violets up in his forge was convinced that their scent, which he himself could not perceive, had a calming effect on restless horses.

As a result of the growing interest in herbal and homeopathic remedies for many horse problems, a range of products has now appeared on the market including aromatic oils and feed additives claimed to calm and settle horses. Many of the essential oils originally used in the preparation of horsemen's drawing oils were imported from the east and are no longer available, and the substitute oils offered in their place do not have the same potency. Although some of the proprietory brands of drawing oils now on the market are of a chemical composition, most are herbal based and, like the feed additives, include such ingredients as ginseng, chamomile, marjoram, passionflower and hops.

Some horsemen used to hang bunches of hops up in the stable to calm horses, and hop pillows have been used for centuries for human insomniacs. Valerian, another favourite ingredient of modern preparations, is the plant from which the drug, valium, is derived. While some oils if rubbed on the hands of the horseman may have a sedating effect on the animal, and others may just smell attractive to the horse, their real secret more probably lies in what their strong odour really conceals. It is generally acknowledged that a horse can smell a nervous handler. Fear in a human, like excitement, can produce adrenalin, an organic chemical, which causes higher blood pressure and a faster heart beat, and a horse's keen sense of smell can detect adrenalin in the air.

Man also naturally produces pheromones, secreted chemical substances which can influence the behaviour and attitude of others of the same or, in this case, different species. Successful horse tamers like Rarey and Magner were fearless and, because they naturally exuded the 'smell of success,' they were scathing of the use of scents and oils because they did not need to conceal their true feelings from the horse. Less skilled or courageous horsemen needed the support of what were in effect artificial pheromones, and optimistic horsemen claimed that the confidence-boosting smell of dominance worked on women as effectively as it did on horses.

Even items of equipment like Magner's Patent Breaking Rig have been revived for modern use and found to be time-saving and cost-effective by some present-day breakers, especially in the United States. One such user is Knott's Berry Farm, a western theme park in California and part of the third largest amusement park in America. A stable of forty-two horses is kept for working in the four-horse teams that pull the five original Concorde coaches, and new recruits are broken to drive with the aid of an appliance they call the 'merry-go-round', and which is simply a tubular steel copy of the Magner rig mounted on old car wheels. Having watched a young horse receive his initial harness training in the device, a witness wrote

> Once between the tubular steel shafts with the lead rope and traces fastened, the horse was made to move forward, assisted by a helper pushing against the arm of the rig. Before long the horse was made to keep the merry-go-round turning by his own efforts, and so he learned for the first time to pull with the collar and traces.

TELEPATHY AND INTUITION

Understanding the horse's mind is integral to many allegedly new taming and breaking systems. Some practitioners claim to be able to understand how an animal feels or is thinking by locking into the horse's energy levels and reading them telepathically. If the horse is afraid, uncertain or confused, the person feels the same way, and this facilitates initial handling and training by being aware of the horse's comprehension, attitude and learning capacity. Others use the psychological approach in a more scientific way.

Linda Tellington-Jones's equine awareness method is a holistic training approach for the mind, body and spirit of the horse which has many supporters and can claim many successes. It enables people to learn how to attain cooperation with their horses through understanding them rather than by dominating them. Said to be based on a profound knowledge of the psychological and physiological needs of the horse, it uses signals that the horse can understand like gestures, postures, movements and the use of the voice, to develop the horse's self-confidence. Touch is a key element in the system. Understanding equine behaviour patterns enables trainers like Californian Pat Parelli to train horses with minimal physical contact and little or no tack but by the utilisation of eye contact and communication through body language, and other horsemen have achieved great success by imitating horse language to communicate with their animals, even if they did it subconsciously. Many excellent breakers have intuition, and their actions are instinctive rather than the premeditated responses of a learned or taught system.

A number of breaking methods, including those practised by Ray Hunt and Owen Brumbaugh, share common ground with the methods of Rarey, Beery and other tamers, the common components being

(1) isolation of the horse from all distractions so that the horse is compelled to concentrate on the handler
(2) the use of non-threatening approaches, and retreats, to the horse so it does not feel intimidated
(3) quiet, calm and deliberate movements, and the continual use of the voice in a soothing manner
(4) placing the horse in a position in which it is dependent on the handler for relief from whatever action the handler is imposing on it.

Around these basic criteria, various trainers developed their own themes and ideas.

One such system was first demonstrated in Australia in 1914 by Kell B. Jeffery, and developed in the 1970s by Maurice Wright and also by Des Kirk who has since practised the Jeffery Method, as it is still known, with great success. The system is based on rewarding the horse for desired behaviour and is achieved through an 'advance and retreat' strategy with respect for his flight distance. The horse is put in a rectangular pen about twenty-five feet by fifteen feet, and a rope with a free running noose is looped around his upper neck right under his jaw where his windpipe lies. The horse is then 'lunged' by having the handler stand at right angles to the horse's front legs and as the horse leaps forward to escape the rope tightens on its throat and momentarily pulls it off-balance before the slip-loop is released. The horse is 'lunged' alternately on both sides by the handler quickly stepping to the right and left in front of the horse as the rope is slackened. Thus the horse is 'punished' with the tightening of the rope and being unbalanced when he tries to plunge away from the handler, but rewarded by the easing of the rope when he stands still or turns in towards the trainer. A few 'lunges' and the horse generally knows what is required of him. In contrast, traditional lungeing teaches a horse to move away from and around the handler.

The next stage is to approach the horse to gain his confidence, and this is done by keeping the rope just taut as the handler moves forward watching the horse carefully. Horses will naturally run away from humans, and the flight distance varies from horse to horse. A tame and quiet horse has a nil flight distance, but that of a horse on a rope is the point of man's approach at which he jumps back, rears or moves sideways. Immediately this happens, the handler should retreat and take the pressure off the horse. By a gradual process of advance and retreat, the handler will eventually get close to the horse, thus invading his personal space. Using firm movements, the neck or shoulder should be touched, but not the muzzle or chin which are very sensitive areas and 'personal' to the horse. Keeping the rope taut with one hand, the trainer should slip his other arm over the horse's neck and lean up against him, then touch him all over with firm, long strokes, speaking in a soothing voice all the time. If the horse jumps he should be 'lunged' again. The handling process is intended to build up his confidence with the trainer, who should hook his elbow over the horse's withers and apply his weight to prepare the horse for mounting. If the horse moves away, firm discipline with the rope is essential.

To accustom the horse to the saddle, a quiet schoolmaster horse is brought into the pen to give the pupil confidence, and he is saddled and bridled, using a jointed Fulmer snaffle. The young horse is then left in the pen on his own with the saddle on and encouraged to move around which might cause him to buck vigorously, but if he realises the saddle will not come off he is unlikely to buck later on when he has a rider on his back. He can then be mounted, still with the lunge rope on for control, and he is unlikely to object to being ridden or even urged forward. Pulling with the lunge rope to either side to unbalance him slightly is likely to make him move should he show reluctance. Once backed, he learns to respond to the rein aids through the employment of a simple draw-rein system, and in a few days he can be ridden outside the pen with safety, the whole process being based on building up the bond of mutual confidence.

MONTY ROBERTS' METHOD OF STARTING HORSES

Perhaps the most widely acclaimed alternative method of breaking horses is that associated with the extraordinary and skilful American, Monty Roberts, and referred to as 'starting horses' rather than breaking them, a term he abhors. The system has been developed over a lifetime of studying horse communication, and it has impressed even the most die-hard of traditional horsemen and produced some unquestionable results. Monty Roberts has a wealth of experience to draw on. The son of a professional Californian horseman who produced horses for rodeo and film work, Monty did stunt work as a child including standing in as a riding double in such movies as 'National Velvet' and 'My Friend Flicka'. He also rode in horse shows and rodeos, winning a total of four World Horse Show championships and two further championships on the rodeo circuit, one of his most memorable wins being the World Championship Cutting Horse Competition on a quarter horse called Johnny Tivio in 1965. Although his father broke horses by the traditional western methods and Monty was brought up in this environment, he began using his advance and retreat system while still in his teens and proved its success by spending four days in the desert, at the end of which he rode back on a mustang he had tamed by his system. Since then Monty Roberts has 'started' over ten thousand horses and established a world-wide reputation through his demonstrations around the world as well as his work with two-year-old Thoroughbreds at his centre near Santa Barbara in California.

Following his 'discovery' in California by Sir John Miller, at that time the Crown Equerry, Monty Roberts was invited over to England where his demonstrations included one at the Royal Mews at

Windsor in front of The Queen who provided several of her own young horses just brought up from grass at Hampton Court as guinea-pigs for 'starting'. Her Majesty was reported to have been greatly impressed with what she saw. Indeed, Roberts states that without Her Majesty's support he may never have gained the recognition he has had for his work. His system is based on the tenets of absolute trust, cooperation, and bonding between the horse and its handler. The horse is never forced to do anything; he is given options.

The concept of advance and retreat

At his farm, Roberts uses a solid-sided circular indoor pen as this aids the horse's concentration, but he has successfully demonstrated his methods in a pen with metal mesh sides with the public seated around the outside. An unbroken horse is turned loose in the pen and by taking on an aggressive stance to the horse, his eyes on the horse's eyes and his shoulders square to the horse's head, Roberts encourages the horse to begin cantering around the ring. Standing at the

Monty Roberts ready to 'start' a horse in front of spectators.

Driving the horse away.

The horse shows submission ready to 'join up'.

Monty Roberts and horse at the moment of 'join up'.

centre of the ring, the trainer keeps the horse moving around him by throwing out a lunge rein to land behind the horse's hind feet. While the horse is circling, Roberts stands at the centre, continually turning to face the horse and remaining equidistant from the animal at all times. A key element of this system is the successful interpretation of equine behaviour and, from the flight impulse of moving away from the trainer at the start, the horse communicates by lowering its head as if to graze and by licking and chewing. After several more laps of the ring with the horse beginning to turn its head towards the trainer, Roberts 'advances' by stepping forward to intercept the horse which turns in the opposite direction. Roberts immediately also turns to intercept the horse in the new direction until the animal comes to a standstill. At this point, Roberts turns his back to the horse and walks away slowly in 'retreat' mode. When Roberts moves away from the horse, it hesitantly follows him in a gesture of acceptance of companionship, stopping when he stops, and moving on again when he does. In Roberts' own words, once 'join up' has been achieved, the rest of the training is 'just academic'.

Kelly Marks, who teaches Monty Roberts' methods to students in England, using body language to prepare a horse to 'join up'.

Important attributes of the system include not impinging on the horse's option of flight, and also allowing the horse to 'join up' in its own time. From the trainer's angle, concentrating on the horse to pick up the signals of communication and making the appropriate responses through human body language is very important. Monty Roberts calls this speaking the language 'Equus'. An assistant brings a saddle with stirrups and a bridle into the pen and places them in a heap in the centre of the pen where the horse is allowed to examine and sniff them before it returns to the trainer, who has stepped back against the wall. Although the horse has never had tack on before, Roberts is able to saddle and bridle the horse without tying the animal up. Occasionally the horse will leap forward, buck or career off, especially when the girth is tightened, but the trainer stands still and the horse comes back to him for reassurance. Eventually a rider is brought in and given a leg-up to lie over the saddle. Great care is taken not to hurt the horse's mouth and while the rider is legged-up into a normal sitting position with both feet in the stirrups, the horse is held by a headcollar under the bridle rather than by the reins. The horse is led forward with the rider talking to it reassuringly and, encouraged with a little leg pressure, it moves off around the pen, eventually trotting and even cantering in both directions. Surprisingly, the join-up process has negated the natural reaction of the horse to dislodge the 'predator' on its back, and few horses buck with any serious intent. The whole procedure is almost always accomplished in less than thirty minutes.

Learning the Roberts system

Kelly Marks, the United Kingdom protégée of Monty Roberts and an advanced teacher of his unique method, runs training courses in the 'join up' method for people who want to learn a new approach to the handling of horses. Her considerable previous experience as an instructor, showjumper and champion lady jockey enabled her to evaluate and compare conventional breaking methods with the advance and retreat technique, and she is now totally won over to the latter. As well as 'starting' young unbroken horses, she works with older animals in a remedial capacity, including traumatised race horses. Her work, like the system itself, is gaining converts although many traditionalists are sceptical until they have seen the results. A bonus of the system is that horses started in this way are more receptive to further training and therefore more likely to reach their full potential. Magazine articles, videos and television documentaries about Monty Roberts and his work have brought the system to the attention of a wide audience and, although the system can be learnt by most people with a sound basic knowledge of horsemanship and who are receptive to learning, failure to recognise and understand the horse's communication signals can only lead to disappointment.

The long-term effects of starting horses with this system are good. Michael Clayton, whose three-year-old homebred gelding, Jonjo, was started by Monty Roberts at one of his demonstrations, believed the system

> saved time in the initial stages of backing the horse but all other essential stages of training, schooling, and developing the horse were precisely the same as for any other horse, and I can detect no difference between this horse's development and others we have backed and broken by slower, more traditional methods.

He added that with part-breds like Jonjo there is seldom trouble at the start but thought Monty Roberts' methods 'especially suitable for Thoroughbreds of great sensitivity'. People in racing circles have certainly shown great interest in the advance and retreat system, and Kelly Marks, like many others, believes that this system of starting horses will not only have a great future but that it will gradually replace many old-fashioned methods.

Each year, 1,000,000 horses are broken in world-wide by a diversity of methods. In years to come, horse-breaking techniques are unlikely to remain static as new generations of horsemen question the traditions of the past and introduce new discoveries and understanding to the training of horses. Successful horse breaking is, and always has been, fundamental to the employment of the horse in man's service for, as Buffon wrote, 'The noblest conquest ever made by man was that of the horse.'

Select bibliography

Anderson, J. K., *Ancient Greek horsemanship*, University of California Press, 1961.

Bowra, C. M., *Classical Greece*, Time-Life Books, 1965.

Beery, J., *Mail course in horsemanship*, 1908.

Berenger, Richard, *The history and art of horsemanship*, London 1771.

Boniface, J., *The cavalry horse and his pack*, Hudson-Kimberly Publishing Company, 1903.

British Museum, Trustees of: Guide to the specimens of the horse family exhibited in the Department of Zoology, 1922.

Browne, W., *Browne, his fiftie yeares practice*, John Piper, 1624.

Casson, Lionel, *Ancient Egypt*, Time-Life Books, 1965.

Cavendish, William, Duke of Newcastle, *A general system of horsemanship*, 1743.

Catton, Bruce (editor), *American heritage*, American Heritage Publishing Company, 1969.

Clutton-Brook, J., *Horse power*, Harvard University Press, 1992.

Denhardt, Robert M., *The horse of the Americas*, University of Oklahoma Press, 1947.

Dobie, Frank (ed.), *Mustangs and cow ponies*, Southern Methodist University Press, 1940.

Druid, The, *The post and the paddock*, Warne and Company.

Dent, Anthony, *The horse through fifty centuries of civilisation*, Phaidon Press Ltd, 1974.

Evans, George Ewart, *Horse power and magic*, Faber and Faber, 1979.

Felton, W. S., *Masters of equitation*, J. A. Allen, 1962.

Greenwood, George, *Hints on horsemanship*, Moxon and Company, 1861.

Hadas, M., *Imperial Rome*, Time-Life Books, 1965.

Haworth, J., *The horsemasters*, Methuen, 1983

Hayes, Alice, *The horsewoman*, Hurst and Blackett, 1903.

Hayes, Captain H., *Illustrated horse breaking*, Hurst and Blackett, 1905.

Hyland, A., *Equus, the horse in the Roman world*, Batsford, 1990.

   The medieval war horse, Alan Sutton Publishing Co., 1994.

Jankovich, M., *They rode into Europe*, Harrap, 1971.

Jennings, Robert, *Horse taming made easy*, United States Book Co., 1866.

Jones, Dave, *The Western trainer*, Arco Publishing Company, 1976.

Karl, Philippe, *Long reining*, A. and C. Black, 1992.

Kenrick, V., *Horses in Japan*, Hokuseido Press, 1964.

Lavine, S. A., *The horse the Indians rode*, Dodd, Mead and Co., 1974.

Lawrence, J., *Philosophical and practical treatise on horses*, T. N. Longman, 1796.

Lydekker, R., *The horse and its relatives*, 1912.

Magner, D., *The art of taming and educating the horse*, Review and Herald Publishing House, 1887.

   The new system of educating horses, Warren, Johnson and Co., 1870.

Miles, W. J., *Modern practical farriery, a complete guide to all that relates to the horse*, McKenzie, 1868.

Morgan, N., *Perfection of horsemanship*, Edward White, 1609.

Offutt, Denton, *Denton Offutt's method of gentling horses*, 1846.

   A new and complete system of teaching the horse on phrenological principles, Appleton's Queen City Press, 1848.

Peters, J. G., *A treatise on equitation*, Whittaker and Co., 1835.

Piggott, S., *The earliest wheeled transport*, Thames and Hudson, 1983.

Pluvinel de, Antoine, *The Maneige Royal*, J. A. Allen, 1969 (from 1626 edition).

Powell, Willis J., *The new secret of taming horses*, Cottage Library Publishing House, 1874.

Rarey, J. S., *The art of taming horses*, Routledge and Co., 1848.

Richardson, Clive, *Driving, the development and use of horse drawn vehicles*, Batsford, 1985.

Roe, F. G., *The Indian and the horse*, University of Oklahoma, 1955.

Rudenko, S. I., *The frozen tombs of Siberia*, Dent, 1970.

Seunig, W., *Horsemanship*, Doubleday, 1956.

Sherrard, P., *Byzantium*, Time-Life Books, 1960.

Sidney, S., *The book of the horse*, Cassell, 1874.

Smith, Norton B., *Practical treatise on the breaking and taming of wild and vicious horses*, 1892.

Tarr, L., *The history of the carriage*, Arco, 1969.

Taylor, F., *Telfer's system of horse taming*, 1858.

Taylor, Louis, *Ride western*, Harper and Row, 1968.

Tellington-Jones, L., *The Tellington-Jones equine awareness method*, Breakthrough Publications, 1985.

Thorn, Percy, *Humane horse training*, Hutchinson and Co., 1922.

Trippett, Frank, *The first horsemen*, Time-Life Books, 1974.

Tschiffely, A. F., *Tschiffely's ride*, William Heinemann, 1933.

Tylden, G., *Horses and saddlery*, J. A. Allen, 1965.

Vernon, G., *Man on horseback*, Harper and Row, 1964.

Vesey-Fitzgerald, B., *The book of the horse*, Nicholson and Watson, 1946.

Walsh, J. H. (Stonehenge), *The horse in the stable and the field*, Routledge, Warne and Routledge, 1862.

Wynmalen, Henry, *Equitation*, Country Life, 1938.

Youatt, William, *The horse*, Blanchard and Lea, 1854

Xenophon, *The art of horsemanship*, translated by M. H. Morgan, J. A. Allen, 1979.

Magazines and periodicals used in research include:

New York Spirit of the Times, circa 1830–40

Bit and Spur (USA), February 1906

New York Coach Makers Magazine, November 1858

New York Tribune, circa 1850–1860

Frank Leslie's Weekly

Turf, Farm and Field

The Rider and Driver, January 1897

Punch

Cruiser Courier

Household Words

Index